Observing Young Children
A Guide for Early Childhood Educators in Canada

Third Edition

Sally Wylie

NELSON EDUCATION

Observing Young Children: A Guide for Early
Childhood Educators in Canada, Third Edition

by Sally Wylie

**Associate Vice President,
Editorial Director:**
Evelyn Veitch

**Editor-in-Chief,
Higher Education:**
Anne Williams

Executive Editor:
Cara Yarzab

Marketing Manager:
Dave Ward

Developmental Editor:
Sandy Matos

Content Production Manager:
Sabrina Mansour
Christine Gilbert

Production Service:
ICC Macmillan Inc.

Copy Editor:
Elizabeth Phinney

Proofreader:
Dianne Fowlie

Indexer:
Maura Brown

Manufacturing Coordinator:
Loretta Lee

Design Director:
Ken Phipps

Managing Designer:
Katherine Strain

Interior Design:
Peter Papayanakis

Cover Design:
Dianna Little

Cover Image:
Jim Craigmyle/Corbis

Compositor:
ICC Macmillan Inc.

Printer:
Webcom

**Library and Archives Canada
Cataloguing in Publication Data**

Wylie, Sally
  Observing young children : a
guide for early childhood educators
in Canada / Sally Wylie.—3rd ed.

Includes bibliographical references
and index.
ISBN-13: 978-0-17-644162-3
ISBN-10: 0-17-644162-X

  1. Observation (Educational
method) 2. Early childhood
education. 3. Child development.
I. Title.

LB1139.23.W94 2007   372.21
C2007-906443-4

I dedicate this book in loving memory to my father and mother who let me play, to my three grown children who raised me, to my amazing grandson, and to my husband, whose playful bantering kept the wings in flight.

Brief Contents

Table of Contents

Foreword

Research on brain development and how social and emotional factors affect young children's learning and development has provided a more complex picture of the child than was the case in earlier times. In recent years, we have learned that young children may be more powerful thinkers than we once believed. We are recognizing that there are different kinds of intelligence, and we know more about how social and emotional intelligence can affect intellectual development. We are also now aware that interest can energize learning and optimize achievement in young children.

Teachers are now recognizing a wider range of evidence that signals progress in young children's development. Teachers have to be skilled interpreters of their observations of different kinds of learning. In these ways, documentation of young children's activities and experiences in group settings is becoming an increasingly challenging responsibility for teachers. At the same time, teachers are learning new ways to communicate professional knowledge about children to parents and administrators.

These are interesting times in the field of early childhood education, and this book will help clarify the place of observation, interpretation, and communication in the professional role of the teacher.

Sylvia C. Chard, Ph.D.
Professor of Early Childhood Education
Director of the Child Study Centre
Department of Elementary Education
University of Alberta

Preface

The main purpose of this edition is to assist students in developing the skills and knowledge necessary to conduct relevant, professional, and meaningful observations of young children in the field of early childhood education. The text is designed primarily for college or university students embarking on a career involving young children. *Observing Young Children* includes references to various professions: teachers, early childhood educators, early interventionists, and resource teachers and consultants—all of whom use observation in a variety of ways for a diverse number of reasons. Observation is a language they all speak and understand.

When I first began teaching a college-level observation course, my colleague and I taught it from an American text with an elementary school focus. We then taught the course without a textbook. Neither option provided the optimum foundation our students needed for the field of early childhood education. They needed to read about current, practical methods that are actually used successfully in the field. They needed a text that covered age ranges from infant to school age, to read about references to British Columbia, Ontario, or Nova Scotia, and to learn about Canadian provincial/territorial legislation or standards. They needed to use relevant case studies, figures, tables, graphs, and read examples of work done by other students to see that it was all real and possible for them to do. In short, they needed a text to *guide* them; one they could follow. I hope that this text addresses those needs.

The more we learn about children, the more we discover what there is still to learn. Uncovering the developmental process of a child's early years and making it visible and meaningful to others requires the skills and knowledge of a practised observer. The student-teacher begins to develop observation skills by practising the role of an observer, but once begun, observation skills lead to a lifelong pursuit of learning. A long-time friend once said, "I have learned to see life as I never did before." The personal level of observation that students bring to the classroom evolves into a professional level of observation, which, in turn, influences how they see the world. The more we learn about children, the more we learn to see ourselves and the world. Through observation and documentation educators can co-construct with children and their families knowledge that is alive with what matters to them.

ORGANIZATION AND CHANGES TO THE THIRD EDITION

The basic organization of the text remains the same as in the second edition. The three parts serve to organize the observation process in a logical progression of developmental learning and teaching.

The three chapters of Part One set the stage for Parts Two and Three. Chapter 1 introduces the purpose and value of observation in the field of early childhood education. Brief historical examples demonstrate how observation has contributed to the evolution of child study and represents an important link between historical and present practices.

More importantly, Chapter 1 speaks to the importance of communication with families while recognizing the diversity of family values, structure, and cultures. When a child attends an early childhood education program, his or her family is extended to include centre staff, other children, and the families of those children. Chapter 1 sets the stage for communication between children, educators, and families, and their communities. Changes in Chapter 1 include new examples of academic research with the addition of key subject areas such as: "Your New Role with Parents/Families" and "Family Diversity." The updated approach to diversity and families gives the reader a clearer idea of the author's philosophy.

The title of Chapter 2 has been changed to "Preparing to Observe Children's Behaviour" with the addition of key subject areas, such as "Reasons to Observe" and "Challenges to Effective Observation." The focus is on the active, systematic process of observing children in the playroom and how to prepare for this process.

Chapter 3 prepares students to observe *and* record the activity of young children. Chapter 3 is about writing objectively, examining personal biases, and learning how to unravel what we see and hear from our subjective interpretations. Examples of student work are especially important as they demonstrate the trials and successes of recording the behaviour of active children in a busy playroom. This chapter separates this text from most all other observation texts as it clearly addresses the complicated topic of how to document the activity of young children. It addresses students' lack of confidence in writing, how recording the behaviour of children requires a distinct style of writing, and how to utilize rough notes in English and other languages (ELL), and offers concrete suggestions that address the question of "How Do I Write This?" This substantially rewritten chapter now gives the recording aspect of observation the coverage required to assist students with the challenge of writing observations.

Part Two introduces two major categories of records and contains three chapters full of the different types of records used to document the activity of young children. Chapters 4 and 5 present two different groupings of observational tools. These groupings are not ranked by popularity, but rather reflect qualitative differences. The groupings are not prescriptive, but suggest how the methods could be organized. Examples in these chapters show the depth and vision of educators as they explore new methods that can be used with different age groups, and adaptations for children with special needs and children from newcomer families. Figures, tables, exhibits, and photos illustrate how educators are currently using observation to learn more about children, their families, and cultures. We have added an Advantages/Disadvantages box for each type of record to indicate how each method is most suitably used. New exhibits include student work to illustrate how methods were used effectively to record a child's activity. And new examples have been included to further illustrate pictorial representation.

Part Three encourages the reader to reflect back on Part One, particularly Chapter 1, and consider the families of young children when examining how observations are used.

To assist the novice observer, Chapter 7 introduces two differing models of how observation is used within a distinct framework or philosophy. The Reggio Emilia approach and High/Scope model are introduced to give students an understanding of how observations are actually used and how vital they are in uncovering the growth and development of young children. The role of the educator and the family in the documentation process is also illustrated to remind students of its importance. Chapter 7 includes two ways observation is used in many child-care settings: developing a portfolio and providing the basis for report writing. Both topics have been extensively rewritten to clarify the practical applications.

While Chapter 7 details concrete ways that observations can be used, Chapter 8 answers the question: "What about when the path is not so clear—when no process is in place to indicate what to document or how to plan from observations?" Educators cannot predict if their work environment will provide a systematic process or philosophical approach to documentation. The significant reorganization of Chapter 8 includes alternative methodologies that support and guide educators in their investigation of ways to share information with others. Underscored are the topics of change in the field of early childhood education with the arrival of newcomers to Canada, children with challenging behaviours, and families who are experiencing difficulties navigating the sometimes turbulent waters of parenthood. The discussion of assessment adds value to the topic of observation as it brings additional meaning to what is discovered through observation. Evaluation brings accountability to any observation/planning cycle and translates into quality care—the value of observation.

Part Three answers two important questions: "How can we best use our skills of observation to assist children and families, and how do our efforts to observe and document benefit children and families in our communities?"

The text is organized in the follow way:

- A case study begins each chapter, with an overview of the chapter and a list of learning objectives.
- Each chapter ends with a summary and discussion questions that reflect the learning objectives.
- Advantages/Disadvantage boxes examine the usefulness of several forms of documentation.
- A glossary of terms assists the reader in identifying the key terms or concepts in the chapter and the Additional Readings section provides several references that support the topics in that chapter.
- Global Focus boxes where early childhood education students outside North America reveal their beliefs about children and families are introduced throughout the text. These insights will help provoke discussion and encourage reflection in the classroom. One of the goals of this edition is to present students with a global vision of observation and documentation.
- Web icons appear beside resources and material that are available to download on Nelson's ECE Resource Centre: www.ece.nelson.com

- The Professional Reflections box at the end of each chapter is a distinct feature of this edition. These professional reflections bring the insights and wisdom of a professional, experienced observer. I hope you will enjoy and learn from them.

Instructor's Resource CD

The Instructor's Resource CD that accompanies this text includes an Instructor's Manual with chapter overviews and outcomes, overhead transparencies, Test Bank questions, activities for the classroom, a listing of audio-visual resources and websites, and activities pertaining to the Instructional Video. (ISBN 0-17-647296-7).

Instructional Video

The Instructional Video is a valuable companion resource for all chapters, but is particularly relevant for Chapters 4 and 5. The video is divided into three sections:

Section I—Introduction

Section II—Unanticipated Behaviours

Section III—Targeted Behaviours

There is also a short clip on appropriate and inappropriate setups.
The video is recommended for group viewing but can be used in individual or small group tutorial sessions.

Acknowledgments

I would like to thank the following professionals for their contribution to the Professional Reflections boxes that appear at the end of each chapter. They are:

Chapter 1—Harold Ireton, Ph.D., University of Minnesota (retired), and author of *The Child Development Review*.

Chapter 2—Claude Painter, M.Ed., Instructor of Early Childhood and Special Education Degree(s), Langara College, British Columbia.

Chapter 3—Carol Paasche, Professor Emeritis of Early Childhood Education, Seneca College, Toronto.

Chapter 4—Beverlie Dietz, M.Ad.Ed., B.Ed., Coordinator, Special Projects, Loyalist College, Belleville, Ontario.

Chapter 5—Dr. Ingrid Crowther, Adjunct Professor, Athabasca University, Alberta, and author of *Creating Effective Learning Environments*.

Chapter 6—Theresa Lu, Master of Science (Child Development and Early Childhood Education) and Assistant Director (Academic Programmes), the Regional Training and Resource Centre in Early Childhood Care and Education for Asia.

Chapter 7—Karyn Callaghan, M.Ed., ECE,C., Professor of Early Childhood Education, Mohawk College, Hamilton, and manager of the Artists at the Centre Project.

Chapter 8—Marion Mainland, B.A., M.A., College of Psychology of Ontario, DPS/DISC (Diagnostic Inventory for Screening Children).

To these individuals I offer a thank you for your support and willingness to share your professional experiences with the readers of this book.

Emotional support is often what is most needed in order to persevere and complete a project. First, I wish to thank my family, friends, and colleagues, both near and far, for their ongoing support. Thanks in particular to my colleague Muriel Axford, with whom I have partnered in various ventures over the years and whose solid comments, criticisms, and praise I have come to trust. I also wish to thank two steadfast professors in the Mohawk College Early Childhood Education Department who have provided feedback, support, and encouragement during this edition: Shirley Bainbridge and Karyn Callaghan. Lastly, but very importantly, a thank you to the Continuing Education students at Mohawk College who showed courage by giving permission for their assignments to be published as excellent models of learning for other students. Their names can be found throughout the examples in the text.

Thanks also to Steve Nease, cartoonist, and Dolores Ellul, graphic artist, for their creative talents, as well as the parents and children who shared their faces with us in photographs.

To the students of early childhood studies, I thank you, as you have always been the inspiration—this book is for you.

My appreciation is extended to the diligent staff of the editorial and production departments at Nelson, whose expertise and organization kept everything on track throughout the entire process. Their professionalism and cheer made deadlines bearable! I wish to thank Sandy Matos, Developmental Editor, for her unwavering patience and support of this edition; Cara Yarzab, Acquisitions Editor, for her support and professionalism; and Dave Ward, Marketing Manager, for his attention to and focus on this edition. I would also like to extend my thanks to Sabrina Mansour, the Content Production Manager, Loretta Lee, Manufacturing Coordinator, Elizabeth Phinney, Copy Editor, and to Gunjan Chandola and all the production team at ICC for their hard work and support during this process.

I also wish to thank the individuals, agencies, and organizations who gave permission for their contributions to be used in this text. Special thanks are due to the generous permissions I received from those currently in the field, who really are making the invisible visible for us all! The more we uncover and share about the exciting world of children, the more we will appreciate what is truly important in their lives and in ours. On behalf of the children and their families, I thank you for your commitment and dedication!

About the Author

Throughout her professional career, Sally has been an early childhood educator, resource teacher, elementary school teacher, consultant, program advisor for the Ministry of Community & Social Services and the Ministry of Children and Youth Services, and professor in early childhood studies. She has partnered with the Regional Training and Resource Centre in Early Childhood Care and Education for Asia on a number of projects, including a video conference with the ECE students from Ngee Ann Polytechnique in Singapore and the Humber Institute of Technology and Advanced Learning. This video was highlighted in the article "Video Conferencing: A Pebble in the Water" in the Fall 2003 issue of the Canadian Child Care Federation's *Interaction*. Sally currently teaches in the ECE Continuing Education Department at Mohawk College of Applied Arts & Technology. After her family, her other sustaining interest is aviation; she has been working for air shows in Canada and the United States for the past 20 years.

WHAT IS OBSERVATION?

Observation is the most important investigative tool we have to discover what we can about how young children grow and develop. Observation has been the means of acquiring the immense body *B.Whos.* of knowledge we currently have on child development. Observing young children and recording their behaviour is considered essential practice in every quality child-care setting. Welcome to this exciting process of discovery!

Chapter 1 will introduce you to the role of student-teacher–observer and some of the topics to consider before initiating your own observations of children in a group setting. Some key discussion topics include acknowledging diversity in child care, communicating with families and centre staff, and developing an awareness of the areas and principles of child development. You will discover that conducting observations is not only a highly personal learning experience, but also a professional responsibility of all early childhood educators. Chapter 1 introduces you to the role observation has played in the development of early childhood education (ECE), with brief historical examples along with those of the present. These brief references demonstrate how observation has contributed to the evolution of child study. For example, Jean Piaget's observations formed the basis of one of the most influential child development theories related to the field of early childhood. This section of Chapter 1 helps to remind us that we now serve as an important link between historical and future practices.

Chapters 2 and 3 set the stage for the novice observer to begin the hands-on process of observing and recording children's behaviour. The focus of Chapter 2 is observing; that of Chapter 3 is recording.

Chapter 2 examines the actual process of beginning to observe young children in the playroom. The process illustrates how initial decisions can be made, such as how, when, where, and, most importantly, why you will observe. Observing young children is more than just sitting and watching children; it is an active, systematic process involving specific skills and knowledge.

Chapter 2 defines observation; a definition that will guide the reader throughout the text. Key concepts lay the foundation for ensuing chapters. The issues of consent and confidentiality complete the chapter, with examples of how information is exchanged while respecting rights and privacy.

In Chapter 3, prepare to observe *and* record children's behaviour. Chapter 3 examines the use of language in recording observations and how, as a teacher of young children, you will become more aware of the function of language. Starting with the process of learning to write a physical description of a child introduces us to the dilemma of what to write and how to write it. How will the parents feel about your description of their child? In order to write objectively, we need to examine our biases and clearly understand some of the judgmental errors teachers make when recording their observations. When a child sits under a table by herself, what does it mean? You will have to unravel the objective facts from your subjective interpretations. When you begin to examine your thoughts and ideas about what you observe, you will become more aware of your biases and values. This process is vital to becoming an early childhood educator who interacts fairly with all children and their families.

Learning *how to observe* children—what to look for and listen to—and *how to record* that information are two of the most fundamental skills you will develop as a professional in the field of ECE.

Chapter

1

AN INTRODUCTION TO OBSERVATION

PHOTO: Paul Till

Imagine for a moment that you are in a child-care setting. It is your first field placement as a student teacher in an ECE program. You have just set up a creative activity for the preschool children. You feel excited and hope that the children will be interested. You want to see what they will do and how creatively they will use the materials.

Here comes a child. What does he look like? Does he look interested? He looks around. He does not say anything but smiles as he leans over the table and pats the container of pom-poms, gives the shallow bowl of glitter a little shake, then sits down. What are you going to do or say?

How did you know children like Liam would find the set-up appealing and the materials eye-catching? How did you discover that children at Liam's age can creatively work with such materials as glitter, glue sticks, pom-poms, pipe-cleaners, markers, and feathers without dumping them, chewing on them, or pulling them all off the table? What skills will Liam acquire, practise, or begin to master while engaged in such activities as this one? What has your role as an early childhood educator been so far? Depending on how you interact with Liam and the other children, you will influence their behaviour. Will they understand your expectations? Will they respond to your comments and physical presence? While participating in the children's play and learning, you will observe, talk, stand back, stop and watch, listen, sit down, make suggestions, give supportive comments, stop, look around the room, respond to questions, and observe.

This interactive process occurs throughout the day with Vincent and Sophie and Liam and others. It occurs at the creative table, on the floor with the blocks, near the cubbies during transition time, and, at some point during the day, probably everywhere in the centre. During this time, you are constantly observing the children, individually as well as a group. Watching and listening, initiating, or reacting during the day are kinds of observation. This ongoing observation allows you to perform your many functions as an early childhood educator, from facilitating and assisting to directing, from providing to sharing—discovering what is necessary and when to meet the needs of the children in your care. These roles and responsibilities are why many student teachers say, "I just went home and flopped on the couch; I was so tired at the end of the day!" Welcome to the many-faceted role of the early childhood educator and the field of early childhood!

From our observations, we can begin to appreciate how children learn, the effects of socialization and culture on the child's personality and behaviour, and how the environment influences behaviour, attitudes, and learning. From our experiences in working with children, we can see why observing and recording their behaviour is vital to the ongoing documentation of children's growth and development.

Overview

The focus of Chapter 1 is primarily to introduce you to the purpose and value of observation in the field of early childhood. The purpose refers to the function of observation in any theoretical model or philosophy involving young children. In this chapter, you will begin with an idea of how observation is used in the playroom to understand individual children. We will also examine the value of observation—the role it has played in the development of the various child development theories we have today.

After reading this chapter, you should be able to:

- Explain the purpose and value of observation in the field of ECE.
- Describe how observation is an integral part of any program or philosophy that involves teaching young children.

- Appreciate the diversity that exists within families and child-care settings.
- Discuss the importance of sharing observations of children with their families.
- Understand the historical role observation has played in the development of child development theories and philosophies.
- Explore how observation plays a role in maintaining and developing quality child care in Canada.

Two Levels of Observation

In the opening scenario, two levels of observation are occurring: personal and professional.

Personal Level

The personal level of observation refers to your present abilities. Since you were born, you have been observing the world. Some of you are probably astute observers of the world around you, others, perhaps more casual about your surroundings. Observation skills also allow you to read others' behaviour. Sometimes, we look at a friend or family member and say, "What's wrong?" How do we know that something is bothering that person? Usually, it is the subtle nonverbal communication or the tone/pitch of voice. We observe other people and make a personal judgment about how they are feeling at that time. These skills have been enhanced by your years of education, your past and present jobs and interests, and your family and friends.

Through those observation skills, you have developed your own ideas, opinions, and values. In turn, these lifelong experiences have created certain expectations. Before you began your ECE program, you probably wondered about what your classes and experiences with children would be like. You were, no doubt, excited to begin your studies for many reasons.

Many students who enter the field of early childhood state that they love children, that they want to change the world and the way to do this is to begin with children, or that they want to help children become the best they can be. Entry-level students say that they have much to share with the children or ideas they want to teach. Student-teachers usually come into the field with some idea of what to expect from children.

When the second-semester students at Ngee Ann Polytechnic in Singapore were asked what they expected to observe during their observations at their new placement, they said that they thought the children would be:

- Very curious
- Have lots of energy
- Talk a lot
- Have honest and open opinions
- Be expressive and unpredictable

- Have fast-changing moods
- Be very creative and adventurous

Do the student-teachers in Singapore expect to see children much the same way as you do? Would you basically agree with most of their statements? It is an interesting exercise to find the similarities in diverse cultures; you can learn a lot!

You do not have to attend college to be able to tell someone what you saw a child do on the playground. However, in order to *frame your observations* in the context of human growth, development, and experiences and then *appropriately interpret* their significance to others, you *do* need formal education and mentoring. Early childhood educators must not only know how or what to observe but also be able to interpret and use those observations to communicate meaningfully with others. These skills represent the second level of observation.

Professional Level

When Liam approached the table to smile, touch the materials, and sit down, how old did you guess Liam to be? Two? Three? Five? Did the description of some of the materials give you clues? Your image of Liam approaching plus some descriptions of his behaviour and the materials presented in the creative activity probably were enough hints for you to form the conclusion that he was not a toddler but could be between three and five years old.

Given such limited information, that conclusion was probably as accurate as it could be. What did you have to know to draw even such a basic conclusion? First, the behaviours that are most typical of a certain age group—from your own experience or from what you have learned about child development—would tell you that. Second, the materials that are set out for this creative activity (glitter, feathers) require good eye–hand coordination, along with the certainty that they will not be tasted! Perhaps you know that as children get older, they can learn the properties of things without having to taste them. In your class curriculum discussions, you will learn what materials or set-ups are most realistic for certain groups of children. As an observer of children in Liam's group, you would be aware of the relationship between the children's learning and the environment. The educational courses offered in your ECE program combined with training opportunities to apply your studies in field practice settings will be two significant factors in your ability to provide quality programs for young children.

Central to your abilities as an early childhood educator will be your professional skills as teacher–observer. Developing observation skills will be a significant part of your role as an educator. These skills—along with your understanding of child development, curriculum, families, and communities—will give you a solid foundation as you develop your career. The process of observing and recording children's behaviour offers you a knowledge base as well as opportunities to develop your own skills in a way that is meaningful to you. Begin with a commitment to learn and you will graduate from your program with confidence—ready to take an active role in the community.

Developing the Role of Student-Teacher–Observer

For a student-teacher, linking academic course knowledge to practical application opportunities takes time. As you learn, you will develop ways to apply newly acquired knowledge to your new role as teacher–observer in the playroom. To develop in the role of teacher–observer will mean keeping an open disposition and positive attitude toward learning new things in new ways (See Exhibit 1.1).

As an early childhood educator, your observations will be filtered through the lenses of your personal and professional philosophy, values, and experiences. These observations will include your subjective judgment; so, it will be interesting for you to discover these **biases** and compare your judgment errors with those of inexperienced—and experienced—teachers.

If you are conducting your observations in a child-care setting as part of an assignment or part of your field placement, you may find those first few observations challenging to do. Why? Partly, you are adapting to a new role as a student-teacher–observer. Also, you will need to develop a new set of writing skills. Almost everything in the playroom will be unfamiliar. Where do you start?

EXHIBIT 1.1 FORMER STUDENTS' FEEDBACK

When I first took the Observing and Recording Children's Behaviour course, I wondered why it was important. Until I went out to field practice the first time, I honestly thought it was not that important. When I was observing children for assignments, I found what some children do fascinating. Today, as I work in the field and watch children, I realize how important it is to observe children properly. By observing children, you learn many wonderful things about their capabilities. It is important for the parents to have this information so that they are aware of what their child can and cannot do. To observe a child comes naturally to me now; I do not realize I am doing it, until I go to tell a parent that their child drew a circle or knew his colours. *—Cheri*

Observation is a very important skill to have as an early childhood educator. As a teacher in an infant room, I observe the different stages of development that an infant goes through. These observations are important because you are able to see if the child is developing age-appropriately. It also allows you to tell the parents what new development happened.

Through observation, you can see changes in a child's behaviour. These changes can be because of changes in the home or in the classroom environment. *—Adell*

SOURCE: Cheri Hoar, Adell Graham

Orientation

When you attend a field placement in a child-care centre as part of a postsecondary program, the probability is that you will have an **orientation.** The college/university orientation will be instrumental in understanding your role and responsibilities while attending a child-care setting. When you arrive at a child-care centre, you will be given another orientation that will acquaint you with the philosophy of the centre, its policies and procedures, and other information relevant to that organization. Once you have completed all the necessary forms—for both the centre and the college/university—you will be logistically ready! But before you begin the excitement of this new venture and your observations, *stop*!

Code of Ethics

The orientation process will include discussion regarding the **Code of Ethics** (See Exhibit 1.2) and issues of confidentiality. *These discussions are of utmost importance.* Student-teachers must realize when entering into any child-care setting that the lives of the children and their families and those of the staff are not to be discussed inappropriately or frivolously. Many institutions/centres ask students to sign a Pledge of

---

EXHIBIT 1.2   CODE OF ETHICS

- Child-care practitioners promote the health and well-being of all children.
- Child-care practitioners enable children to participate to their full potential in environments carefully planned to serve individual needs and to facilitate the child's progress in the social, emotional, physical, and cognitive areas of development.
- Child-care practitioners demonstrate caring for all children in all aspects of their practice.
- Child-care practitioners work in partnership with parents, recognizing that parents have the primary responsibility for the care of their children, valuing their commitment to the children, and supporting them in meeting their responsibilities to their children.
- Child-care practitioners work in partnership with colleagues and other service providers in the community to support the well-being of children and their families.
- Child-care practitioners work in ways that enhance human dignity in trusting, caring, and cooperative relationships that respect the worth and uniqueness of the individual.
- Child-care practitioners pursue, on an ongoing basis, the knowledge, skills, and self-awareness needed to be professionally competent.
- Child-care practitioners demonstrate integrity in all of their professional relationships.

SOURCE: Courtesy of the Canadian Child Care Federation

Confidentiality stating that the student-teacher will *not* discuss the events of the centre or the persons involved. When a centre posts its Code of Ethics, the staff are telling everyone that they support the values and principles laid out in the Code. More importantly, they state their intent to work toward fulfilling these **tenets** on a daily basis. These principles apply to everyone who is involved at the centre, and that includes you, the student-teacher.

Essentially, the Code of Ethics is about respect. Demonstrating respect to children means listening to them, recognizing them as human beings with valid feelings and ideas, and talking to them about things that interest them. Having a genuine conversation with a child communicates a readiness to learn about the uniqueness of each child rather than being a detached commentator who uses such phrases as "Good job" or quiz questions such as "What colour is that? What shape is that? What sound does it make?" Use your observations to really uncover the distinctiveness of each child.

PHOTO: Courtesy of Sally Wylie

Remember, when a student-teacher becomes an observer of a child in a centre, then the Code of Ethics applies in practice, as do the provincial/territorial regulations. Parental permission must be obtained before any research is conducted on a child. The issues of consent and confidentiality will be covered in further detail in Chapter 2.

Different Philosophies: The Special Role of Observation

As you have learned from other ECE program courses, many different philosophies are practised in the field of early childhood. These philosophies, in turn, are reflected in policies and procedures—what a centre does. Even observations, which are **generic** in nature and setting-independent, take on a special role in each setting. They play an integral role in all philosophies. For example, child-care settings that adopt a High/Scope approach will use observations very differently from a centre that primarily uses a theme-based curriculum. The documentation developed from observations in a Reggio Emilia centre will again be different from the ways observations are used in a Montessori School or centre that has developed an **eclectic** approach to their program. No matter which approach, when you conduct your observations, find out which methods of observation are utilized in that setting. Even though all educators in differing programs observe, they will use different forms, have different expectations, or utilize specific types of records. Observations do not represent a particular philosophy; they instead reflect a philosophy. As this text suggests, there is more than one way to document the activity of young children. This flexible approach is necessary given the tremendous variety of child-care experiences across Canada as noted in Alan Pence's keynote address at a national conference in Calgary (see Exhibit 1.3).

Your New Role with Parents/Families

Make the acquaintance of the parents/guardians of the children in your room. Initially, you could observe staff and parent exchanges during drop-off and pick-up times as they are good learning opportunities. Establishing a **rapport** with families, even if it involves only brief greetings during the day, is a useful way to begin relationships with families. These exchanges also provide opportunities for you to develop your communication skills in your new role as teacher–observer. Begin by mentioning something commendable about a child's interactions with others or convey a brief happening of the day. Establishing a friendly bond of communication will then make it easier for you to ask for permission to conduct observations on the child.

Getting permission to conduct observations on a child from the parent/guardian is a fundamental practice in child care. If centre policies do not make it possible for the student-teacher to obtain permission directly, the playroom teacher may assist in this. However, talking with family members can be very beneficial and insightful. Parents are often delighted that their child has been chosen for this special attention. Often, the parent may ask for a copy of the observation as it is of great interest to the parent how another person views his or her child. Look for further details on the topic of obtaining consent and confidentiality in Chapter 2. Also, in this chapter and throughout the text, look for ways families are included in the process of observing and recording children's behaviour. Families are the primary receivers of our observations; we observe and record the activity of young children to uncover and share with families the joys, interests, and skills of their children while they are in our care.

The Essential Partnership

The best interests of the children bring families and teachers into an essential personal and professional partnership. Sharing information from observations with parents is about creating relationships. These relationships are founded on a **reciprocal** learning process. Early childhood educators, like many other professionals, maintain a sensitive balance between providing a quality care service and responding within an emotional and personal relationship. Parents entrust their child to the teacher's care, and the teachers accept that responsibility with an attitude of mutual respect, as noted in Exhibit 1.4. "Showing respect means that programs and early childhood educators are **child-sensitive,** that is, they notice that children are unique, acknowledge this as important, and use this knowledge as a significant basis in planning the total program. 'Respect' may be a more descriptive term than the frequently used 'child-centred', which may seem rather one-sided or totally indulgent toward children. Respect demands responsiveness" (Gestwicki and Bertrand, 2008, 78).

SOURCE: Courtesy of the Child Care Information Exchange 03/01.

Relationships: From, To, and With

When a child *first starts the program,* the sharing of information begins. The child's family is the first observer of the child; the family has much to share. Teachers want to know *from the parents* what they can learn about the child *and* the family. The interest shown communicates respect and a willingness to learn and understand. Parents, in turn, want to know about the setting, the teachers, the program, and the policies. These initial exchanges and other daily practices strengthen bonds of trust and support. Truly, the early years are the most opportune time for children and their families to experience acceptance outside the home and to develop respect for the **diversity** that exists within child-care settings in Canada today. Each child-care setting reflects in some ways a **microcosm** of the community it serves. Child care is an environment rich with opportunities for learning. Here is where children, staff, and family relationships grow; becoming more aware daily of one another's expectations, development, and priorities.

> Children learn what is expected of them and what to expect from others through the cultural messages passed on from parents, grandparents, and other significant adults. These messages shape a child's understanding of everything from touch, positioning of one's body, what is regarded as mannerly, and how one thinks, senses time, and perceives space to beliefs about what is important and how to set immediate and lifelong goals. The ideal is for families and caregivers to be involved in a joint process that ensures that children thrive within the respective cultures. In the process, children may become bicultural. It is important, however, to assure that becoming competent in another culture adds to what a child already has and does not replace the cultural traditions of the family or origin. (Capone, Oren, and Neisworth, 2004, xi, xii)

Family Diversity

Every family is a complex unit that is rich in diversity. Awareness of the diversity of family structures, ethnic backgrounds, and linguistic and cultural differences of the greater society means that early childhood educators are always challenged to create and respond to new ways of communicating with children and their families.

> "In serving culturally diverse communities, keep in mind that not all parents share the same ideas about how, where and when they should be involved in their children's schooling. Parents may also face barriers, such as limited time or limited proficiency in English. On the other hand, they, and their ethnocultural communities, may represent substantial resources that schools can draw on to assist English language learners and to enrich the cultural environment for everyone in the school." (Many Roots, Many Voices, Ministry of Education, 2005, 44)

Acknowledging the fact that a child's family and culture influence that child's uniqueness is an important step in beginning the exchange of learning between educators and families (See Exhibit 1.5). Sharing information with parents is really about a commitment to

- listening to and valuing the families of each child,
- recognizing that parents may have another point of view regarding their child, and
- working to create an open, meaningful, reciprocal learning process.

The awareness that each child is unique in herself/himself contributes to an interest in the child *and* the family. When educators understand what families are trying to accomplish with their children, they can look for ways to support them.

EXHIBIT 1.5 CELEBRATING DIVERSITY

An integral part of respecting children is accepting and celebrating their diversities. In nurturing diversity, teachers need to assess their own values and attributes when developing and implementing a bias-free approach to their work. This approach must include not just cultural sensitivity but totally inclusive practice that incorporates ability, age, appearance, beliefs, family composition, gender, race, socioeconomic status, and sexuality. Teachers need to be able to critically evaluate such materials as books, teaching aids, and films and to replace those that promote stereotypes with more sensitive materials.

SOURCE: Wilson, Lynn. *Partnerships*. Toronto: Thomson Nelson. 2005. 103.

EXHIBIT 1.6   FAMILY DIVERSITY

Dual-Parent Families

Single-Parent Families

Same-Sex-Parent Families

Parent with Special Needs

Child with Special Needs

Grandparent Raising Child

Divorced Parents that Remarry

Inter-racial Marriages

SOURCE: Illustration courtesy of Dolores Ellul

Diversity can also refer to the structure of the family. Some different family structures are represented in Exhibit 1.6. These examples of family diversity do not refer to **ethnicity** but, rather, to the groupings of families.

Today, many children are cared for by either one parent, grandparent(s), or extended family members. The child may be picked up and dropped off by a designated friend or relative. Throughout most of this text, the terms "family" and "the parent" are used interchangeably. This reflects the reality that parents may not always be the primary caregivers as they struggle to balance other roles and responsibilities outside the family. This thought is echoed in the many texts I have read, child-care settings I have visited, and professionals with whom I have spoken: as the world changes, so does the configuration of the child's home life.

Observing Children at Play: Uncovering Children's Learning

When you work with children, there will be no two days alike. Even when a timetable/schedule is constant, the activity within that time frame is rarely predictable. If the schedule changes, for example, if it is too hot or too cold to play outside, the children's behaviour will certainly change. Some children handle change with great ease, while others insist that everything in the day has to be the same as it was the day before. That is all worth noting.

No two children will be alike. You may be in a room with children from several different cultures. Some children may talk to each other in their own language, and you may not understand one word. That is an interesting observation on the first day of your placement! You may come from a different background from the children in the group, and so, you may be bewildered by some of their behaviours. Hopefully, you will ask questions and share your observations with the teachers, and learn what is unique about each child.

While you are observing the children, they will also be observing you. Children are good observers. They will tell you, if they can, that they like your hair or your glasses or your clothes. They might even tell you to go home! Do not take it personally. You are in their "house." Their reactions are in response to *their* observations. You are new to them. No doubt, the children who are verbal will go home and tell their families about you. I remember when my children came home from child care, they talked about the new teachers in *their* room. Child-care relationships extend to include everyone in the child-care setting, including you, and therefore expand the possibilities of relationships and discoveries that are made.

Observations of Children during Play

Children at play will be the main focus of your observations. Play is a personal and **intrinsic** process. Play is what children do to please themselves. It has often been said that play is the work of children. Play is a time of ordering, inventing, imagining, pretending, and discovering! Children structure their own vision of the world, and their roles within it. Remember that in play, children demonstrate what they know how to do, what they understand, and what they want to master and learn. The information you record while conducting your observations during children's play is one of the most important functions of an early childhood educator. Observations can uncover the most amazing thought processes, the creative discoveries of how children see the world, and the wonder-filled ways they convey their feelings about life. These observations will help you to understand each child and the dynamics of the group interactions. When educators listen, watch, and record children's play in an area, such as the dramatic play centre, they may observe them with their dress-up clothes and hear their comments about the shoes or where they are going. From their dialogue, their mannerisms, and interactions with others, they can tell us about their home life, and their dreams and frustrations. On the basis of these observations, the children's play can be expanded by introducing new ideas or expanding on their ideas.

Observations can be used as feedback to the children about their interactions with one another. This practice of narrating what a child is doing, such as "Are you feeling sad because Bridget took your Lego pieces, Josie?" helps children understand how they feel or how others may be feeling or why certain events happened. Perhaps your feedback will help a child put into words what he or she is trying to express. If so, those observations will facilitate the child's social and emotional development. How does that make *you* feel?

If, while painting, a child looks up at the flickering of a fluorescent light and asks, "Miss Lisa, is there lightning in there?" it is a good teaching/learning opportunity for both of you. These spontaneous, "teachable" moments contribute to the overall understanding of this child. What have we learned from just this one sentence? This child has a good understanding of weather phenomena, and he or she can speak in sentences using questions. Documenting an observation like this one is also an excellent sharing opportunity with the child's family. These casual, spontaneous indicators of a child's character are some of the most important observations you can make and share. Why? Parents miss out on these moments of their child's play while they are at work/school, and the child's day, therefore, can sadly become invisible to the parents. Your observations can make those parts of the day visible to the parents and can make the child's thought process tangible to them. In this way, not just the products such as paintings or cut-outs or colourings go home with the parents, but also the documentation of the process; how they were done or what thoughts helped to create the art work, such as Justin's story in Exhibit 1.7.

Observations can also be shared with other children. For example, if two children are playing in the sandbox outside and they appear to be having difficulty sharing the toys, you could join them and tell them what you have observed: "Marva and LeAnne, I saw both of you trying to fill your pails with sand from the same spot. Both of you were digging, and it looked like you were getting in each other's way. Is that what I saw? What would you like to do? What can you do to help each other?"

In group settings, children hit and hug, yell and whisper; they learn to include and deal with exclusion. They struggle with conforming to other people's ideas and priorities while trying to express their own. Observations about these everyday occurrences are made even more significant when documented. Noting who a child seems to like and how she investigates a new

SOURCE: Courtesy of Sally Wylie

EXHIBIT 1.7   GHOSTS IN THE OLD HOUSE

Beginning with chalk on coloured paper, Justin invents a story about his former house.

Justin: "We have a new house. Grandma lived with us in the old house. There are ghosts in the old house."

Justin draws a large rectangle and begins to fill it with vague shapes.

Justin: "This is the smoke, and here is the fire, and these are two ladies. I'm going to make ghosts now. Now eyes . . . very big. So they see. They just need eyes. Ghosts have to be orange."

Have you ever seen a ghost?

Justin: "I found a little ghost, not a very big one."

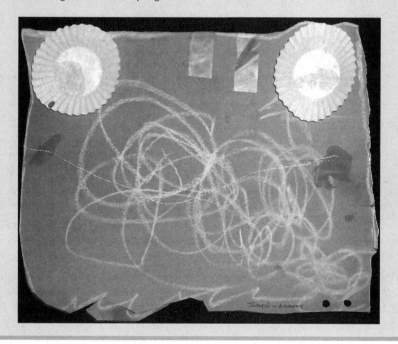

SOURCE: Photo and text courtesy of Jason Avery, Artists at the Centre.

toy is important. So, too, is listening to and documenting the evolution of a child's story while he is painting. These are all examples of relevant occurrences. When documented and shared, they uncover or disclose something unique about that child. When shared with parents/families, they bring forth a family response and then, possibly, encourage them to share their observations and a treasured bond of communication has begun. You can bring to life important information about the child and his or her day. How rewarding!

Sharing information will most certainly take place with other adults as well. Teachers in the room, the staff across the hall, or the supervisor/director are just some of the staff you will be interacting with in the centre. They will enjoy hearing your observations during the day. These comments tell them that you are interested in the children, that you are engaged in the centre, and that what they do is important to you. Believe it or not, they look forward to *your* observations. While you are a student-teacher, parents may not come to you with their questions. However, you will want to observe how a teacher responds to the parents' questions, such as "Do you think that Sophie acts selfish when she is playing with other children?" or "Did Siat have a good day today?" These questions are not rhetorical questions, but real questions that can persist in a parent's mind. A teacher can assist parents by sharing their observations and documentation and collectively generate some plausible answers. When this is done, not only has information been shared, but the parent has been listened to and the parent has listened to the teacher—back and forth, to and from and with—every day. Slowly an essential relationship develops to the benefit of all concerned.

Understanding Child Development through Observation

If you visited an infant room, the reason for observing might be to note carefully the changes in each infant, some subtle and others quite obvious (first steps), in order to share information daily with the family. Infants cannot tell their parents or care-givers how they felt during the day, what they did, or why they were not hungry, and so, the teachers' observations are extremely important. Significant changes occur in these early months of life and continue into toddlerhood. The presence or absence of certain behaviours may be cause for concern. Changes in patterns of behaviour or rates of change also indicate that growth and development are (or are not) occurring. Your understanding of child development is another essential part of your training in ECE, along with your observation skills. Table 1.1 lists examples of key behaviours that are typical of a child's first five years.

Relating the behaviours of each child in your group to what is known about child development of that age group is vital to your role as teacher–observer. Parents will ask you, "Is that normal for a three-year-old?" Having an idea of what is typical for most children of a certain age will help you answer a question like this. Relating your observations of behaviour to the areas of development also gives you another way to frame your answers.

Areas of Child Development

What are areas of child development? One explanation is that they represent groupings of similar, related behaviours, skills, attitudes, and growth that typically occur in a pre-dictable pattern. For example, the developmental area of fine motor includes such skills as pincer grasp, palmar grasp, dexterity, and coordination of fingers for a specific task. How these groupings are determined and how and why they are organized into areas of development is quite complex and beyond the scope of this text. Be prepared for variations of how these areas are represented as you read various texts during your studies. For example, some texts refer to areas of child development as **domains.** You will note that the areas of development in Table 1.1 and Exhibit 1.9 are indicated quite simply as:

Gross motor	Fine motor
Self-help	Cognitive
Speech and language	Social-emotional

Referring to them as domains or sectors, or areas of development, does not change the fact that these terms all relate to this topic. Other texts refer to developmental areas in other ways, such as grouping gross motor and fine motor skills into simply "physical development" or grouping self-help skills together and calling them "life skills." Adopting the term "developmental area" does not mean that the term "domain" is wrong or vice versa; the terminology is just different. For example, Table 1.1 and Exhibit 1.8 show a different organization of developmental areas. Be prepared for these variations as you progress with your studies.

It is your professional responsibility as an educator to be aware of the jargon and terminology and what it means in the field of early childhood.

When observing a child and recording your observations, you will want to use the areas of child development as a **guide.** What does that mean? It means that when you record your observations, you will use these developmental areas as the framework or guide to interpret or give meaning to what you have discovered about a child. For example, let us say you wrote down some observations of Jamal. He is three years old. You observed him playing in the block centre. If you organize all your information about Jamal under the headings of each developmental area, you will be able to cover all aspects of Jamal's development more clearly.

EXHIBIT 1.8   JAMAL'S DEVELOPMENT

Gross motor	Fine motor	Self-help
• Lifts big blocks with both hands	• Pushes cars under bridge	• Gets blocks off shelf
• Squats in front of the shelf	• Lines up six cars in a row	• Asks peer for some cars

Cognitive	Social-emotional	Speech & language
• Rebuilds blocks when they fall	• Plays with blocks for 20 min.	• Talks to self while playing
• Builds a "garage" and pretends he is a race car driver	• Shares blocks with peers	• Makes various car sounds

---

EXHIBIT 1.9   AREAS OF DEVELOPMENT

- Cognitive
- Speech and Language
- Fine Motor
- Socialization (socioemotional)
- Self-Help
- Gross Motor

Guidelines and Rates of Development

Let us go back to some questions a parent might ask. Supposing a parent realizes that her son is not bringing home the volumes of artwork he used to and asks: "Is that normal for a three-year-old?" Is it normal for a child to suddenly stop making things and bringing home artwork? How would you answer? Relating a child's behaviour in terms of typical growth and development frames your answer in a professional manner: "Yes, Mrs. B., many children in the group will go through periods when they do not appear interested in painting or making crafts. They are just too busy learning new things or developing relationships within the group. At this age, their play begins to include other children in more complex ways. Peter and his friends have just discovered other things to do for now!"

Check Table 1.1. It would appear Mrs. B.'s son is displaying behaviour typical of children in this age range. Perhaps this explanation is the reassurance Mrs. B. required. Children not only go through phases of what they like to do, they also develop according to their own rate of development. For example, one toddler in a group may be pointing at things and imitating sounds but only has a vocabulary of 20 words, and yet another toddler in the same group may be labelling objects, using abbreviated sentences, and have a vocabulary of over 50 words. This variance in behaviours can be attributed to a wide variety of factors, such as experience, temperament, and environment. Each child develops at his or her own rate.

TABLE 1.1	CHILD DEVELOPMENT IN THE FIRST FIVE YEARS				
Age/Mos.	**Social**	**Self-Help**	**Gross Motor**	**Fine Motor**	**Language**
Birth	Social smile	Reacts to sight of bottle or breast	Lifts head and chest when lying on stomach	Looks at and reaches for faces and toys	Reacts to voices
	Distinguishes mother from others	Comforts self with thumb or pacifier	Turns around when lying on stomach	Picks up toy with one hand	Vocalizes, coos, chuckles
					Vocalizes spontaneously, social
6 mos	Reaches for familiar persons	Feeds self cracker	Rolls over from back to stomach	Transfers toy from one hand to the other	Responds to name—turns and looks
	Pushes things away he/she does not want		Sits alone, steady, without support	Picks up object with thumb and finger grasp	Wide range of vocalizations (vowel sounds, consonant-vowel combinations)
9 mos	Plays social games, peek-a-boo, bye-bye		Crawls around on hands and knees	Picks up small objects—precise thumb and finger grasp	Word sounds—says "Mama" or "Da-da" as name for parent
	Plays pat-a-cake	Picks up spoon by the handle	Walks around furniture or crib while holding on		Understands words like "No," "Stop," or "All gone"
12 mos	Wants stuffed animal, doll, or blanket in bed	Lifts cup to mouth and drinks	Stands without support	Picks up two small toys in one hand	Uses one or two words as names of things or actions
	Gives kisses or hugs	Feeds self with spoon	Walks without help	Stacks two or more blocks	Talks in single words
	Greets people with "Hi" or similar	Insists on doing things by self, such as feeding	Runs	Scribbles with crayon	Asks for food or drink with words
18 mos	Sometimes says "No" when interfered with	Eats with fork	Kicks a ball forward	Builds towers of four or more blocks	Follows simple instructions
	Shows sympathy to other children, tries to comfort them	Eats with spoon, spilling little	Runs well, seldom falls		Uses at least 10 words
	Usually responds to correction—stops	Takes off open coat or shirt without help	Walks up and down stairs alone	Turns pages of picture books, one at a time	Follows two-part instructions

(continued)

TABLE 1.1 CONTINUED

Age/Mos.	Social	Self-Help	Gross Motor	Fine Motor	Language
2–0 yrs	"Helps" with simple household tasks Plays with other children—cars, dolls, building	Opens door by turning knob	Climbs on play equipment—ladders, slides	Scribbles with circular motion	Talks in two-three word phrases or sentences
2–6 yrs	Plays a role in "pretend" games—mom, dad, teacher, space pilot	Washes and dries hands Dresses with help	Stands on one foot without support Walks up and down stairs—one foot per step	Draws or copies vertical (/) lines Cuts with small scissors	Talks clearly—is understandable most of the time Understands four prepositions—in, on, under, beside
3–0 yrs	Gives directions to other children.	Toilet trained	Rides around on a tricycle, using pedals	Draws or copies a complete circle	Combines sentences with the words "and," "or," or "but" Identifies four colours correctly
3–6 yrs	Plays cooperatively, with minimum conflict and supervision. Protective toward younger children	Washes face without help Dresses and undresses without help, except for tying shoelaces	Hops on one foot, without support	Cuts across paper with small scissors	Counts five or more objects when asked "How many?" Understands concepts—size, number, shape
4–0 yrs		Buttons one or more buttons	Hops around on one foot, without support	Draws recognizable pictures	Follows a series of three simple instructions
4–6 yrs	Follows simple game rules in board or card games	Usually looks both ways before crossing street	Skips or makes running "broad jumps"	Draws a person that has at least three parts—head, eyes, nose, mouth, etc.	Reads a few letters (five +)
5–0 yrs	Shows leadership among children	Goes to the toilet without help	Swings on swing, pumping by self	Prints first name (four letters)	Tells meaning of familiar words

SOURCE: Gayle Mindes, Harold Ireton, and Carol Mardell-Czudnowski, *Assessing Young Children*, New York: Delmar, 1996, p. 34. Reproduced by permission of Dr. Harold Ireton.

Norms and Developmental Guidelines

The Ages and Stages maturational approach to child development was popularized by Arnold Gesell. He believed that all children evolved or matured through certain sequential developmental ages and stages. "Arnold Gesell made detailed observations of growth and development in the 1920s and 1930s. He outlined **norms** for physical development. Gesell felt that the first six years of life were the most important for physical development. His normative approach gained great popular acceptance" (Read, Gardner, and Mahler 183). However, he was quite concerned that people would see them as necessary milestones, rather than guidelines. He voiced apprehension about his developmental guidelines being seen as some kind of strict set of behaviours to be achieved at or before a certain time.

Using any developmental, sequential approach can be extremely helpful in explaining behaviour, but it is not a prescription. Use the areas of development as a guide, but *only* as a guide. Each child develops at her or his own rate and learns about the world through her or his unique family, friends, culture, and child-care environment. Children five years of age may play the piano, dance, play soccer or chess, or have the sensitivity and perception of someone far older in years. Other five-year-olds may not demonstrate many of the skills typically shown by this age for a variety of reasons. Expect a diversity of skills and knowledge within your group of children. Use your understanding of child development to help parents appreciate their child's own unique abilities.

> "Teachers bring to the partnership another point of view. As child development professionals, they see the child in relation to normal milestones and appropriate behaviors. They notice how each child plays with other children in the group—what seems to challenge Mickey and when Ramon is likely to fall apart. Unlike parents, teachers see individual children from a perspective that is balanced by the numerous other children they have taught. They observe how the child behaves with a variety of adults, sensing children's ability to trust others adults through interactions with them at school. When parents need help for themselves or for their child, teachers become resources" (Gordon and Browne, 2007, 273).

Principles of Development

Principles of development have been developed to explain how children grow and learn. Child studies over decades have generated a knowledge base of research, theories, and practices, which we can say embodies main principles of child development. These principles have been founded primarily on the collective observations of teachers, sociologists, psychologists, parents, and many others. See Exhibit 1.10 for an example.

1. Domains of children's development—physical, social, emotional, and cognitive—are closely related. Development in one domain influences and is influenced by development in other domains.

2. Development occurs in a relatively orderly sequence, with later abilities, skills, and knowledge building on those already acquired.

3. Development proceeds at rates varying from child to child as well as unevenly within different areas of each child's functioning.

4. Development and learning occur in and are influenced by multiple social and cultural contexts.

5. Children demonstrate different modes of learning and different ways of representing what they know.

SOURCE: Adapted from Carol Gestwicki, *Developmenally Appropriate Practice*, Second Edition (1999).

History of Early Childhood and Observation

How Long Have People Been Observing the Behaviour of Young Children?

Some of the first recorded observations, which still have an impact on what we do and how we think about children, were made by people who were keenly interested in discovering the how, what, and why of children's learning. These observations have been significant because the observations were recorded. They now represent the foundation of a study or discipline in an area previously uncharted.

When you are in an ECE setting, take a good look around. The curriculum, the environment, and the role of the teacher will have been inspired by one or more philosophies. Current ECE programs are based on decades of theoretical discussions, practices, and research. Observation has played a key role, as you will discover in the following section.

Unique Observations: Itard and Piaget

The two researchers who are often associated with unique observations are Jean-Marc-Gasparad Itard and Jean Piaget. Both lived during very different times: Itard in the 1800s and Piaget in the 1900s. These men observed and recorded behaviour for different reasons, but both, with their descriptive observations, contributed individually to the study of how children learn and develop.

Before the 1800s, Itard, a French physician, worked with children with hearing impairments. Although his work and writings of the day were well recognized, he will probably always be best known for his studies with a young child, Victor, who had lived in the wild and was said to have been raised by wolves. Itard took charge of Victor and worked with him for years. Itard's observations were some of the first documents to demonstrate an interest in and acceptance of a child with extreme behaviours and disabilities. Itard's book, *The Wildboy of Aveyron,* was his most famous work.

One of Itard's students was Edouard Seguin. Seguin used the work introduced by Itard to create an education program for the children whom most educators of the day had passed over as being "useless idiots." Seguin's teachings, in turn, influenced the opening of schools in the mid-1800s for children with developmental delays. Some of the recorded practices and programs for children with special needs that we consider quite modern are adaptations of the documented original ideas of such thinkers as Itard and Seguin. Seguin also influenced others, such as Jean Piaget and Maria Montessori, who became key figures in early childhood psychology.

What Piaget Discovered

In the early 1900s, another Frenchman, Alfred Binet, was given the task of devising tests to assist school personnel in determining which students were not capable of succeeding in the regular classroom. All children were being considered for public classrooms, and the French government wanted to **segregate** those who were trainable and those who were educable. So, Binet began devising tests that determined which children would enter the regular classes and which would not.

At that same time, a Swiss epistemologist (a person who studies knowledge), Jean Piaget, met with Binet. Piaget was interested not so much in how children obtained the *right* answers but in why their problem-solving strategies were consistently getting *wrong* answers in the same kinds of ways. He wanted to understand how children learn and how the brain "digests" incoming information. Piaget came to the notion that not only do children think in organized ways but also that they think in ways that are qualitatively different from those of adults!

Piaget took a very unique approach to developing his theories—he based his research on his observations of his own children and others' children. In one of his texts, *The Origins of Intelligence in Children,* you can read his original, precise observations of his children. On the basis of 183 observations, he discusses, among many things, flexibility in thinking, classification of objects and events, and symbol acquisition. You will no doubt become more aware of his documented observations and learn how they have influenced contemporary educational practices more profoundly than have those of any other theorist.

However, not all theorists were impressed with the inferences derived from Piaget's observations. Similarly, they were not interested in having behaviour described in Freud's terms and concepts of id, ego, and superego to explain personality development. From the beginning of the 1900s, some theorists became dissatisfied with the abstract concepts of Piaget and the **introspection** of Freud, believing them to represent unscientific methods of determining development.

Observation and the Language of the Behaviourists

The growing industrialization of the Western world revolutionized how people worked, socialized, and viewed success, setting the scene for the behaviourists. This school of scientists concerned itself with explaining and measuring behaviour. Two of the major behaviourists were John B. Watson and B.F. Skinner.

Watson is considered the founder of behaviourism. He was influenced by the famous Nobel Laureate Ivan Petrovich Pavlov. You probably associate Pavlov with drooling dogs and classical conditioning. Interestingly, however, he was not concerned about the educational issues of the day but about how the digestive system works. As a physiologist, Pavlov wanted to determine the effect of saliva on the digestive system. He experimented on dogs because he could afford them as study subjects. He did not set out to create a new model for learning, but his studies were seized upon by the academic community and heralded as a new way of explaining the learning process. One of the main observation tools covered in Chapter 4, ABC analysis, is based on Pavlov's classical conditioning studies.

John B. Watson and B.F. Skinner posited that a conditioning process might be the answer to explaining all behaviour. Their assumption was that all behaviour is the result of environmental learning. If behaviours were rewarded, they would likely be repeated. Negative reinforcements, such as taking away a privilege, were seen to deter certain behaviours. Much of their work in the 1950s has influenced how we even define the behaviours we observe today.

The Legacy of the Behaviourists

Much of the vocabulary used to describe the process of conducting observations of early childhood stems from the work of the behaviourists. In this text, our definition of **behaviour** is based on the methodical, impassionate work of Watson, Skinner, and other scientists of the behaviourist school. Describing behaviour with a precise, scientific approach, separate from conjecture, is partly the legacy of the behaviourists. In Chapter 2, you will learn key vocabulary and concepts directly relating to this division of clear description and subjective interpretation. Their interest in what causes behaviour has also influenced parents' and teachers' use of stickers, candy, or other rewards for good behaviour. Using a reward system to change undesirable behaviours is a common strategy used by adults (see Exhibit 1.11). Can you think of ways in which your family may have influenced your behaviour with a reward system? Fundamentally, the credo of the behaviourists was that a response followed by a reward is more likely to be repeated. In Chapter 4, you will become acquainted with one of

EXHIBIT 1.11 CANDY! CANDY!

"If you're really good while we're at Uncle Joe and Aunt Jane's house, we'll stop on our way home and buy you some candy. But you have to be good, or no candy for you!"

SOURCE: Courtesy of Dolores Ellul

the recording methods used for this purpose. In the debate over whether learning is governed more by our genetic nature or influenced by our environment, the behaviourists clearly believed that learning is a relatively permanent change in behaviour that develops as a result of experience. Are your education and training as a student-teacher governed to any extent by the legacy of the behaviourists?

The behaviourists changed how we see, measure, and, more importantly, define behaviour. In this text, our definition of "behaviour" is based on the methodical, impassionate work of Watson, Skinner, and other scientists of the behaviourist school. Are behaviourist theories of learning, then, the underlying philosophy of this text? The answer is no, but this book recognizes the value of defining behaviour in ways that permit the observer to describe, reflect, comment on, analyze, and draw conclusions based on her or his observations. This text takes an eclectic approach that draws on a variety of methods and philosophies and recognizes the role of observation in all of them.

The Child Study Tradition

The child study tradition began in Europe and was then embraced by key educational movements in the United States; many educational settings began using the developmental approach to learning.

The Child Study Movement was pioneered by a number of Americans, such as G. Stanley Hall. He established a centre for child study at Clark University. A few of his students were John Dewey, Arnold Gesell, and Lewis Terman, all of whom were major contributors in the field of studying and measuring children's learning. The Child Study Movement is significant, as many researchers began to use observation for developing their child-related disciplines. For example, Gesell, a developmental psychologist, designed a measure of infant development that distinguished infants with "normal" development from those with **atypical** development. This measure or scale was based on the observation of hundreds of infants.

Early attempts in teacher training "began in the 19th century, when some psychologists studied children, often their own, through recording their activities. This technique was applied to the study of children in educational settings just after World War I, when it was pioneered by early proponents of a developmental approach to curriculum.

> "Although early childhood teachers accepted the principle of record keeping based on observations, the practice failed to become widespread because the skills were not taught at most institutions preparing teachers" (Cohen and Stern 9).

SOURCE: D. Cohen and V. Stern, *Observing and Recording the Behavior of Young Children*. New York: Teachers College Press, 1978.

This brief dash into history is only a glimpse at how observation has been part of the great theoretical struggles in education and research into young children's development. Taking a quick look at the role of observation in determining what we know about children today helps us to see where we've been (Exhibit 1.12) and that may assist us in where we are going. The field of early childhood education is constantly evolving, and as we continue into the 21st century, there will be more change yet to come!

Observation in Professional Research

Observation has always played an important role in the research and development of new theories. For example, finding patterns of similar responses among children led Piaget to conclude that children develop different constructs of learning at different ages and stages.

Formal observation has been a valuable tool in establishing the difference between popular thinking and legitimate investigation. In the clinical-research model, observation is used as a means of collecting data for a specialized topic of study that may clarify our understanding of children. One example is Harvard University's Dr. Jerome Kagan, whose focus has been the shy, inhibited child. His stature as a professional researcher is well known. He has received many awards for his research over decades into the behaviour of young children. A good example of his formal research was highlighted in a lecture at McMaster University in Hamilton where he shared several factors that may account for the variation among children. From the eight possible factors he described, the four described in Exhibit 1.13 were noted to have the most documentation in scientific evidence/studies.

EXHIBIT 1.13   KAGAN'S FOUR FACTORS INFLUENCING PERSONALITY

1. Inborn temperament: This area refers to the genes/DNA/basic biological and chemical composition that makes a difference in the temperament we are born with.
2. Birth order: First-born children ask, "What do you want me to do?" seeing authority as generally benevolent. Later-born children think adults have clay feet and are quick to embrace revolutionary ideas.
3. Parents: Parents influence how valued (or unvalued) a child feels. What is the currency of value in the home? How restrictive or permissive are the parents?
4. Identification: Children identify with family first, then group, then culture. The more distinctive the model, the more powerful is the identification.

SOURCE: Courtesy of Dr. Jerome Kagan

Formal observation plays a major role in legitimizing the ideas, methods, and variables of the research process. As shown in Exhibit 1.14, researchers tend to study a topic in a detached, factual, non-participatory, and objective manner that is quite different from the style of the teacher–observer in the playroom.

Formal settings refer to settings in which the environment is constructed for a specific purpose, such as testing or a research study. Formal observation methods are

EXHIBIT 1.14   EXAMPLE OF ACADEMIC RESEARCH

We know that "teachers' collaborative relations with parents and work in a family context do not come about naturally or easily" (Powell, 1998, p. 66). From the very first teaching assignment many teachers find themselves struggling in working with families. Some have ethical concerns; others just lack knowledge, skills and strategies (Powell, 1989; Keyes, 200). Professionals have repeatedly challenged the field to provide both teacher and administrator training in working with parents (Epstein, 1989; Powell, 1998). In the last few years teacher education programs have responded by developing a range of activities to accomplish that preparation (Acosta, 1996; French, 1996; Koerner & Hulsebosch, 1996; Morris, 1996; Silverman *et al.*, 1996) This theoretical framework, a systemic model that considers both complexity, dynamics and interrelationships (Senge, 1990) would also make an important contribution towards preparing teachers to work more effectively with the diverse parents they now encounter in schools.

SOURCE: Keyes, Carol R., "A Way of thinking about Parent/teacher Partnerships for Teachers", International Journal of Early Years Education, Vol. 10, No.3, 2002, page 179.

SOURCE: The Association For Childhood Education International, ACEI Position Paper, *Childhood Education*, 73, np. 3 (Spring 1997), p. 165.

usually conducted by professionals with extensive training and education, such as child psychologists or researchers in educational facilities.

Informal settings refer to the settings that are familiar, natural, and known to the child, such as daycare, before- and after-school programs, nursery school, or private home care. This textbook is about the informal observations made in these settings. Teachers can choose to be involved with the children they are observing or to observe unobtrusively from a distance.

Dr. Lilian G. Katz, professor of Early Childhood Education at the University of Illinois, addresses this notion of a two-tier system of observations and questions the lack of communication between those who are working in the field with children in informal settings and those who are doing research in formal settings. It seems that Dr. Katz would like to see more dialogue between the two groups. Perhaps early childhood educators need to be more aware of new theories and research (see Exhibit 1.15), and the theorists need to take some cues from educators about what research topics are truly worth pursuing.

The Role of Observation in Determining Quality Care

What role or responsibility does government play in maintaining legislative standards in child-care settings of each province/territory? Who ensures that standards are being met in daycare, drop-in centres, or in private home care? What role does observation play in determining the quality of care?

In Canada, each province or territory establishes standards and guidelines for child-care settings. These standards cover the ratio of adults to children, group size, space per child, fire safety, number of toilets and sinks, health and hygiene practices, staff qualifications, and so on. Most child-care services are under the auspices of the provincial/territorial social services ministries. Each ministry regulates quality and accessibility through its arrangements with publicly funded and private daycare settings.

Although standards and regulations differ among provinces and territories, several key topics are agreed upon by all. Two examples are custodial care and educational training. The custodial aspect of group care refers to sanitary and safe conditions. An example of safe conditions would be ensuring that all staff have a minimum of first aid and CPR training. Educational training refers to programs, curriculum, and staff qualifications. Examples of educational training are as follows:

- Appropriate programs based on the individual needs of children
- Individual and group activities in programs
- Meeting appropriate developmental levels

All provinces and territories agree that educational training should be covered under standards and regulations. Quality care, as defined in the three examples, is a fundamental requirement.

In meeting the needs of the child in the group on the basis of the age and developmental levels of the group, teachers demonstrate their commitment to a professional code of standards. In order to maintain a quality program, educators rely on their knowledge of child development, appropriate programs, and awareness of the diversity among children and their families.

Developmentally Appropriate Practice

This approach is also reflected in the National Association for the Education of Young Children (NAEYC) guidelines for developmentally appropriate practice (DAP) approach to curriculum and learning in the United States. The basic assumption underlying the philosophy of developmentally appropriate practice is the idea of individual appropriateness; each child is a unique individual, and therefore, teaching practices must reflect that uniqueness. The first position on developmentally appropriate practice was adopted in the United States in 1986 by the NAEYC. From that initial position, subsequent publications evolved to further explain what appropriate practices actually meant, as well as elaborating on the standards of quality programs. With the 1997 revision of that first position statement, the role of *cultural context* in a child's development and learning is now acknowledged as one of the essential conditions for teachers in their decision making.

These three main kinds of information (Exhibit 1.16) will be the basis for constructing your observations. Knowledge of child development is important so that you can make appropriate interpretations about a child's behaviour: for example, "Coleton's language skills are developing appropriately for a two-year-old." Your observations will reflect the unique strengths, interests, and needs of each child in the group. Learning about the child's family will help you further understand the child's social and cultural influences. Quality care of children, appropriate programming, and parent-teacher-child relationships can all be reflected in the observations made in the child-care setting.

Even though standards and regulations may seem like abstract concepts to you right now, the point is that quality care begins in the playroom. Your observation skills are an integral part of ensuring quality care.

Observation: Assessing, Evaluating, and Appreciating

If observing is also monitoring, evaluating, and assessing, then observation plays a key role in early childhood education.

- By assessing the environment and health and safety standards, vigilant teachers contribute to children's emotional and physical health.
- By observing and recording children's behaviour, teachers contribute to the growth and development of the children in their care.
- By evaluating the curriculum, they ensure appropriate programs.

By monitoring their role in relation to children and their families, the community, and their profession, early childhood educators maintain the quality programs we have come to expect for our children.

In a **pluralistic,** democratic society, teachers of young children know they have valuable opportunities to promote social harmony and chances for social learning. Perhaps that is one reason you have joined the ranks! Having sensitive, committed teachers who are aware of each child in the group is essential to achieving an atmosphere of trust, acceptance, and caring. Discovering the uniqueness of each child is the greatest joy and challenge of every teacher. Observation skills are the key to unlocking those discoveries.

Summary

If we return to the scenario at the beginning of this chapter, we can reflect upon the purpose of observation in the playroom. Observations reveal how each child grows and develops, how children interact and play together, how the environment may influence behaviour, and the importance of the role of the teacher–observer. From this chapter, you have learned that observations have played a major part in the development of child-related philosophies and practices. Whether in the context of clinical research or an informal daycare setting, observation is the foundation for what we learn about children. This process is vital to becoming an early childhood educator who interacts fairly with all children and their families. In the scenario at the beginning of the chapter, the student-teacher hoped the children would benefit from the activity and interactions. Through observations and that one expectation, the student-teacher was contributing to the standards of quality care for all the children.

PROFESSIONAL REFLECTIONS

What children do in their early years is truly wonderful. To fully appreciate all that they are doing and learning, early childhood teachers need tools for observing children directly and obtaining parents' observations of their child. I prefer to talk about appreciation, rather than assessment, for the following reasons: to appreciate means to value or admire. Appreciation also means being fully aware of something (or someone) with a heightened perception and understanding of that person or thing.

The early childhood teacher stands at the centre of the appreciation process. Her observations are critical because they are based on getting to know each child and appreciating the child's development in relation to her knowledge of young children's development.

Parents' observations are critical because they know their child best . . . for a longer time and in a wider variety of situations. Teachers need to know how parents see their child and identify their questions and any concerns. Are they satisfied with or worried about their child or about how they are doing as parents?

Parent conferences that are parent centred as well as child centred provide the best means of answering these questions and creating effective working relationships with parents. Start with the parents' perceptions and questions and then add your own observations. When parents feel included, they will welcome your thoughts and suggestions.

—Harold Ireton
University of Minnesota

KEY TERMS

atypical	ethnicity	norms
behaviour	formal settings	orientation
bias	generic	pluralistic
child-sensitive	guide	rapport
Code of Ethics	informal settings	reciprocal
diversity	intrinsic	segregate
domains	introspection	tenet
eclectic	microcosm	

DISCUSSION QUESTIONS

1. What are some of the reasons for and values of conducting observations in a child-care setting?
2. Why is it important to share with parents the observations of children in group care?
3. How has observation as a practice helped develop various theories and philosophies?
4. In what ways does the process of observation contribute to the standards of quality in early childhood settings?
5. Why is observation an integral part of any program or philosophy that involves teaching young children?

ADDITIONAL READINGS

Eliason, Claudia, and Loa Jenkins. *A Practical Guide to Early Childhood Curriculum.* 8th ed. New Jersey, NJ: Pearson Education, 2008.

This text in its initial chapters covers the topics of the historical importance of early childhood education, the values of play, developing partnerships with parents, and curriculum planning. The chapters on planning the curriculum are of particular interest as they serve to further expand on the concepts presented in this text.

Gestwicki, Carol. *Developmentally Appropriate Practice: Curriculum and Development in Early Education.* 3rd ed. Albany, NY: Thomson Delmar, 2007.

This text provides essential information for nurturing the development of children from birth to age eight years. The concepts and practices of developmentally appropriate practice are thoroughly discussed. The important component of the philosophy and practice is the notion of individual appropriateness. Observation plays a key role in planning for emergent curriculum.

Mooney, Carol Garhart. *Theories of Childhood: An Introduction to Dewey, Montessori, Erikson, Piaget & Vygotsky.* St. Paul, MN: Redleaf Press, 2000.

The text itself is about 100 pages and could be a handy primer for someone interested in these theorists, who have had such an impact on our perceptions of how children learn and how adults guide them. The text is an easy-to-read overview of the key concepts of each theorist.

Wilson, Lynn. *Partnerships: Families and Communities in Early Childhood Development.* 3rd ed. Toronto: Thomson Nelson, 2005.

This textbook focuses on the partnership of early childhood educators and families. It supports and illustrates concepts briefly introduced in Chapter 1. It examines in detail the changing face of Canadian families, building effective partnerships, and ways to involve and communicate with families. The text also discusses the types of families we may meet, such as teen families, multiracial families, and immigrant and refugee families.

Chapter

2

PREPARING TO OBSERVE CHILDREN'S BEHAVIOUR

PHOTO: Courtesy of Play and Learn Nursery School.

"When I first started really observing children," said a second-year early childhood studies student, "I began to see that when children sit, for example, on the floor during group time, they don't just sit. I used to think that if a child sat in group time, that's all he did. Then I began to notice how he would look around and up at the ceiling and at his friends. He would pull at his shoe, his clothes, wipe his face on his sleeve. He would alternate his attention from the teacher to himself, to the other children, and back to the teacher. He would rock forward with his upper body, then from side to side. Sometimes, he seemed interested, sometimes he appeared distracted by any little thing going on around him. Even a little piece of fluff on the carpet in front of him seemed to be of interest to him.

"What I couldn't understand at first was why observations like this were important; or why the teachers jotted things down during the day. Then, one day, in my field placement, I sat in on the planning time and I discovered that the teachers used this opportunity to discuss the children in the group: their progress, program ideas, suggestions for guidance behaviours, and so on. I was impressed when they planned their curriculum and used the observations they had gathered on the children to make changes or adaptations to meet their needs."

Overview

This chapter asks the classic questions of who, what, when, where and how as they pertain to the observation process. But, the most important question is why: "Why observe young children?" You'll also want to know some of the challenges involved in conducting observations of young children in the playroom. In preparing to observe, confidentiality is a subject of primary importance and will be examined along with the maintenance of children's records and files. Chapter 2 defines observation by what it is and what it is not. In this chapter you will become familiar with some very important concepts that are fundamental in answering the question: "What is it that we are observing?" They are:

- the differences among behaviours, characteristics, and internal conditions;
- separating our objective observations from our personal inferences; and
- identifying two key styles of conducting observations.

Understanding these key concepts will lay the foundation for the ensuing chapters and prepare you to conduct meaningful, accurate, and effective observations.

After reading this chapter, you should be able to:

- Define the concepts of behaviour, internal conditions, and characteristics.
- Make basic decisions about why, who, where, what, how, and when to observe.
- Identify challenges to effective observations and possible ways to problem-solve for solutions to these challenges.
- Explain the reasons and procedures for consent and confidentiality and the role these play in obtaining information about a child.

Defining a Systematic Process of Observation

Everyone has a general idea of what is meant by the word *observation*. It suggests that a person observes, watches, sees, and takes in **stimuli** from the immediate environment primarily through the sense of sight. Yet, observation is really a generic term for using all the senses, including the other senses: hearing, smell, touch, and taste. When asked for our observations on a bakery, for example, we will probably comment on more than just what we see: we will remark on the wonderful aroma upon entering the bakery and certainly describe the tastes!

Early childhood educators will say that their observations are even more than that. Since young children communicate much of what they think and feel through their bodies, teachers have to develop the expertise to "read" behaviours; that is to say, interpret what the child is communicating in terms of child development, and then convey that information to others.

Observation is a systematic process of watching and listening to children and recording their behaviour in a meaningful way for future use.

The definition begins with a very important word: *systematic*. Systematic means there is some kind of order, method, or practice and a rational connection among related events. It is the opposite of hit or miss, maybe yes or maybe no, or any other random choice-left-to-chance. Systematic implies that there is a way to do things; it suggests that organization is involved. That organization may be imposed: "These are our procedures, and this is who you will observe," or be your decision: "I am interested in observing Farah and her interactions with her peers." The main point is that in your role as a teacher, you will need to systematically observe each of the children in your group so that no child is overlooked.

Observation, then, is a systematic process. What is a process? It is an ongoing series of events that has already started but has not yet finished. A process proceeds in time, usually changing as it evolves. The process of observing can refer to the actual observation you are making on a specific child at a certain time, or it can refer to the entire lifelong practice of observation. As with almost any process, such as developing observation skills, learning always takes place along the way, even for an experienced teacher.

One function of a systematic process of observation is to ensure that *all* children will be observed and their behaviour will be recorded. By being systematic in your approach, you will be quite certain you have given equal attention to all the children in your group. A simple example would be to determine whether all the children had an opportunity to participate in a special activity. Suppose you are celebrating a special event (Remembrance Day, Diwali, Christmas) and each child will participate by making a special piece of artwork. Using your observations, you will make sure each child has the opportunity to fully complete his or her project. In this instance, a checklist system would confirm participation.

Perhaps you want to systematically observe each child at play to get an idea of how he or she interacts with others. It may take a while, but by observing two or three children a day, you will eventually document each child's activity. This approach helps prevent the all-too-common case of paying more attention to some of the children and virtually none to others. If the information the teacher has been observing is of a checklist nature (i.e., can tie shoelaces, wash hands independently, run without falling), it is easier to identify and record. Even then, mistakes are made, such as checking off a behaviour beside one child's name when, in fact, another child accomplished the behaviour. Suppose you are observing a highly complex activity, such as a child's play in the dramatic centre. Suppose also that on that day you do not feel well. What you observe may not be what you record days later. Subjective feelings may cloud your memory of what actually happened. "We need to know why we want to observe, be very attentive while we observe and record, keep our information organized, and then reflect and think about what we have learned so that we can use it in our planning and teaching" (Peterson, 1996, 97).

Being systematic in how you observe and record requires practice and self-discipline, but the results are worth the effort. These sound practices help develop a positive working relationship with parents and coworkers. In particular, it is comforting to parents to know that their child's progress is noted and, more importantly, their child's daily activity is documented and valued.

The Process of Watching and Listening to Children

Watching or observing young children is not a passive activity. Watching young children is very different from watching television or a video. Why? The teacher plays a very active role, being totally engaged with the children throughout the day. The adult in the playroom is responsible for the children and their well-being. Children communicate using their bodies to express themselves: a frown, a finger curling a strand of hair round and round, shoulders shrugging, a loud, long sigh. What does it all mean? "The most powerful communicative interactions come from your careful observations of how the child experiences the world and what he or she attempts to communicate" (Klein and Chen, 2001, 153). What behaviour is relevant to observe? These are good questions.

Listening is part of observation. Seasoned teachers say they can take the pulse of their group by just stopping to listen to the tone of the room—without looking up from what they are doing. Where the sounds are coming from, their intensity, or the lack of noise all tell teachers what is happening in the room. Children, too, use the rhythm of the sounds in the room to detect that all is well or to alert them to stop their play to look around. Educators listen to the tempo of the group as well as the sounds of an individual child. Listening is an important activity.

In her article, "To Speak, Participate and Decide: The Child's Right to be Heard," Kim Wilson states:

> In quality early learning and child care programs practitioners and parents are partners, sharing their observations of the child to gain a broader perspective of the child's thoughts, feelings, talents and areas where he might need extra support. With this information, parents and practitioners increase their understanding of how they can help the child to reach his potential. To be "heard" refers to the child's right to speak, participate and decide. The child has the right to be "heard" during all types of activity. This mans that adults are listening, observing and respecting the child's viewpoints when she is speaking, gesturing, playing, creating and choosing. (Wilson, 2006, 31)

Once children are engaged in play, it is important to make further observations about the following:

- What were the choices available to the child in the playroom (on that given day)?
- How did the children use the materials? Any surprises from the observations?
- What were some of the play-based choices the child made?

From the findings of these observations, teachers could evaluate

- what the children learned and enjoyed, and
- what activities influenced their choices or use of materials.

Further observations offer teachers opportunities to uncover how children respond to something new, such as the example in Exhibit 2.1.

Observations, then, form the basis for another set of observations. We continually **monitor** and observe the children, the environment, and the curriculum on a daily, weekly, and monthly basis.

A systematic process can also refer to a *cycle* of observation. This cycle would begin with observations upon enrollment with further observations conducted peri-

---

EXHIBIT 2.1   FREE WILLY—AN OBSERVATION OF CHILDREN'S LEARNING

With the arrival of new fish in our classroom, the children have been very curious as to how the fish eat, swim, and sleep.

Thanks to the school, we were able to receive cut-outs of whale puppets that the children were able to pull apart and fold into their very own "Free Willy."

Using their small motor skills, the kindergarten children carefully folded along the lines until they had successfully completed making their whale. "Oh cool! Look at mine!" exclaimed Marquise. Pretty soon, the kindergarten room had turned into a pool of swimming whales, as the children moved their whales in an up-and-down motion, making sounds like "Psh, Psh, Psh," as heard coming from Sydney. "That's the splashing sound," she confirmed.

Erica and Sarah were busy in the quiet area building a bed for their whales as they used the Jenga and alphabet blocks to create a cozy sleeping area for their pets.

Rebecca had set her whale on a chair in the dramatic area and was placing a plate of eggs, grapes, and bread for her whale to enjoy. For most part of the day, the children showed enjoyment and curiosity about whales as they continued to personalize their whales with names, and Jalesa, Shadaya, and Teresa coloured their whales in a variety of different colours.

The children gained an understanding of the world around them as they played with the paper whales.

SOURCE: Documentation by Josephine Lopez and Vince Custodio, and Essen Chavez, 2002.

odically thereafter until the child leaves the program. In Chapter 8, we will discuss other ways of using a cycle of observation.

Searching for an Accurate Definition of Behaviour

To define behaviour and talk about it, an operational definition is needed so that everyone is measuring behaviour the same way. A clear definition should be easily read, repeated, and paraphrased by others. Behaviour has been defined by (Cartwright and Cartwright, 1984, 4) as "anything that can be *seen, heard, counted, or measured.*"

Imagine the following behaviours:

- Stamping feet
- Hanging head down
- Swinging legs
- Sucking thumb
- Running in circles
- Staring into space

Just a few words make it possible to visualize a child doing these things and possibly even to make inferences about how he or she might be feeling or thinking or why he or she is running around in circles.

Young children express themselves with their bodies. For example, toddlers perceive not only with their eyes but also with their hands and their bodies. Toddlers love to put things into containers and take them out again. They try things out, then practise them over and over until they master whatever it is they are trying to do. Young children explore and discover their world using all their senses to understand concepts of over and under, round and soft, sticky and squishy. As adults, we often forget how important the process of discovery truly is for children because we have already assimilated this information. We can observe toddlers' behaviour as they climb in and out of a cardboard box, puffing and grunting, grimacing and tugging at the box. When the teacher says to Jacob, "Can you climb *out* of the box?" and he does, Jacob's behaviour tells us that he has learned about the word "out."

Since young children communicate much of what they think and feel nonverbally, it is even more important to be aware of this "silent talking" to best understand what each child is "saying." You cannot see sadness, but you can hear crying. You cannot see imagination, but you can hear a child in the drama centre telling another child to "make some dinner for the baby," or watch children race across the playground pretending to be horses.

On the basis of Cartwright and Cartwright's definition of behaviour, sadness and imagination cannot be behaviours because we cannot see them. Behaviour is something that can be seen. We can see a child crying. We can hear a child proclaim, "My dinosaur is sad today." We conclude from these behaviours that sadness and imagination exist as internal states.

Internal Conditions

Internal conditions are unobservable, internal states of being that are cognitive, emotional, or physiological. Some examples of emotional conditions are disappointment, pleasure, fear, happiness, distrust, apprehension, excitement, and frustration. Some cognitive conditions are thinking, problem solving, remembering, and classifying.

Physiology refers to the body's functioning, taking into consideration physical condition; for example, being tired, energetic, or achy. Physiological conditions refer to internal states that cannot be directly observed, such as a sore throat or a headache.

At this point, we have defined two important concepts: behaviour and internal conditions. Decide which of the following are behaviours and which are internal conditions:

- Jumps
- Said
- Happy
- Stumbles
- Frustrated
- Hungry
- Thinking
- Painted

PHOTO: Paul Till

Four of these words are conditions. Consider the word "frustrated": what would you need to see or hear in order to infer that a child is frustrated? If you describe the behaviour using such words as "yelled and threw the puzzle on the floor" or "sighed heavily" or "mumbled, 'I just can't do this puzzle. I'm so upset,'" you may conclude that the child seemed frustrated. Can you see or hear "said," "stumbles," and "painted"? Yes. What about "hungry"? That is a physiological condition because it is an internal state that is not observable. If you were hungry, how would other people know? You would probably tell someone. How does an infant express hunger?

This is why observing young children is so important. Much of what we do with them on a daily basis is to interpret what they are "saying" and try to respond to their wants and needs while clarifying their world for them. The early childhood educator also needs to clarify to other adults involved how he or she arrived at these conclusions. Responding to and communicating with an infant who appears upset involves many vital skills, including relaying that information to the parent or caregiver.

Characteristics

The usual behaviours of a child are often referred to as the *characteristics* of that child. Characteristics are patterns of behaviour or sets of traits that distinguish an individual from others. Some examples of characteristics could be:

- Easygoing
- Affectionate
- Reliable
- Considerate

For our purposes the term "characteristics" will not refer to physical traits, such as brown hair or blue eyes, but, rather, to behaviours. It will refer to characteristics or traits of personality. Characteristics can also refer to a predisposition to behave in certain ways. What is a characteristic of a good friend of yours?

The Three Concepts: How Are They the Same/Different?

Behaviours are different from characteristics and internal conditions. Behaviours can be seen, heard, measured, or counted.

Characteristics and internal conditions must be *inferred*. An *inference* is a logical conclusion based on given information or, in this case, on groupings of behaviour. In other words, you would have to observe the behaviour in order to make an inference. Inferences add personal judgment. An inference adds another dimension to the observation so that now your observations have created the possibility to ascribe a characteristic to a person or to surmise that some internal condition is occurring. For example, if a child is crying on the bus, we infer that "The child is upset" = internal condition. On that same bus, look around, and form immediate impressions about others on the basis of their appearance and behaviour. We observe a man move over to make room for a pregnant woman and think, "He's a considerate person." We have learned to use our background knowledge and accommodate new information to make inferences. Let us see if we can analyze the three concepts discussed thus far.

Indicate which of the following are behaviours, internal conditions, or characteristics:

- Breaks toys
- Grins widely
- Nervous
- Pushes wagon
- Easygoing
- Patient
- Sore throat
- Affectionate

"Breaks toys," "grins widely," and "pushes wagon" are behaviours. "Sore throat" is an internal condition. "Nervous" could be a condition (that is how you are feeling right now, but no one is aware of it), or it could be a characteristic of someone. "Easygoing"

EXHIBIT 2.2   AMBIGUOUS WORDS

Some words can describe an internal condition or a characteristic, depending on how they are used in a sentence. The following words are examples:

Content
- She appeared content to sit on her teacher's lap. (describes an internal condition inferred by the observer)
- She seems very content with life. (describes a characteristic as it refers to a pattern of behaviours or overall disposition)

Aggressive
- He seemed aggressive with his friend on the playground. (describes an internal condition inferred by the observer)
- One of the teachers thought Marcie was an aggressive child. (describes an overall predisposition or set of traits that typifies that person)

Anxious
- Dominic appeared anxious to begin the new story. (describes an internal condition inferred by the observer)
- Antonella's mother says that she is an anxious child. (describes a characteristic as it refers to a pattern of behaviours or overall disposition)

All three words are inferred on the basis of specific behaviours.

and "affectionate" could be terms which describe characteristics. "Patient" could be either a condition or a characteristic. See Exhibit 2.2 for more examples.

Characteristics and Labels

What is the difference between a characteristic and a label? Children learn to classify people, things, and events to bring meaning to their world. As adults, we continue this process. Often, in the process of ordering and classifying zoo animals, types of cars, or varieties of flowers, we further classify things in the categories of "like" and "don't like." We affix personal values to them. Some people, things, and events are valued more than others. When we ascribe negative values while classifying, we are **labelling.** Labelling is often used in a demeaning manner. Great care must be taken to define the characteristics of a child and to avoid assigning negative labels to him or her. For example, see Exhibit 2.3.

Our years of everyday experience assist us in interpreting everyday events. When interpreting a young child's behaviour, you will want to be as accurate as you can in making reasonable judgments about that behaviour. For example, you may see Anthony gazing out of the window at the rain. You observe him tracing the drops of rain with his finger as they trickle down the window pane. What inference could you draw from this one observation?

Is he sad, curious, daydreaming, or just waiting for his dad? The more clearly we differentiate between what we are observing and our conclusions or inferences, the more effective we will be at communicating that information to others.

As a teacher, you will want to gather many examples of behaviour in order to be as accurate as possible. Drawing inferences from one sample of behaviour is rarely good practice and can result in misunderstanding. For example, let us assume you just started

---

EXHIBIT 2.3 CHARACTERISTICS AND LABELS

There is a fine line between describing people in terms of their characteristics and negatively labelling them. Listed below are some words that have negative connotations. Other words are offered as alternatives. Can you think of others?

Label	Alternatives
skinny	thin, slender
bossy	assertive
noisy	boisterous
selfish	egocentric
babyish	immature
rude	outspoken

working at ABC Nursery School. When you enter the preschool room, you observe Milena screaming at the top of her lungs and hitting Sladjana over the head with a doll, and the teacher running toward them. What would you infer from this? Suppose that after the ruckus settles down, you find out that Sladjana took from the cubbies Milena's favourite doll, which she just got as a birthday present. Maybe the teacher mentions that she has never seen Milena acting that way before. Now what do you think?

When examining behaviour, we need to consider many variables before we arrive at conclusions. Again, establish a good practice of observing children on a regular basis. Be familiar with a range of appropriate observation methods. Judiciously observe and record behaviour in a meaningful way. Remember, your goal is to obtain accurate, objective, and relevant information that is needed. As a rule, it is better to have less data that are reliable than to have volumes of unreliable data.

Changes in Behaviour: Settings, Stimuli, and Time

Children act differently in different settings. A setting can be anywhere behaviour occurs: the playground, the cloakroom, or on a field trip. The setting can also include the equipment and materials, the physical set-up, the children and adults present, and the events that are peripheral to the situation. Teachers know that children often behave differently when taken out of the daycare centre on a field trip. Children who are usually shy become very outgoing and excited, while other children who appear quite confident in the classroom seem afraid and cling to their favourite teacher. The change in behaviour does not "fit" some children's usual pattern of behaviour.

It may also be important to note what triggered a certain behaviour. Let us go back to the example of Milena hitting Sladjana with a doll and screaming. As we suggested, the stimulus for Milena's behaviour may have been Sladjana's taking the doll from the cubbies. What started the chain of behaviours can be a variable itself. This stimulus may trigger an isolated behaviour or may set off behaviour that fits a pattern.

Often, you will hear teachers on the playground say such things as "Okay, who took the ball away from Sammy?" or "Stop fighting over the bike. Who had it first?"

SOURCE: Courtesy of Steve Nease

What the teacher wants to know is what the sequence was. Who was first? When the teacher finds out, he or she may be closer to determining what, when, and *why* certain behaviours occurred. In Chapter 4, analyzing the effects of stimuli on behaviour is discussed thoroughly (event sampling/ABC analysis).

Time as a Variable

Time is a major variable. Consider the behaviour of preschoolers starting nursery school (first group experience) in September. Do you think their behaviour will change by the following April? By then, they will know the routines, understand the expectations, and have made new friends. Those children who cried for mum will not be crying anymore. Many children who appeared shy initially will be chatting busily with their friends.

Though young children do not have a strict sense of time the way adults do, most of them do have a sense of "what comes next" in terms of their general day. I remember asking a preschooler, Kenny, if he knew what time he ate supper at home. Kenny replied, "After the cartoons is done." What happens at certain times of the day helps "set" children's internal clock. An interesting example of the influence of time on young children's behaviour involves the change to daylight savings time in the spring and the change back in the fall. For many children, one hour makes a *big* difference. Even infants will establish a feeding schedule of their own and be quite predictable in terms of their behaviour, beginning to fuss to remind adults it is time to eat!

A child's behaviour can also vary from morning to afternoon. Teachers will say that variations in an individual's behaviour could stem from family practices at home or the child's disposition. The beginning of the week versus Friday afternoon also makes a difference in the behaviour of some children. Ironically, time is one of the main variables of behaviour, yet it is a concept not totally understood by children. It is good to remember that some children are just like adults in that some are "early birds," while others are "night owls." Identifying with children's experiences helps us relate to them and to understand better what they are thinking or feeling.

Of course, there are other variables besides time, setting, and stimuli. These three broad categories were presented at this point to illustrate the notion that records of behaviours at different times, in different settings, with different stimuli will increase the probability of your inferences being more accurate and reasonable. Patterns of behaviour will begin to emerge, even if the pattern is constant change. Recording patterns of behaviour gives us the information we need to plan and evaluate the children's growth and progress, appropriate curriculum, teaching strategies, and the environment, and allows us to talk professionally with the parents and caregivers of the children.

Recording Behaviour in a Meaningful Way for Future Use

"Recording children's behaviour in a meaningful way" implies that you have collected information with a particular purpose in mind. Having a purpose means that some initial decisions have to be made. Writing in a meaningful way takes the recipient of the information into consideration. Haphazardly making notes that are illegible, undated, and subjective has little value to others. That is to say, as a writer of observations, you are documenting information so that others will benefit; you are writing for others. "For future use" tells us that you will *act* on the information and not file it away to be forgotten. Choosing what is meaningful and writing or recording it in such a way that the information is useful represent a major focus of this book and a large part of your role as an early childhood educator. Hopefully, you will value not only the joy of discovery but also the rewards of communicating your discoveries to others and seeing the difference you can make in people's lives.

Whether you are a student-teacher in your field practicum, a new teacher, or a teacher who has been in the field for many years, basic decisions have to be made. The difference in approach to that decision-making process is the level of experience people have in making these decisions. These decisions involve the questions of why, how, when, where, and what to observe. Let us take a look at some of the decisions that you could make along with your colleagues or supervisor.

Asking the Questions: Why, How, Who, When, Where, and What

Why Observe Children?

What will be your reasons for observing? Stop and consider a short list of reasons why you want to observe young children. Check your reasons with the reasons given below.

Reasons for Observing Young Children

Why do early childhood teachers want to observe? Why are observations so important? Let us begin by listing some of the main reasons for observation.

- *To observe children's growth and development.* Teachers know that children develop at different rates and in their own way. They know that each child demonstrates specific interests, styles of learning, knowledge, and skills. For each child, teachers observe and document important information. For example, a teacher may write down the questions Ahmed asked, such as why leaves curl up when they change colour in the fall. These questions indicate a keen interest in nature, curiosity, and a desire to learn. The teacher may want to note Kate's reluctance to sit on the carpet with the floor toys and other children. Perhaps there are reasons why Kate seems to shy away from this social area and activity. The teacher may also record notes about how Samuel, 20 months old, picked himself up after he tried several times to stand by holding onto the toy shelf. The teacher may want to note his persistence and his problem solving, and how he coordinated his body movements to attempt this task. In Exhibit 2.4, the observer documented the intense concentration of Nicholas (roughly two years old) while he painted for 35 to 40 minutes.

EXHIBIT 2.4 NICHOLAS PAINTING

Nicholas is roughly two years old and paints with great focus. He is persistent and undeterred by the action in the room. (This was an especially busy day with many new faces.) This session went on for *35 to 40 minutes,* with the only break occurring at about the 30-minute mark. At this point, he left the easel to sit at the round table and draw with pencil and paper with the same undivided attention we saw at the easel. He returned to painting when his pencil drawing had filled the page.

Nicholas was shown how to hold the brush and suffered this interruption with pioneer spirit. This photograph of Nicholas could have been taken at any point during his painting session as his attention was unwavering.

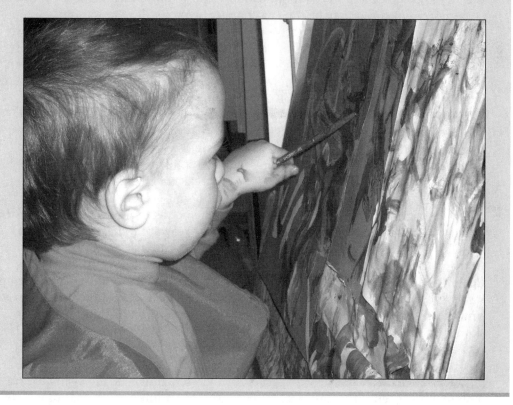

SOURCE: Photo and text courtesy of Jason Avery, Artists at the Centre.

- *To observe the group as a whole.* There are dozens of reasons why teachers monitor the interactions of their group of children. They may want to discover where children tend to spend most of their time. Teachers also like to get a sense of their group in terms of who typically plays alone and which child usually plays with others, who leads and who follows. Teachers keep track of the growing relationships and socialization between children for a variety of reasons; one of the most critical reasons is to share information with parents. Teachers also need to watch the group to make sure that a child is not being bullied or is not becoming too consistently aggressive with others. Seasoned teachers will tell you that the dynamics of a group changes over time, especially when a new child arrives or leaves the group. As mentioned earlier, effective teachers watch for and listen to the ebb and flow of the group's activity; it tells them when the group is working well together or hints at unrest within the social experience.

- *To determine how children play with certain toys or equipment.* Early childhood educators are ever vigilant to what children say and do when they are playing, as well as how they invent new ways to play with ordinary objects. This information tells them about how children learn, what they understand, and how they feel about the toys and equipment in the room. For example, children who ignore or misuse certain props means it may be time to change the props. Teachers also pay attention to how children use the creative or sensory materials. Some children love to plunge elbow-deep into sand or water, yet other children will hold onto the very tip of a container so as to not touch the sand or water. The behaviour of children while manipulating materials or playing with toys reveals a great deal about their personalities as indicated in Exhibit 2.5 – A different kind of Intelligence.

- *To observe for the safety and well-being (social, emotional, and physical) of each child in the group.* Some educators consider this reason a health-and-safety issue: one that speaks to supervision skills, rather than a topic involving observations. Yet, to supervise a playground or playroom, you need solid observation skills. Health and safety encompass emotional and psychological as well as physical well-being. Teachers notice who seems to be low on energy or out of sorts. They will notice the body language and facial expressions of children and determine whether or not the child is "himself/herself." Observations clearly are relevant to health and safety.

    Observing for the rules of safety indoors and outdoors is yet another role of the teacher–observer. Watching to see if the children sit down before going down the slide or use their walking feet indoors ensures the children are playing safely. Observation of children's behaviours and appropriate follow-up prevents unwanted consequences. For example, if Matthew persists in sliding headfirst down the slide, he will be redirected elsewhere in the playground by the teacher-observer. Setting limits and following through mean using your observation skills to see if the children are listening to directions and playing safely.

- *To evaluate staff development.* During your field practicums, you are evaluated on a number of criteria. This feedback gives you information on the areas in which you perform well and areas to improve. These field practicum competencies such as "Gets down to child's level when talking" will be observed if demonstrated, and recorded and evaluated. Teachers, too, are evaluated by their supervisors in terms of job performance. Staff development is based on the observation of key performance indicators.

- *To evaluate themselves as a group.* Teachers set goals and plan together. "Teams of teachers help each other gain perspective on the class, an individual, a time of

EXHIBIT 2.5   A DIFFERENT KIND OF INTELLIGENCE

To a casual observer, four-year-old Judy might seem a wallflower among more gregarious playmates. She hangs back from the action at playtime, staying on the margins of games, rather than plunging into the centre. But she is actually a keen observer of the social politics of her preschool playroom, perhaps the most sophisticated of her playmates in her insights.

Her sophistication is not apparent until Judy's teacher gathers the four-year-olds around to play what they call the Classroom Game. The game—a dollhouse replica of Judy's own preschool classroom, with stick figures that have for heads small photos of the students and teachers—is a test of social perceptiveness. When Judy's teacher asks her to put each girl and boy in the part of the room she or he likes to play in most—the art corner, the blocks corner, and so on—Judy does so with complete accuracy.

And when asked to put each boy and girl with the children he or she likes to play with most, Judy shows she can match best friends for the entire class.

Judy's accuracy reveals that she has a perfect social map of her class, a level of perceptiveness exceptional for a four-year-old. These are the skills that, in later life, might allow Judy to blossom into a star in any of the fields where "people skills" count, from sales and management to diplomacy.

That Judy's social brilliance was spotted at all, let alone this early, was due to her being a student at the Eliot-Pearson Preschool on the campus of Tufts University, where Project Spectrum, a curriculum that intentionally cultivates a variety of kinds of intelligence, was then being developed. Project Spectrum recognizes that the human repertoire of abilities goes far beyond the three Rs, the narrow band of word-and-number skills that schools traditionally focus on. It acknowledges that such capacities as Judy's social perceptiveness are talents that an education can nurture, rather than ignore or even frustrate. By encouraging children to develop a full range of the abilities that they will actually draw on to succeed, or use simply to be fulfilled in what they do, school becomes an education in life skills.

SOURCE: Daniel Coleman, *The Nature of Emotional Intelligence*. Copyright © 1995 by Daniel Coleman. Used by permission of Bantam Books, a division of Bantam Doubleday Dell Publishing Group, Inc.

the day. Observations can be a means of validating one teacher's point of view. By checking out an opinion or idea through systematic observation, teachers get a sense of direction in their planning. Such an assessment implies self-assessment. A team that looks at what their program is or isn't accomplishing and how their program may be affecting children values the reflective process and professional level of teamwork that goes with it" (Gordon and Browne, 2007, 204–205).

- *To use a variety of methods, which helps to ensure a fair overview of information.* Using a variety of recording methods, such as those in Chapters 4, 5, and 6, helps to ensure a fair overview of the child. By using a mix of documentation methods, you will achieve a more balanced picture of the child than that achieved by

SOURCE: A.C. Benjamin, "Observations in Early Childhood Classrooms: Advice from the Field," *Young Children* (September 1994). Copyright © 1994 by the National Association for the Education of Young Children.

relying on one type of assessment or type of record. The use of a variety of methods will be discussed again in Chapters 7 and 8. Here it is mentioned to reinforce the reasons for observing young children. Obtaining information in a number of ways will assist you in gaining a more thorough understanding of a child. A teacher's background in typical growth and development is necessary to determine the appropriate methods to use (see Exhibit 2.6).

- *To discover the variability of skills/temperament within each child.* When young children are acquiring new skills, knowledge, and ways of figuring things out, you will see a wide range of competence during the learning process. Children display a wide variety of subtle differences from one time frame to another. Children can demonstrate variability in their personal behaviour even hourly or daily! This is all the more reason to keep an open mind about the discoveries that unfold in any setting with young children. As we discussed earlier in this chapter, such variables as time of day, setting, and a change in routine can produce behaviour that is atypical for a child. Just when you think Rebecca is mastering getting on and off low equipment or chairs independently and with ease, she surprises you by falling repeatedly while trying to climb over the sandbox ledge. Similarly, children react differently to different people, welcoming some with smiles and rejecting others by walking away.

- *To involve parents in the process of discovery.* Parents are interested in your opinion. They want to know how their child gets along with other children, whether he or she is "normal" for his or her age. They want opinions based on knowledge and objective information. They also want to tell you about their child; they are the ones who know their child best. They want to compare observations. "Parents who have become child observers get really excited about what they are discovering. . . . As they share their findings with the teacher and the teacher responds by sharing observations with the parent, their relationship changes dramatically. They become true partners in education and care" (Beaty, 2006, 425).

- *To observe who is happy and having fun and who is sad, upset, lonesome, or frustrated.* Teachers get to know the children in their group very well after a time and form strong relationships with each child. This relationship allows teachers to see subtle yet possibly significant changes in the child. The moods of the child will be important information for the parents or caregiver. These daily observances such as in Exhibit 2.7, Amy and her construction, are important in the shared rearing of children in day care.
- *To observe the environment and make adaptations to it.* Teachers use their skills to evaluate the environment. Behaviour is influenced by the context or surroundings. Observing how children use and respond to their environment is part of a teacher's role. The playroom can be arranged to suit a particular group of children

---

EXHIBIT 2.7   AMY AND HER CONSTRUCTION

Amy applies tape and tissue paper to a sheet of construction paper. We talk about the colours she is using and hold the individual pieces of tissue up so they are backlit by the window.

What are you thinking about?

Amy: "The wonder of the time when I see the colouring rainbow." Pause. "A blue is wiping off the purple."

Why?

Amy: "Because the purple is mean to his sister." Pause. "The red was drying off because of the green blue. The Pokemon (inaudible) but I don't want to watch it. It will burn my tongue."

Brenda: "That's great work Amy!"

Amy: "And I put an extra heart in."

SOURCE: Photos and text courtesy of Jason Avery, Artists at the Centre.

by enlarging the space for floor toys. Better use of books and audiotapes can be encouraged by relocating them to a space away from a busy area. By watching the children interact with their environment, definite patterns may emerge: some parts of the playroom may be heavy traffic areas because several popular activities are occurring side by side. Observing how the children interact with the environment gives teachers ideas for possible changes or adaptations. Basing curriculum materials and equipment on children's interests, strengths, and needs avoids a narrow program focus.

EXHIBIT 2.8   STANDARD FOUR—OCCUPATIONAL STANDARDS FOR CHILD CARE PRACTITIONERS

The ability to use observations to assess children's skills, abilities, interests and needs

Required skills and abilities	Required core knowledge
Child care practitioners are able to:	Child care practitioners know:
a) use observation in an objective, non-judgmental way to assess children's skills, abilities and interests;	1) methods for the observation of children;
b) use observation to evaluate if the environment is appropriate, comfortable for and accepted by the children;	2) methods for recording, sharing and using observations of children; and
c) use observations to plan developmentally appropriate experiences that are respectful of the children's culture; communicate the results of their observations to others in a factual way that also helps to identify goals and/or jointly plan program experiences; and	3) the factors to take into account—such as a child's developmental level, past experiences and cultural background—when interpreting observations.
d) use observation to determine whether program experiences are appropriate useful and accepted by the children, and to modify them if necessary to better meet the children's interests, abilities and developmental needs.	

SOURCE: Doherty, Gillian, "Occupational Standards for Child Care Practitioners", Canadian Child Care Federation, 2003, page 19.

- *To maintain occupational standards.* Occupational standards in Canada have been developed to define acceptable professional behaviour and knowledge. See Exhibit 2.8 for the occupational standards developed for child-care practitioners as they pertain to the use of observations in child-care settings.

Throughout this text, we will revisit these examples of why teachers observe and explore new examples of how observations are used in the playroom. Certain chapters will focus on specific methods and reasons for observing and recording children's behaviour.

How to Observe Children

Once you have determined your purpose or reason for observing, you will need to decide what types of records to use. Your purpose for observing will influence, or even determine, the types of record-keeping methods you use. The observation tools you choose can be designed and developed yourself or can be modified versions of commercial observation tools. This topic is so complex that Chapters 4, 5, and 6 are devoted to exploring the various records used in early childhood education.

How does one go about the actual act of observing?

Spectator Mode

Observing and recording children's behaviour from a detached and uninvolved position allows the teacher to be a spectator to events in the playroom. Some centres are fortunate to have an observation room where a teacher or parent can comfortably observe the playroom without affecting the behaviour in the room. Most clinical and college laboratory school settings have the luxury of such a vantage point, and for staff and parents, the advantages of an observation area are numerous (Chapter 6 covers this topic in detail). Parents often say that it is a treat to stand back and watch their child just for the pleasure of seeing her play without the child knowing that her parents are there watching.

Taking on the spectator role allows you to stand back and look at the big picture. While you may be observing a specific child, other children's behaviour or the teachers' behaviour may also get your attention. Perhaps you did not realize how much time one of the teachers spends cleaning up the sink area, going through cupboards, rearranging artwork, and generally spending time on the environment, rather than with the children. Until you step back, you may not see how much influence one set of behaviours has on others in the room.

Taking the spectator role allows you to focus clearly on a child and to take your time recording your observations. Exhibit 2.9 offers a good example of documentation by a spectator of children's activity.

During a dedicated observation time, the teacher–spectator should not be counted on to assist in the playroom (see Exhibit 2.10). Teachers say that this system, when well communicated, ensures a safer and more adequately supervised room

EXHIBIT 2.9   CURTIS AND A FRIEND

Curtis and a friend set about making a cell phone. They use a small cardboard box, some buttons, and a straw to represent an antenna. Curtis manages assembly, while his friend knows the constituent parts. Their collaboration is fluid and even allows for wide-ranging chit-chat.

When his accomplice leaves, Curtis shifts the newly made toy to his own purpose.

Curtis: "I turned it into a walkie-talkie. There's a speaker here and a button here."

Who will you talk to?

Curtis: "It's just pretend."

Would you teach Justin how to make a walkie-talkie?

Curtis: "Sure. I'm a great teacher."

Being a great teacher and being an A+ student, Justin quickly completes his own walkie-talkie. Without missing a beat, he realizes a flaw. If he has only one walkie-talkie, he will be unable to communicate with his mother.

Justin: "I'm making one for my mom."

He creates another in an instant and delivers it to Mom. He is now free to try out the pretend devices with Curtis from opposite sides of the room. Interference or low batteries mean the two have to get very close to hear each other.

SOURCE: Photos and text courtesy of Jason Avery, Artists at the Centre.

because everyone is clear about who is doing what. Teachers also say that letting the staff and the children know that they will be occupied with observing is a more honest approach. Instead of divided attention and distractions all around, observation can be done with full attention. In this way, misunderstandings—"I thought *you* were watching the drama centre"—are less likely to occur.

Most student-teachers have opportunities to engage in spectator-mode observations since these are usually part of their assignments or field placement expectations. These same students may also comment: "My cooperating teacher doesn't do observation at all! I never see her sitting and writing things down." The student-teacher may not be aware that the more experienced teacher is observing but, in many subtle ways, using a variety of strategies. These methods may be less overt because they are modified to meet the style and purpose of the observer. After years of experience, you too will have developed your own techniques of being an efficient observer of young children.

Participatory Mode

The participatory mode refers to observing while participating in the playroom. This means that, while you are sitting at a cognitive table and assisting the children with a matching game, you are also observing one of the children in the group while making notes. This type of observation requires multitasking! At first, it may seem impossible to observe, write, and still be aware of the children around you, talk to them, and so on. Yet, experienced teachers will tell you that the participatory mode most certainly resembles what occurs daily in the playroom. Being able to function in all these roles, rather than being just the observer–spectator, is the most realistic scenario in early childhood education. Add to that the occasional visitor to the playroom, the telephone ringing, and other day-to-day occurrences, and a teacher may not have the luxury of playing one role at a time.

During your studies in early childhood education, you will have opportunities to observe children in a playroom. Initially, you will likely conduct your observations using the spectator mode. This style allows you to focus on what you are observing without interruptions. However, as part of your education, you will also hopefully be asked to complete certain activities while observing a child for a particular reason. This participatory style will give you an idea of the skills required by an early childhood educator, the challenges that may present themselves, and the opportunities to problem-solve and develop confidence. Beginning to observe and record simultaneously represents quite a learning curve. Writing with descriptive language—paying keen attention to specifics and detail while in a busy playroom—takes concentration. Yet, once you have had the opportunities to practise, observing becomes easier, and increasingly, your observations will become significant in your ability to communicate clearly what you have discovered about the children.

Who Will You Observe?

Your decision to observe a particular child will involve others. Since playroom teachers observe all the children in their groups, they will be good resources. Talk to them. Perhaps a new child has started at the centre, and the staff has not had much time to observe him. You may want to be part of the team by collecting initial information, such as with what toys he or she plays, and with whom he or she is friends. Staff may know which parents might be pleased or reluctant to have you observe their child. Make sure to take into consideration the wishes of the parent/caregiver, and get permission before beginning the process.

Whom would you choose to observe in a playroom setting: the shy, withdrawn child; the rough-and-tumble, active child; or the quiet, independent child?

When to Observe

Timing is a critical element of observation. When will you have time during the day? When is the best time? Are some times better than others?

As with other decisions, the teachers of the preschool room may want input so that you can achieve your intentions as a team. It is a good idea to be clear about whom you will be observing and when. As a team, decide which time of day would be most appropriate. Remember that your observations will be most valuable when conducted during free playtime.

Keep in mind that there will never be an ideal time, so do not wait for it. Learn to create opportunities to observe, and have your notebook nearby so that you are prepared. Then, as you are sitting next to the preschoolers as they rummage through the block centre, piling up brick blocks and laughing as they push them over, you are there, ready to document their play.

Where to Conduct Observations

Finding a place to observe can be as complex as finding the time to observe! If you want to be a spectator, you might want to try a spot away from a child or a group of children. This distance will allow you to focus on the task at hand. Try not to be so far away that you cannot hear the conversations. When you begin your field placement or assignment, first look around the playroom to find the places (more than one) that will work for you.

To start off, make yourself as **unobtrusive** as you can. "The great advantage of observation over other forms of assessment of young children is that it is nonintrusive. It does not interrupt children's play or other activities; indeed, it can often be done without the children even being aware that someone is watching what they're doing." (Billman and Sherman, 2003, 2). You do not want the children to feel that you are staring at them. Children's behaviour often changes when they sense that they are being watched. You could appear to be quite busy without signalling that you are observing. The main idea is to be part of the normal rhythm of the room. If you are in a centre where observation is an integral part of daily life, then your observation will not be an extraordinary event and will probably go unnoticed by the children.

What if one or more curious children do approach you to ask what you are doing? What do you do? Try not to make eye contact, answer their questions very briefly, and tell them you will be able to play with them when you are finished. Give them suggestions for things to do until you are ready to join them. Ask for help from your team members. They'll be happy to assist! If all else fails—especially if you are working with toddlers—put aside your materials and try again later.

What to Observe

What will you observe? Everything the child is doing? That sounds easy enough, but is it? If you said, "I want to see with whom Kuldip plays," your observations would be straightforward, as it is easy to jot down who Kuldip's playmates were during the day.

Suppose, however, that you wanted to record *how* she played or state your opinion as to *why* she behaved as she did. Then you would need to determine whether what you observed was actually behaviour or whether you inferred certain characteristics or internal conditions. You would use clear, descriptive language to record your observations of how Kuldip carefully attached one of the cars to another. Then, as she looked up and smiled, you might make some interpretations about how she felt. Watching her manipulate the tiny cars and talk to her friends at the same time, you might also be able to comment on her fine motor and communication skills.

PHOTO: Courtesy of Eglinton Public School.

What you are learning about observation has you already looking at children, and maybe everyday events, in a different way. These new skills will help you apply what you may be learning in other courses, such as child development and curriculum development. Integrating your knowledge with emerging observation skills will contribute to your growing sense of confidence and professionalism.

Challenges to Effective Observation

Before continuing, we need to confront the fact that some teachers do *not* systematically observe and record children's behaviour. Why? Teachers and student-teachers have identified some of the challenges to systematic observation. The following are some of the challenges indicated. Please note the problem solving suggestions under the caption "Problem Solving and Teamwork" on page 62.

The Time Challenge

In theory, observation appears to be invaluable—an essential process to ensure a quality program. In reality, it takes time to record the observations of young children's busy activity. Lack of time is the main reason given for not documenting observations. Many teachers say that the role of an observer in the classroom competes with other roles, such as curriculum planner, administrator; liaison person with parents, visitors, and volunteers; room supervisor; and, most importantly, caregiver to the children. Each of these roles takes time and effort. Reflective observation may occur simultaneously as the teacher facilitates play in the dramatic centre or assists a child struggling with a puzzle. Finding time to record these observations before they are forgotten, however, requires an even greater time commitment.

Almost every issue revolves around time; how *best* to utilize time to serve the interests of the children. The issue is making observation a priority and then making sure that time is found to do it. Observation should be seen not as an alternative activity but as one that needs to be included as part of best practices. In some centres, program time is given to teachers to document their observations. However, if documenting the information at a later time is only an occasional event, rather than a systematic process, it really does not represent best practices.

Other Challenges

Here are further challenges to conducting observations in the playroom:

- *Lack of teamwork.* In order to observe and record children's behaviour within a busy schedule, coworkers need to determine who will conduct observations in the daily program. Responsibilities need to be identified, rotated, or shared. If those responsibilities are shared unequally, then problems may result within the team. Perhaps some teachers fail to see the relevance of observing or do not understand how the observations will benefit the child. If some teachers document observations while others do not, these inconsistent staff practices may be noticed by parents as a concern. There are many other situations that develop in relation to the observation process. Can you think of others that impact on the lack of teamwork in any playroom or centre?
- *Not part of philosophy or practice of the setting.* Almost all child-care settings practise some methods of observation. It may be, however, that the observations are expressed as comments of the day. They are made casually, shared informally, and seen more as everyday occurrences than as observations; for example, "He slept for two hours today," or "She didn't seem herself today—she hardly ate any lunch." These comments, although valid information, are feedback about the routines of a child's day. They do not represent a systematic process of observing and recording children's behaviour. How can you find out if a centre/organization has developed a philosophy or practices regarding the observation of children?
- *Challenges of everyday events.* Teachers are busy people! They may plan to observe each day, but because a coworker left early, or the Humane Society representative came in to show animals to the children, or it was Sammy's birthday, the observations may not get documented. Special events and certain holiday times of the year usually preclude systematic observation. Early childhood teachers say that these events require a dedicated focus, and they are too busy to observe and record. Yet, it is often these events that yield the most surprising discoveries about children.
- *Unfamiliarity or lack of training.* Some teachers and student-teachers say that being unfamiliar with observation methods prevents them from starting or continuing to observe. They feel that they may be doing it wrong or are not sure what is expected. If a person feels that writing is not one of his or her strengths, then

that person may be reluctant to begin the process let alone share his or her observations. How a teacher/student-teacher feels about his or her writing skills has a bearing on the willingness to document and share information with families.

Problem Solving and Teamwork

Perhaps you will encounter these or other challenges to conducting observations of the children in your care. These challenges, however, can be overcome with a willingness to resolve the issues, good communication skills, a sense of humour, flexibility, and a good grasp of what can be realistically accomplished! Being willing to work together as a team to develop skills and confidence will ensure steady growth personally and professionally. Trusting yourself and others to want to work for the common good of the children is the best place to start.

Although this text offers no magic answers or a list of all-inclusive strategies, here are some suggestions to begin the problem-solving process with your team:

- *Include the families.* Parents want to know what their children are doing at the centre and appreciate information, cooperation and sharing in decision making. They like to know that they can contribute as well. Find ways to encourage parents to become part of the documentation process.
- *Examine the schedule.* Will slotting someone in to cover for 15 minutes a day of observation be realistic? When team teaching, who will facilitate group time and who will observe? How can the day be made to accommodate reflective observation? As a student-teacher, you are in an ideal role to be able to assist teachers in their construction of the daily observation process.
- *Work out a plan to observe.* Teachers could identify *observation time* as a discussion item for the staff meeting agenda to discuss the strategies involved in developing a plan of observation. Being proactive rather than reactive will create new opportunities and reasons to observe.
- *Think about and discuss the tangible benefits of observation.* What are the benefits to the children, families, teachers, and the community? How can these benefits be communicated to the parents and families of the children in the centre as well as the community?
- *Share your interest.* Your enthusiasm for your role as teacher-observer can be communicated to your colleagues and other professionals. Meet with parents and colleagues to discuss ways in which the observation process can further illustrate the exciting growth and development of the children in your care.
- *Communicate!* Discuss your schedule, your professional goals, your philosophy, your values, your talents, and the areas in which you lack skills. By acting professionally, monitoring your own behaviour, and clearly expressing your personal and professional goals, it is possible to lay the groundwork that is necessary for a group of people to work as a team. You could start by saying, "I'd really like to find more time to observe some of the children." Find people who agree with you and are willing to work out possible ways for you to achieve your goal.

Ways in which directors/supervisors can promote and support systematic observations are as follows:
- Set aside time for weekly, biweekly, or monthly staff meetings.
- Ensure that each staff member comes to the meeting prepared to discuss individual children, the group, and the curriculum and shares this information with the supervisor/director.
- Discuss time management and staff scheduling to ensure everyone has adequate time to observe individual children or groups of children.

- *Research!* Find effective ways that others are using observation to create exciting programming or document the progress of individual children. Check out the websites of local centres/programs or national organizations. What are ECEs in other countries doing to document the activity of the children in their care?
- *Observation can be made a priority.* This can be done at the supervisory or administrative level in the child-care setting. Through a mission statement or centre policies, the philosophy of the centre is defined and will state as goals or specific **pedagogy** what role observation has in the program. There are many ways in which directors or supervisors can promote and support systematic observations (see Exhibit 2.11). Instead of waiting for the professional responsibility of a teacher, however, we need to motivate ourselves.

Making the Best of Special Moments

Whether you are a student-teacher or a teacher, you will get to know the children in your group and begin to observe the daily changes in their growth and development. Experienced teachers will take advantage of every opportunity to make the best of special moments. They will make a special effort to record developmental milestones such as first steps, first words, learning to use the potty, and first cuts with scissors. They will document these milestones for the parents and for themselves. Special times can be recorded with photographs and an album prepared for all the children and families to see. Centre staff can document a child's collaborative efforts on a particular group project. Teachers may spend time with a child documenting the child's artwork for later inclusion into a portfolio. A teacher may, like the example in Exhibit 2.12, provide special creative opportunities for children to spark interest and explore new experiences.

Probably the most important documentation kept on young children are records of the so-called ordinary things that occur throughout the day. These recorded events make the invisible visible; through the observations, parents can "see" the behaviours or circumstances that they normally would not see during the day.

EXHIBIT 2.12   SOPHIE PAINTS HERSELF

A teacher at the centre has provided Sophie with a photograph of herself at the easel and has pointed out the variety of skin-coloured paints available. Sophie begins with a faint oval and places a bold stroke for her mouth about a third from the bottom using the same tan colour.

Sophie paints an oval symbol for an eye and then spends a bit more time trying to create eyelashes.

She switches to yellow and at either side of her figure places what she refers to as fingers.

This is followed by a dress.

During this time Sophie has worked only from her memory of what a portrait should be. Distractions in the room threaten to end the session and she moves to leave, only to glance at the photo and return to add teeth.

Another check reveals the need for hair. It is only after the addition of legs to the figure that Sophie can at last join the others in play.

SOURCE: Photo and text courtesy of Jason Avery, Artists at the Centre.

Perhaps it is a short record of how their child helped another child to stop crying on the playground. Parents love to hear how their child assisted the teacher or helped peers; it reaffirms to parents that they are doing a good job of parenting. Your observations will carry the visibility of actions to the parents; family members will themselves interpret how they feel or think about the content of the observation. Having records of these important events reminds us all that what children say and do are valued and important.

Consent and Confidentiality

As a professional in any child-care setting, you need to be well aware of the subject of consent and confidentiality. Compliance with the college policies and those of the child-care setting you will be attending is mandatory.

As well, each province and territory, through the appropriate government ministry, sets out standards and guidelines regarding consent and confidentiality. These recommendations suggest a system for exchanging information between the parents/guardians and the centre. "Records are covered by legislation dealing with privacy and an individual's access to information. A record is defined as almost any form of information, including letters, daily logs, case notes, memos, drawings, videotapes and computer files. Therefore, a record includes all agency records, from the most informal to the most formal" (Valentino 14). Each agency's or organization's policies and procedures are guided by this legislation and usually noted in their parents' manual or office documents. In addition, federal legislation, such as the *Freedom of Information Act* and the *Bill of Rights,* must be considered, as this legislation guarantees confidentiality and the rights of the individual. Each licensed child-care setting must follow the advisories but may interpret how the consent forms it uses will be phrased.

Centres will have separate consent forms for each child (see Exhibit 2.13).

Some children, if they are enrolled in two different programs, will have specific consent forms, as in Exhibit 2.14. The consent form gives the centre permission to receive and transmit information from one centre to the other.

Whether you are a student-teacher or a new teacher, you should be made fully aware of the centre's policies and procedures before you begin your new position. You need to be advised as to what information you may access and what records and files are strictly confidential. If this information is not forthcoming, it is your responsibility to ask so that you are apprised of the policies and procedures.

EXHIBIT 2.13   AUTHORIZATION FOR RELEASE OF INFORMATION

This form may be used to exchange information when the child is attending more than one program. Please complete and sign this permission form to allow this exchange of information.

I/We give permission to ABC Nursery School and Canadiana Public School to exchange information about my child. This consent form covers the time period from September 7, 1999, to June 20, 2000.

_____   _____
Name of Child   Date of Birth

_____   _____
Signature of Parent/Guardian   Date

_____
Witness

EXHIBIT 2.14 **AUTHORIZATION FOR EXCHANGE OF INFORMATION**

This form authorizes a professional from the child-care centre to obtain information on a child.

I/We hereby authorize ABC Nursery School through its representative

_____

(Supervisor/Director)

from any educational, social, and/or medical authority on

_____   _____

Surname   Given Names

I/We hereby further authorize ABC Nursery School to convey to any educational, social, and/or medical authority information on

_____   _____

Signature of Parent/Guardian   Date

_____

Witness

Office Files and Working Files

Every licensed setting maintains its records according to a set of ministry expectations and centre policies unique to that centre. Many centres have what they refer to as their office files and their working files. The office files are kept in the main office in a secure, locked filing cabinet. Typically, office files can contain such information as medical records, referral forms, intake information, and financial records. Student-teachers do not have access to these files—only the supervisor/director and/or designated staff members have this access. Parents have access *only* to their child's file.

Working File: Portfolio

A working file could be a folder or portfolio that is kept for each child. This file is not an actual file but a folder containing a variety of information. The working file may have one piece of paper in it or dozens, but access to it is generally not restricted. The information could refer to areas of program focus or the interests and skills of the child. The portfolio could contain artwork, photos, and observations. However, just because this information is not stamped "confidential" does not mean that it is left out for all to see. On the contrary, every effort should be made to keep portfolios or any kinds of records on a child within the child's folder and to keep the folders in a designated area. This practice respects the privacy of individuals and limits the possibility of papers going astray. Portfolios will be explored extensively in Chapter 7.

To ensure that parents and guardians are aware of any observations you may complete on their child while you are a student-teacher, an introductory letter may be given stating your name, the name(s) of your instructor(s), and the purpose of the observations. This letter could be shared with the centre supervisor, involved staff, and the parents. Not all settings will require a letter in their exchange of information procedures, but most parents like to know who is working with their child and what information on their child is exchanged. Parents are usually aware of the student-teachers and appreciate their contribution to their child's experiences. The letter offers an opportunity for the student teacher to interact personally with parents and try a new role. See Exhibit 2.15 for an example of a permission letter.

Be sure to explain to parents/caregivers that your observations are part of your studies. If they would like to read your observations, have your professor read them over first and give you feedback. Perhaps some changes may be required to avoid misunderstandings. The supervisor or teachers of the centre, knowing the parents as well as the children, will also be able to offer the benefit of their experience regarding the wording of your observations. You will want to present your information as accurately and professionally as possible. Getting input from others will be an excellent

EXHIBIT 2.15   PERMISSION LETTER

Dear Parent:

The students of Northern College are required to complete a series of observations on children for my course, First-Year Early Childhood Education. The purpose of the observations is to familiarize the students with the process of gathering objective information and interpreting that data in a mean-ingful way. This requirement is part of the students' training in the field of early childhood education.

On behalf of the Early Childhood Education Department of Northern College and our student, _____, I would like to request your permission to have your child participate in these observations.

If you have any questions, please do not hesitate to call me at the college at 202-567-6789.

Thank you for your support and cooperation.

Sincerely,
A. Member
Early Childhood Education Department
Northern College

learning experience as well. Remember *never* to transmit written information to parents without the approval of the early childhood educator or supervisor in charge. Again, be aware of the agency's policies and procedures regarding consent and confidentiality.

Summary

Behaviour is what can be observed. This chapter defined the systematic process of those observations by separating behaviour from internal conditions and characteristics. In so doing, you will understand how this process is linked to the separation of objective observations and personal interpretations. Making decisions regarding how, why, what, who, when, and where to observe are essential to the appropriate practice of conducting observations. The discussion of the importance of consent and confidentiality included various authorizations necessary in sharing information.

PROFESSIONAL REFLECTIONS

I can remember how, as a child, I enjoyed watching one of my aunts paint landscapes. I used to sit close by her, watching in fascination as she mixed paint colours from her palette and spread them in exciting compositions across her canvass. Years later in my life, I recall phoning her to announce that I was taking a watercolour class, and I asked if she could offer me some tips. She advised that I should spend time observing the colours of the sky and the vibrant colours of nature. At first I thought this would be easy enough until I discovered the shades and hues of nature's colours are endless. My aunt helped me look at the world with a new perspective.

Observing young children in my professional practice evolved in a similar fashion. As a student of early childhood education, I have vivid memories of my instructors encouraging me to observe young children in much the same way that my aunt encouraged me. They helped me appreciate that a child walking across a room did not do so simply by placing one foot in front of the other. Rather, he/she might be tiptoeing, skipping, pausing to reach for a book or crouching to look under a table, all the while making his/her way across a room. It was difficult for me at first to "tune in" to the diverse mannerisms of the children I observed, let alone keep note of their actions. Yet, now I understand how invaluable it was for me to develop my observational skills. I value this ability as it is one of the most important tools an early childhood educator can rely on to ensure the implementation of a quality curriculum.

–Claude Painter
Langara College

KEY TERMS

ambiguous words	monitor	stimuli
labelling	pedagogy	unobtrusive

DISCUSSION QUESTIONS

1. What are the differences among behaviour, internal conditions, and characteristics? Why has this chapter taken such care to point out the differences between them?
2. Why is it important to think through the initial decisions of what, why, when, where, and how to observe?
3. What are some of the challenges to conducting observation and some possible solutions that are relevant to your current experiences?
4. Why are the procedures for obtaining consent from parents important in the field of early childhood education? What role do these procedures play in the observation process?

ADDITIONAL READINGS

Elliot, Barbara. *Measuring Performance: The Early Childhood Educator in Practice*. Albany, NY: Delmar Learning, 2002.

This text is, for the most part, a self-assessment tool that is organized into sections containing vital competencies basic to the development of those who care for young children. Although this text is designed for this purpose, it also serves as a reminder that observation is not only essential in recording the behaviours of children as well as those of the caregivers of those children. There is a preface commentary on brain research, and the analysis of the complex role of the early childhood educator is an interesting read.

Gestwicki, Carol, and Jane Bertrand. *Essentials of Early Childhood Education*. 3rd Can. ed. Toronto: Thomson Nelson, 2008.

An essential text for anyone considering the field of early childhood education, especially the research updates from previous editions on quality care. The text is both informative and introspective so readers will clearly understand the need for careful professional preparation for this field.

Goleman, Daniel. *The Nature of Emotional Intelligence*. New York: Bantam Books, 1995.

This book is for anyone who is interested in how temperament, personality, character, and morality evolve and affect life's lessons and, ultimately, the society in which we live. If the book raises more questions than it answers, perhaps it has succeeded in its purpose—to get us to think about how we have learned life's lessons and how our early experiences may form the blueprint for our future emotional life.

Wilson, Kim. Canadian Child Care Federation. "To Speak, Participate and Decide: The Child's Right to be Heard." *Interaction* 20.3 (2006).

The entire edition is devoted to the topic of a child's right to be heard. Listening to children is a main focus of this text. In this article, active listening is about valuing a child's expression, contributing to their self-esteem, and role-modelling caring and respect. Kim Wilson's article stresses the importance of listening as a human right, a responsibility of adults, and a way to nurture citizenship.

Chapter Three

◆ **3** ◆

PREPARING TO OBSERVE AND RECORD

PHOTO: Courtesy of Alwynn Pinard

Two first-year early childhood education students are loading their books and papers into their backpacks. Their first class of the day is Developing Observation Skills. They've been in class for an hour; for the second hour of class, the instructor has directed them to the lab school observation deck to conduct their first observations of children. "What are we supposed to be doing? I don't get it," says Daniel.

"I don't know for sure, but we're going down to the lab school to watch the children," replies Janelle. "I don't know what we're going to do *exactly*—she said we'd be writing down what we see the children doing. Sounds easy to me."

Later on, after the class has had the opportunity to try two one-minute observations and one five-minute observation, the students gather together to share their first attempts with the instructor and one another. The instructor asks, "What did you learn about your observations today? I'm not looking for any particular answer. Just throw out ideas about what you just experienced." The following are some of the comments:

- "I couldn't believe what a child does in the span of a few minutes!"
- "There was so much going on, I didn't know what to write down."
- "When I looked down to write and then looked up again, my child had moved from his chair to the water table, and I never saw him go!"
- "What are we supposed to do with these observations now? I can't read mine!"
- "I couldn't think of the right words. I didn't know what to call some of the toys they play with, and I couldn't think of words fast enough to describe what she was doing."

As the discussion continued and students tried to read what they had hurriedly written down, they commented on how much they had actually recorded. If more than one student had watched the same child, they compared observations. They talked about how interesting it was that when three people had observed the same child, although they all recorded some similar things, each person picked up on something that the others had not. Janelle asked, "How do you know what's important to write and what isn't? Daniel noticed that the boy scratched his arm a lot. I never saw that. Compared with Daniel, I hardly have anything written down. I'm never going to get this!"

Overview

The content in Chapters 1 and 2 laid the groundwork for understanding the actual observation process. Chapter 1 discussed the importance and value of observation in any child-care setting. Chapter 2 defined the systematic process of observation and key concepts.

Chapter 3 is about getting started. It is primarily about developing special observation skills that are critical to the role of teacher–observer and highlighting how your language will adapt during this process. This chapter examines how language usage, combined with observation skills, produces knowledge about young children. What has been observed, and what will be recorded? Whether your documentation represents a few lines that accompany photographs or comments attached to a chart or a narrative such as an Anecdotal Observation, there must be congruence between what was observed and what is recorded. The process of observing and recording children's behaviour is one of discovery. The most important discovery is what you learn about children. However, while documenting what is observed you will also begin to understand how writing is a process of discovering your *own* thoughts.

This chapter will be most effective when used in conjunction with opportunities to observe. These opportunities to practise and apply your knowledge will help you to grow in skills and confidence. It takes time to develop your own observing/recording style. As you progress, compare your first efforts with other later observations. Doing so will allow you to see how your skills and abilities have improved. Learning how to observe and record your observations comes with time and practice. Over time each person's observations become as unique as their fingerprints. In this chapter, we will begin to understand the process of knowing what to write and finding the right words to say it.

After reading this chapter, you should be able to:

- Adapt your language to the new role of teacher–observer.
- Recognize that writing is an acquired skill as well as a process of discovering your thoughts.
- Develop an awareness of common forms of judgmental error or bias.
- Write detailed, descriptive observations using action verbs, adverbs, and adjectives.
- Compose a physical description of a child.
- Become familiar with basic guidelines associated with the observation process.

Getting Started

Adapting Language in a New Role

I remember, as a child, watching my father read the newspaper. I would point to a word and ask, "What does that say?" When he told me, I would look at the squiggles on the page and think that he must be magic in order to read. I thought I would never learn how. When I began to read, and to write, I too mastered the "magic" of squiggles. More importantly, I gained confidence in my ability to do so.

In your role as a teacher–observer of young children, you will become reacquainted with language usage: verbs, adverbs, nouns, and adjectives; and begin to recognize the importance of oral and written communication skills in the field of early childhood. Your confidence, too, will develop as your documentation improves.

Students report that they can actually see an improvement in their written skills, which gives them another benchmark for their success besides tests and assignments. Instead of reproducing existing knowledge in the form of assignments or tests, students begin to develop a new set of skills starting with a blank page!

Remember our definition of observation?

> *Observation is a systematic process of watching and listening to children and recording their behaviour in a meaningful way for future use.*

Recording their behaviour in a meaningful way implies that this information will be accessible, useful, and written in a clear and descriptive manner to be shared with others. So, let's take a look at adapting our language in our written work so that it is meaningful in the new teacher–observer role.

Adapting Your Communication Style in Child Care

Adapting your language with children will represent a shift in your communication style. Instead of the casual conversations you engage in with peers, you have to think through not only what you are going to say to children but also how you will say it. Instead of saying, "Hey, you guys, stop throwing sand on the floor," you will need to use the children's names rather than slang and state your expectations positively: "Aisha and Maribeth, let's keep the sand in the sandbox. Sand is not for throwing. We can throw the beanbags and balls instead when we get outside." Adapting your language and monitoring your messages is a critical part of developing your communication skills in child care.

Finding the words children understand challenges us to look beyond the words we normally use, to rethink concepts, and to reframe them in words children can relate to. This doesn't mean talking down to children or using baby talk: it means talking to children differently than you talk to your peers. For

SOURCE: Courtesy of Steve Nease

example, if you tell a toddler "Bring that over here," you might get a blank stare. Why? Children need concrete descriptions. Because toddlers don't understand what "that" refers to or where "here" is, rephrasing the sentence using concrete descriptors will clearly convey what is expected. "Joey, bring me the ball." Another example to illustrate how understanding was achieved through rephrasing took place in a kindergarten setting. When asked if a young girl could draw a picture of a woman, she replied, "No." When the same request was made, but with one different word, "Can you draw a picture of your mommy?" the girl responded with a smile and began to draw immediately. Adapting language or rephrasing using concrete words or descriptors makes a big difference in the process of communication with young children.

What does this adaptation of language in the playroom have to do with observation? Being aware of language usage with young children, we communicate using key words that are descriptive yet concise. When we conduct observations, we also use key words and descriptive words and try to focus on what behaviour is important to record. Our adaptation of language in the playroom influences us as we look for, listen to, and record information that is meaningful. We begin to use key words with children, and we write down key words when observing them. In the opening scenario of this chapter, one of the students' comments was, "There was so much going on, I didn't know what to write down." As we will see in this chapter, the more opportunities you have to record your observations, the more you will understand how the process of writing helps to discover your thoughts. For example, Danielle's rough notes demonstrate what she recorded during her observation. When she had time to copy her rough notes and reflect on what she had written, she was able to clarify the meaning.

Danielle's reflection on her own work transformed her rough notes that only she could read into a good copy that was easy for others to read and understand. Repetition and practice allow us to become better at not only knowing what to write down, but also using key words to express our thoughts. The more you practise, the more efficient you will become at writing down what you have observed. See Figures 3.1A and 3.1B for samples of Danielle's notes.

Developing Vocabulary

Learning new words is the process of developing a ***vocabulary.*** Children, as well as adults, have a larger passive vocabulary than an active vocabulary. That simply means that we understand and know more words than we generally use on a daily basis. Documenting children's behaviour (what we see and hear) means using words in a descriptive way that we may be unaccustomed to using. A conscious effort must be made to adapt the way we use language, and therefore encourages us to broaden our active vocabulary in our role as educator. Adapting our communication style means learning the definition of new words and how to use these words appropriately in the early childhood profession.

Learning new early childhood topics includes learning new vocabulary. Check out the "Key Terms" at the end of each chapter and the glossary at the back of this text if you find words that are unfamiliar. Developing a new, active vocabulary may not come easy, but it is worth every effort!

Using Descriptive Language

Let's begin with the very simple building blocks of language: verbs, adverbs, nouns, and adjectives. Here's where we can begin to build strong images starting with ordinary words such as "walk" and "talk":

- Alternative verbs for walk: amble, stroll, saunter, clomp, stomp, march, strut, stride, toddle
- Alternative verbs for talk: whisper, state, declare, speak, converse, utter, shout, murmur

Each alternative word creates a different mental image—think of the difference between "limping" and "marching." **Verbs** are action words. Sometimes we can get enough action out of a word that we don't need any other words to get our meaning across. However, if we need to qualify a verb further, **adverbs** are very handy. Many adverbs in the English language end in "ly." Some examples are hastily, happily, and brilliantly. These words add meaning to the action, for example: "walked heavily," or lightly or quickly. Adverbs make the action come alive to help others see what you have seen. For example:

- Adverbs for walk: slowly, heavily, carefully, briskly
- Adverbs for talk: slowly, sharply, haltingly, surely

Using imaginative and descriptive language gives us new words and the ability to further our understanding. **Adjectives** are words that qualify nouns. *Nouns* are words that name a person, place, object, or idea. Young children begin learning language word by word, and a baby's first word is usually a noun. Adjectives state the attributes or qualities of a noun; for example: big, yellow, fuzzy. Adjectives perform the same function with nouns that adverbs do with verbs. Adjectives clarify what we are talking about. Instead of just a chair, we could have

- a highchair, a small chair, a lounge chair, a rocking chair, a folding chair.

  Instead of a puzzle, we could have

- a single-insert puzzle, a floor puzzle, a DLM puzzle, or a multiple-insert puzzle.

A clear description of an item (noun and adjective) helps illustrate for the reader what the child sat on or played with. This object could have a direct influence on the child's behaviour. For example, if four-year-old Nadia takes a 5-piece, single-insert puzzle off the shelf, sits down, and begins taking it apart, she will probably have no difficulty in putting it back together. But if she takes a 35-piece, multiple-insert puzzle off the shelf, you will likely see a different set of behaviours. Defining the kind of puzzle gives us clues and helps us to understand Nadia's difficulty—or lack of difficulty—with the puzzle. These adjectives used to describe materials are not idle words. They serve to clarify for the reader a child's response to materials in the environment. Do you see why using descriptive language is important to the process of documenting what children do or say? Items in the environment influence the activity of young children. Puzzles without all the pieces, torn books, and broken toys influence children's behaviour. In using descriptive words such as "torn" and "broken," clear images are conveyed, helping the reader to understand the consequent behaviour of a child; for example: "He picked up the torn book and quickly placed it back on the shelf."

Recording Observations: Calling out the Game

A single word in itself may not be significant, but a combination of several words can create such a strong image that the reader can clearly imagine the action. Hockey fans who listened to hockey games on the radio will tell you that, based on a commentator's (like Foster Hewitt's) descriptions, they could see Maurice Richard or Teeder Kennedy flying through the opposition to score the winning goal. Through descriptions of the play, listeners could visualize the game unfolding, cheering for their heroes and groaning at the goal scored against them. If you knew the game of hockey and could imagine the rink and the players, all you needed was the voice coming out of the radio and the game was before you.

Putting the words on paper describing children's behaviour is in a sense like calling out the game. If you write the "play" down clearly enough, the reader will be able to "see" what you what you wrote and hear what was said through the dialogue included. Look at this example:

> Marco sat quietly on the carpet with his back to the others in the play-
> room. He sat with legs crossed in front of him. His elbows rested on
> his knees with his hands cradling his head. He leaned forward slightly
> and stared at the puzzle on the floor directly in front of him.

Descriptions like this reveal not only what Marco was doing but, more importantly, the quality of his actions. He wasn't just sitting on the carpet. The adverbs used, such as "quietly" and "slightly," provide more detail, indicating how Marco was sitting. From this brief description, you can perhaps get a sense of what feelings his posture suggested. Maybe he was deep in thought or perhaps he was just tired. All of the words combine together to describe his behaviour. This description, in turn, helps us to make inferences about how Marco was feeling.

Semantics and Pragmatics

Before children attend Grade 1, they have already acquired the grammar, semantics, and pragmatics of their first language. If children have been in daycare, nursery school, or private home care, early childhood educators have been their first teachers along with parents/caregivers and other family members. "The quality of adult–child interactions is ***the*** most single important influence on the child's language development" (Winzer 285).

Semantics is concerned with the meaning of words. While words are learned, so, too, are other forms of communication that often accompany these words: tone of voice, facial expression, and body language. Conversations with people we know tend to be full of body language, sounds, intonations, facial expressions, and code words that have meaning.

To clarify the meaning of the semantics here is an example: the word "Mummy." It is one of the first words a very young child learns and says. Yet, look at the powerful meanings in that one word:

- "Mummy!" Translated: "I want the person who feeds me."
- "Mummy?" Translated: "I'm in my room. Where are you?"
- "Mummmyyyy!" Translated: "I miss you and I want to go home!"

That one word is so powerful, but by itself it is just a word. The tone, strength, and meaning of the word is what is important. Family members, like teachers of young children, tune in to the semantics or meaning of the child's limited vocabulary. Documenting the meaning behind the word is necessary in order for the observation to convey the appropriate meaning. This process of learning and documenting language requires effort and active participation. As we will see in later chapters, the reciprocal nature of adult–child communication can also be the catalyst in uncovering what we may learn from observing young children.

Social interactions give rise to the use of language in a social context—**pragmatics.**

It is in social settings that the child learns how she or he will use language as a means of communicating socially with others. "Hi" and "Bye" are two of the earliest forms of social communication that families and educators model for young children. Waving bye-bye and saying the words convey a strong social message. Greeting people with a "Hi" uses language as a social conveyance. For children to achieve understanding and use of language, there must be a high degree of adult participation and understanding of the language-learning process. This process is important to capture with documentation as noted in Exhibit 3.1.

How can you describe the activity of nonverbal toddlers? Their nonverbal behaviours will influence how you observe and record their activity. Exhibit 3.1 demonstrates one of the ways teachers Brenda and Marija have documented the activity of toddlers.

From these two examples you can readily see that the teachers were able to utilize photographs and written documentation to convey meaning in the toddler's social, yet nonverbal, activity. As well, they also documented the role of the parent and that of the teacher.

EXHIBIT 3.1 DEVELOPING SOCIAL PLAY SKILLS

TOGETHER FOR FAMILIES

Initially engaged in separate activities, Matthew (1yr 10m) and Peter (2yr 6m) experience a non-verbal social interaction. Using the can lid activity as a vehicle, they work toward further developing their sharing and turn-taking skills; Matthew, Peter, and Brenda, the Early Years Facilitator, take turns putting the can lids into the slot, as Peter's mum watches.

Child Development

- Physical, Intellectual, Emotional—Turning, wrist movement, lining up the lid, and fitting it through the hole
- Eye-hand Co-ordination
- Ability to attend
- Social/Emotional development, ability to share and take turns

(continued)

Parent/Teacher/Environmental Influences

- Active participation of teacher and parent
- Verbal encouragement
- Environment provides opportunity for social interaction

SOURCE: Today's Family/Ontario Early Years Program/Together for Families

Getting Started: Writing Your Observations

Writing is a complex process. Even writing a simple shopping list requires a series of steps. What are the steps?

1. Deciding what you need at the store—your purpose.
2. Making a list—format.
3. Writing the items down—documentation.
4. Checking with others—teamwork.
5. Remembering to use the list! Observations are meaningful only when they are used!

The purpose of this brief, well-used example is to demonstrate that even a shopping list isn't simple. There are steps in the process of this familiar task. Writing observations in a clear, descriptive narrative relies on similar steps:

- determining the purpose
- choosing a format/method
- recording your observations
- consulting with others

This basic comparison illustrates the steps in writing that are required no matter how simple the task. This chapter will assist you in clarifying the process of recording the activity of young children and assist you in getting started writing observations.

Writing Observations

Writing observations requires a unique style of writing. It is not like writing an essay or a term paper where you choose a topic, and then follow the tried-and-true stages of successful essay writing. Many books, courses, and workshops exist for people who are interested in writing a successful essay, a good business report, a technical manual, a romance novel, or a short story. Yet, there are few resources available to guide early childhood educators in developing the appropriate writing skills needed for documentation, reports, and forms typical of the child-care field. This textbook attempts to address this need.

Rough Notes

How is note taking in class similar to writing rough notes of observations? The process is similar because you are simultaneously listening and watching (electronic presentation/overheads/chalk notes) while you are taking notes. In this way, taking rough notes for playroom observations are similar to class notes. You are multitasking: watching, listening, and recording. No wonder this skill does not come easily!

Class notes represent your efforts to record important academic information. While taking class notes you have also learned shortcuts, how to highlight certain terms and organize them within your notes. During lectures, students typically receive hints about headings, grouping of information, examples to illustrate main points—cues that are helpful when assimilating new information.

When writing observations as rough notes, there are no such guides (what to write) or cues (how to write it). There is no one to instruct and suggest at the time. You have to rely on yourself to observe and record, and to decide what is relevant to document and what is not. A student wrote: "When I wrote my good notes from my rough notes, I recalled the whole observation and also things that I had not written down originally, such as small things like the expression on the child's face; it all came back to me as I was rewriting."

The first few observations engender uncertainty—uncertainty of what to look for and what to write. With guidance and opportunities to observe, write, and rewrite, students gain skills. As one student wrote, "I found writing from rough notes to good copy very rewarding, as I found that when doing the good copy I had missed some of the interesting things I saw the child do. Observing made me become aware of looking at what a child does in her play at the centre. Observation is an eye opener!"

As mentioned earlier, writing observations is more than a skill; it is a process of discovering thoughts. Exhibit 3.2 offers an example of how a student used her rough notes to reproduce their thoughts into observations that are meaningful and easily read.

Writing with Confidence

Good writing takes time, reflection, the ability to analyze and critique; the willingness to redo what has already been done, and the courage to self-evaluate. For some students, writing is not a comfortable or desirable exercise. Writing may not engender confidence because of a history of previous struggles.

Students in a continuing education night class suggested that a lack of confidence was a bigger issue for some than the actual writing process: "I found it to be very difficult. I wasn't sure how to make it all make sense without dragging my sentences out for too long. I wasn't too certain what was expected. This was my first paper in many years so I agonized whether I was doing it right or not."

"Doing it right" or "not sure what is expected" is a typical concern for students returning to a school environment. Perhaps students are concerned that,

EXHIBIT 3.2 EXAMPLE OF ROUGH NOTES AND THE GOOD COPY

Rough Notes – Part 1

1:40 Moved to circle area — 1 chair

Tried to sit on chair w 2 friends one fell off + cried stood up and watched her cry while teacher helped cryer.

Picks up toys from floor held toy cat undr left arm toy Barbie in left hand and walked around room.

Sat on edge of chair looked all around room

twisted doll leg with right finger tips

yawned.

Good Copy - Part 2

Running Notes

Child's Name: Jane   D.O.B.: March 2004   Age: 2½ years

Observer: Sandra Weddum   Date: Thursday, October 19, 2006

Time	Observations	Comments
1:40	Jane wandered to circle area. There is only one chair (meant for the teacher). Jane tries to sit on it with two friends. One friend falls off the chair and begins to cry. Jane stands up and looks down at her friend and watches as the teacher comforted her.	Interest in friend's folly.
1:45	Jane glances around the room and runs to the cutting table where a toy Barbie and stuffed kitten are on the floor. She picks them up with her right hand and tucks the kitten under her left arm. She holds the Barbie by the hair, in her left hand. Again Jane looks around the room. Jane edges over to a chair and perches on its edge. She continues to look around the room as she twists the Barbie's hair with her right fingertips. Jane grasps the seat of the chair with her left hand.	Appears to have attachment to toys. Seems interested in her surroundings. Perhaps looking for something. Involvement with others?

SOURCE: Courtesy of Sandra Weddum

over the years, they have forgotten how to study, or lack confidence in their own abilities.

For students who have recently immigrated to Canada or who are now returning to school after a period of adjustment in this country, another layer is added to the writing process: translation. Students may write their rough notes of their observations in their own language (or both languages as in Exhibit 3.3), translate them, and then rewrite them in English.

EXHIBIT 3.3 NAYER'S ROUGH NOTES: URDU AND ENGLISH

Rough Notes

The following rough notes are written in both english and urdu.

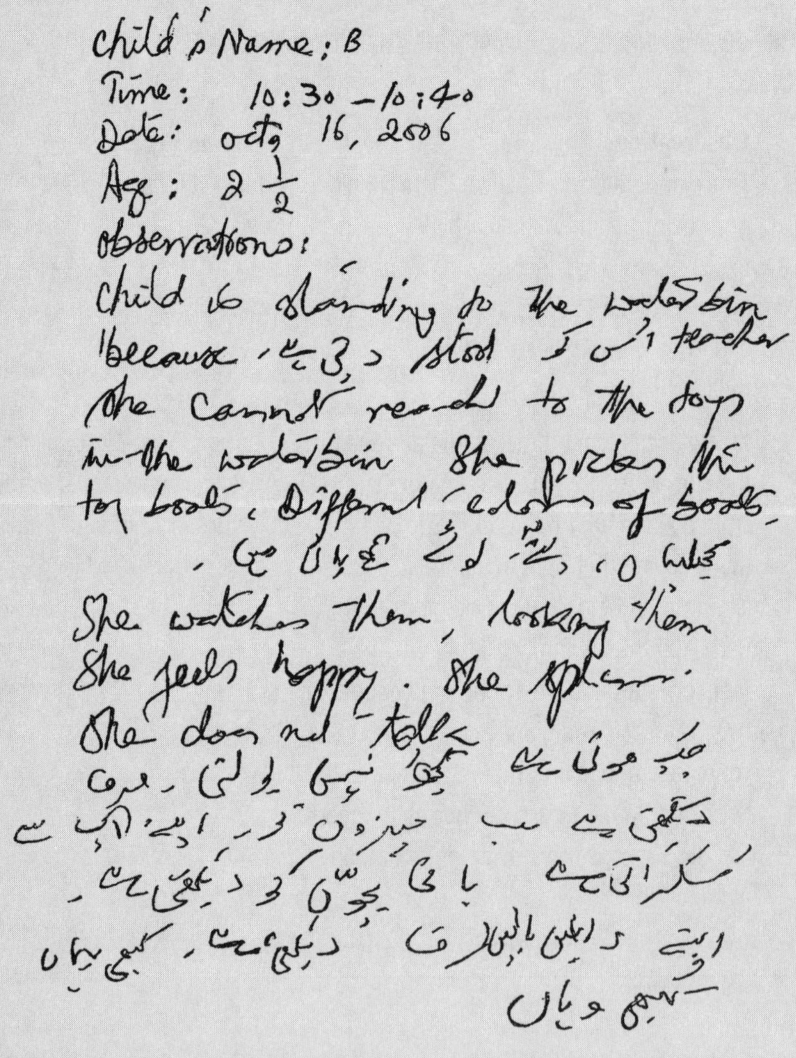

Child's Name: B

Time: 10:30 – 10:40

Date: oct 16, 2006

Age: 2½

Observations:

Child is standing to the water bin because ... stood ... teacher she cannot reach to the toys in the water bin. She prefers the toy boats. Different colours of boats.

She watches them, looking them. She feels happy. She ...

She does not talk.

[Urdu text]

Good Copy

Anecdotal Record

Child's Name: B_____   Age: 2½_____

Time: 10:30–10:40_____   Date: October 16, 2006_____

OBSERVATIONS

Child B is standing to the water bin. She is standing on the stool to reach the toys in the water bin. She touches all the materials that are floating in the water. At first she picks the green boat then she picks the red boat. One of her friends tries to get the red boat but she does not give it to him. He pushes her but she does not react. She keeps herself busy in playing with the boat. Teacher asks her to share. She listens to the teacher and puts it back in the water. She gets a toy fish. She waves her arms up and down, still holding the toy firmly in her right hand. She looks around at the teacher sitting at the other end of the water bin. She does not say anything but smiles as she leans over the water bin. Her peers are talking to the teacher. She listens to them. She mumbles to herself. She moves her body as the boat floats in the water. She is about to fall. She slopes downward. She wiggles but she controls her body. She keeps balance to stop herself from falling. Then her teacher says, "It's story time." She goes to the reading centre.

SOURCE: Courtesy of Nayer Khan

It may take a considerable amount of time and commitment to search for appropriate words. Other students say they think about what they want to say in their own language, then mentally translate it into English and then write it.

Students may require extra supports to achieve written proficiency and competency. In college/university settings, students can access a language lab, apply for peer tutoring, or take an active role as part of an in-class buddy system.

Opportunities to Observe

Opportunities to practise observing and writing your observations is fundamental to developing your writing skills. Observation areas in colleges/universities are specifically designed for the observation of children. In Chapter 6, observation areas are discussed in detail. Another opportunity for students to observe is to attend a designated child-care setting in the community. If neither opportunity is available, the video entitled *Observing Young Children* accompanying this textbook can be viewed in the classroom. This video, through a series of clips, features the behaviours of infants, toddlers, preschoolers, and kindergarten-age children. Some clips provide only the audio portion so that students focus on one modality, which may be initially helpful. Community or lab school live observations combined with video practise sessions provide students with practical, non-graded opportunities to develop their writing skills and work on their confidence.

Learning a New Skill

Initially, all students find developing the skills to effectively record their observations challenging. They struggle with appropriate ways to write down what they think or feel: "The way we say things when writing our observations is not how we'd say them in regular conversations, so we find it sort of clumsy to try to write like that."

Observations are factual, based on what actually occurred. Some of the reasons why learning this skill may be difficult are

- the need for detailed writing using a descriptive vocabulary
- having to observe and record simultaneously
- being unsure about what to observe and record
- lack of confidence in current writing skills

Interpretations are our subjective responses to what we have observed. Writing interpretations can be even more challenging than writing observations, because with interpretations you have to

- analyze the observations.
- interpret why you thought the child did what she or he did.
- apply your knowledge from theories of child psychology and child development.
- frame your inferences in terms of the areas of child development.
- write your inferences in a positive, professional, and user-friendly manner.
- remain open-minded to other possible interpretations.

Developing skills specific to the observation process is a little like learning how to write all over again. We know it's not magic. It just takes work and a lot of practice, practice, and more practice. Being proficient in writing clear observations and interpreting children's behaviour is expected of a graduate of an early childhood education program. Once you become an early childhood educator with your own class, you will see the benefits these skills will bring to the children, their families, and yourself.

Observation Guidelines

Hopefully, at this point, you will have had opportunities, either in the playroom or through the use of video clips, to observe and record children's behaviour. If you are already in a child-care setting, you will have had the opportunity to observe children. Remember those initial decisions we discussed in Chapter 2 that followed the basic, journalist approach: why, how, when, where, and what. These basic questions guided your initial decisions. Here are other important guidelines to consider when documenting children's behaviour:

- *Talk with staff.* Let them know *what* you'd like to do, and find out *when* that may be convenient. Discuss what's best for everyone during that time frame. For example, a good time for you to conduct your observations may be when all staff are present rather than early or late in the schedule when you may be needed to assist if not all the teachers are on site.

- *Choosing a child.* Choosing a child for your observation is important. Some student-teachers choose the child sitting on a chair at the creative table because she's quiet. This choice may appear easy, but if that child isn't active, there may not be a great deal to write about. Most new observers tend to choose a child who is active in the group; this simply guarantees that there will be a lot to write about, and for the beginner, more opportunities to learn.

- *Spectator or participant.* If you adopt the spectator mode, find a place (*where*) to observe that is unobtrusive. Sitting off to the side or in the background will ensure that you are interrupted less often.

    If you are observing while being involved with the children (a participant), plan ahead for how you will go about recording your observations while still interacting safely with the children. Watch your pens!

- *Adding essential information.* As soon as possible, record the child's name and date of birth. Some centres may want you to use only the child's first name, initials, a ficti- tious name, or simply "Child A." Check with your supervisor or director to ensure you are following the centre's policies. Again, to be consistent with centre policies, find out how dates of birth are recorded: as day, month, and year; or year, month, and day; or month, day, and year. It may not seem relevant at first, but when you notice that the child's birthday is December 1, 2006, the child's age could vary depending on how the date of birth is represented: 01/12/2006 or 12/01/2006. How would you know? Asking for clarification will help avoid any misunderstandings.

- *Record the essential information as indicated in the example.* This data is fundamental to accurate records.

Example:

Observer: Sandy   Date: 05 October, 2008
Child's name: Child A Child's D.O.B.: 01 December, 2006
Time: 10:15–10:20

- *Materials needed.* Allow yourself one page for a one- or two-minute observation using plain or lined paper. You will find that you need considerably more pages for a five- or ten-minute observation. Bring more than one pen.

- *Experiment with ways of writing down your information.* Invent shortcuts using abbreviations such as:

LH for left hand,	A = alone	sh= short
RH for right hand,	P = one or more peers	lg = long

or an initial for the child's name, and any other short forms meaningful to you. Writing in sentence form simply takes too long. Jot down key words and abbreviations. When you use abbreviations, make sure you give yourself enough clues so that when you go to rewrite what you wrote, you can understand it. A student said, "I found it challenging to first learn to write in rough/short form.

I thought I would forget what the short forms meant! If I didn't use any short forms, then I missed things in my observation!"

As you practise, you will learn which words are key. Remember that our first efforts at developing any skill are seldom our best. Keep practising!

- *Recording dialogue.* When you are documenting older children or children who are talking together, you will quickly realize the challenge recording their conversations poses. It will be impossible to write down everything that you hear. You might want to try these two methods: tape recording or **paraphrasing.** In Chapter 6, the topic of using tape recorders is covered thoroughly. Paraphrasing means that you are summarizing or putting into your own words the gist of the child's conversation.

  For example, supposing you are interested in observing a four-year-old girl who is sitting at a table creating a picture. While she paints, she says, "You know, last night I watched TV until really late, and then my mom said it was time for bed, so I went upstairs and then I had to brush my teeth and get ready for bed, but I wanted my mom to read me a story so she did, and then I still wasn't tired, so she read me another one." Obviously you won't be able to write down all she said plus document the colours she used while painting, her grasp of the brush and so on, so you could paraphrase what she said in the following manner: "Nina talked while she painted. She told me in sequence what she did last night ending with her telling me that her mother read two books to her before she went to sleep." Telling Nina's story in your own words summarizes the conversation. It gives a sense of what she was talking about. If you are paraphrasing what the child said, then you do not need to use quotation marks. When you are recording a direct quote, use quotation marks such as the example in Exhibit 3.4.

- *Rewriting your observations.* Once you are finished writing your observations, determine when you will rewrite them in detailed form. Do not leave them until the next day or later, or much of what you have written will be lost. Go back over your notes as soon as possible that day and rewrite as much as possible, or at least write out the key words as phrases while they are fresh in your mind. The longer the time that passes before the initial observation and the rewrite, the more that will be forgotten. A student wrote, "I found it helpful for me to put little reminders on my rough notes for things that really stick out. I also tried to write my good copy as fast as I could after the observation so that it was all fresh in my mind."

- **Reflections.** When you are rewriting your notes, stop and reflect. Add the words you know will capture the essence of what you saw or heard. Instead of "walked," you might use the more descriptive words "shuffled along" to describe the action more accurately. You might write "said forcefully" instead of just "said," because the child seemed upset about someone else grabbing the computer mouse. Do not add description just to make a lot of words—make the words count and be meaningful. Does adding words while rewriting change what was originally written? Adding descriptors to what you write is acceptable providing the initial meaning of the observation is not changed. To illustrate this point, look at the examples in Exhibit 3.5.

EXHIBIT 3.4 EMILY AND THE SEASHELLS

Emily brings three shells to the table. She chooses a snail shell and saves the half clam and scallop shells for later. She attaches two lengths of yarn to the inside of the shell.

What are the strings for?

Emily: "Teneyes."

Antennae?

Emily: "That's how they see."

What do you hear when you put the shell to your ear?

Emily: "The sound of the sea."

How did that sound get in there?

Emily: "A bit of water went in the . . . went dee dee dee in the hole."

SOURCE: Courtesy of Jason Avery, Artists at the Centre.

EXHIBIT 3.5 NOTES AND DESCRIPTIONS

Original Notes	Notes with Descriptive Words Added
Smiled. Watched teacher.	Smiled warily. Regarded teacher carefully.
Tapped fingers on puzzle.	Tapped fingers lightly on puzzle.
Shifted in seat.	Shifted slowly in his seat.
Hummed to self. Focused.	Hummed quietly to self. Seemed quite focused.

Which of the four examples changed the most? Which of the four examples changed the least? These four examples may assist you in understanding the influence words have on our interpretations.

Self-Evaluating and Sharing

When you have completed several sessions of observations, take a look at the samples you are writing to find out what is working and what isn't. For example:

- Can you read what you have just written?
- Are you using shortcuts or abbreviations?

- What are some of the good key words you used?
- Did you include contextual information?

Can you see the difference between some of your earlier observations compared to the ones you are currently doing? What has changed? Your ability to evaluate your own progress is crucial to your learning. Develop a willingness and ability to evaluate your current skills against your former skills. As a lifelong learner, an honest appraisal of your own work is important. Only you know where you started with your observations skills and how much you have learned and developed in this area.

Sharing your observation and learning from those of others is important as well. The sharing process benefits everyone. However, *do not compare* your observations with others; for example: "She writes more than I do" or "I should have written it that way." This isn't a competition! Every observation has its own unique perspective, and so it should. To illustrate this point, refer to the four examples of observations of the same child based on a video clip of a boy (Exhibit 3.6).

No one will see the same event in the same way, because what we see is filtered through a personal, unique network of senses and perceptions. However, you may want to discover the kinds of things other people saw or heard, or how they chose to record these events. You can certainly learn from others and they from you!

EXHIBIT 3.6   COMPARISON OF FOUR OBSERVATIONS: THE BOY AND THE SLIDE

1. Child A is sitting in the sand on the end of the slide. He looks around and then picks up his shoes. He slowly walks to the slide. He leans on the slide while standing and slides down holding his shoes.
2. Child A is sitting at the end of the slide, playing in the sand. He took off both of his shoes and then stood up and walked over to the side of the slide. He puts one leg over and pulls himself onto the slide. He then slides down the slide feet first on his belly.
3. Child A is sitting in the sand of the playground. He starts to take off his shoes by first removing his right shoe and then his left shoe. Child A walks over to the blue slide, but only slides down with the left side of his body on the slide. He then picks up his shoes and slides them down the slide.
4. Child A is sitting on the ground outside in the sand. He doesn't have any socks on his feet. He picks himself off the ground and walks over to the slide. He sits down and takes off his shoes. He stands at the slide and puts his shoes on the slide and lets them slide down.

Writing Physical Descriptions

Portrait painters often say that the hardest model to paint is a baby or small child because of the lack of distinctive or defining features. Young children's faces have yet to acquire the lines of time and strong features that are characteristic of adults. One way to develop your observation skills further is to write a physical description of a child. You could practise by writing a description of a child's photograph, a picture of a child in a magazine, or any child you know. It seems an easy enough thing to do. Until you do it. During this process, you will be obliged to consider not only how to actually write an accurate description, but also how to write one that parents/family members would appreciate.

What are some defining physical features? Eyes, hair, and body build are a few with which to begin.

Eyes can be described in terms of colour, shape, and size. They can be expressive, twinkling, sad, or searching, but we have to be careful here: we do not want to wade too deep into the kind of description that becomes an interpretation of what we **think** we see. How would a parent feel if you said her or his child had sad eyes? What are the connotations?

Hair can be described in terms of colour, length, style, and texture. To practise writing physical descriptions, start by brainstorming words, terms, and phrases either by yourself or with a group. Finding words to describe, for example, hair colour can be interesting. One source of words to describe hair colour is the local drugstore where hair colour products are sold. Try finding one that simply says "blonde" or "brown"! What about lips? What about ears? We

PHOTO: Courtesy of Sally Wylie

have to be careful about how we describe children. Saying a child has "big ears" is not terribly flattering. Are the descriptions of ears important to the physical description of a child? Be aware that parents can be sensitive to perceptions expressed about their child. Keeping that in mind, how would you answer these questions:

- How do you describe a child whom you think is obese without actually saying it?

  State the child's weight factually, for example, 14 kg, or in terms of his build, for example, a stocky or sturdy build.

- Should you say fair-skinned or Caucasian? Should you even comment on skin colour?

Skin colour can be described in olive tones or shades of brown. You could describe the child as having a fair, freckled complexion. The answers to these questions are high individualized—as individual as the child being described.

- What if the child has a special need such as Down syndrome? Should you describe his or her facial features?

  Describe the child as you would any other child in terms of hair colour, texture, and colour, and shape of eyes. You may add to the description the fact that this child has Down syndrome.

As you can see, the process of observing and recording is beginning to take on new meaning. Our responsibility to the children, their families, and others is to be fair and equitable even when we are expressing our perceptions of their physical characteristics. In writing a physical description, we are learning how to see anew and to use tact, sensitivity, and professionalism in documenting our perceptions.

Descriptions and Implications

Descriptions of children need to be written in narrative form to capture the essence of the children's physical characteristics. The use of adjectives is helpful in this exercise. For example, "Sabrina has short, dark-brown hair that is thin and wispy. Her big, brown eyes are expressive and sparkle when she smiles. She has a slender build and is of average height for her age. She has olive skin, and her complexion is smooth and clear."

Based on this description of Sabrina, could you find her in the classroom? Would her parents feel that this is an appropriate description of Sabrina? You can use both of these questions as criteria for determining whether any description is fair and accurate. Words often carry negative connotations; for example, we need to be aware of how a parent may react to having his or her child described as "skinny" rather than "slender." What does "skinny" imply? Does "slender" have the same implications?

"Peter has light-blond hair that is thick and curly. He has big, blue eyes with long, dark lashes. He has a sturdy build and is about the same height as others in the preschool room. He has chubby cheeks that have dimples when he smiles." Based on Peter's description, could you find him in the classroom? Would his parents feel that this is a good description of Peter? Perhaps you feel that "chubby cheeks" isn't complimentary. How do you think Peter's parents would feel? It is important to know the parents of the children you work with; in being sensitive and in tune with all parents, misunderstandings are less likely to occur.

Let's look at one last example, a description of Morgan: brown hair, brown eyes, average weight. Could you find Morgan in the classroom? Would her parents feel that this is a good description of her? This description is so brief it sounds like it came from a police bulletin! If this child had been in your preschool room for over a year and this is all you could come up with to describe her, what inferences could be made about your observation skills?

You may never be asked to write a physical description of a child in your entire career as an early childhood educator. However, the likelihood that you may, in some form, need to have acquired the skills in order to do this is higher than you would guess. You will undoubtedly need to describe a child for reasons such as

- a wellness report
- an accident report
- an unusual occurrence report
- descriptors for a resource teacher or other professionals working with the children in your care

Having practised writing descriptions and considering how they would be received by parents or caregivers prepares you for situations where these skills may be required.

Checking for Objectivity

Once you begin observing children, your next challenge will be to develop an awareness of your attitudes and perceptions regarding children and the decisions you make about them. Each decision you make, such as whom or what to observe, is a personal choice and is, therefore, subjective. In choosing what to observe, a personal choice is made. Even if two people observe the same child, very different information could be recorded as seen in the comparison of four observations of the same boy in Exhibit 3.6.

Admitting Error and Bias

If you ask teachers of young children if they have favourites in their groups, they will probably say yes. Human nature is such that we just prefer some people to others. But being the educator of young children, you will need to be aware of your own biases. Admitting a bias—positive or negative—goes a long way in preventing you from treating the children unfairly or unprofessionally.

As a teacher, you must be perceived by all the children to be fair and objective; their trust in you as a nurturing, caring adult depends on it.

Here are some ways of enhancing objectivity in the child-care setting:

- Record your observations in a systematic and legible manner. Store the information in a logical and accessible yet private place. Rewrite any notes the same day you make them. Pen is preferable to pencil.
- Use precise and descriptive language, focusing on action verbs and descriptors to lend detail.
- As a matter of practice, have a coworker observe the same child at the same time. Then, share and compare your observations and interpretations and discuss your findings.
- Get to know the staff you work with—they have biases too. Discuss the children, your feelings, and new ideas. Some early childhood educators tend to favour

SOURCE: Courtesy of Steve Nease

certain aspects of the curriculum, such as creative activities. Be aware of your curriculum biases so that you set up a balanced curriculum for the children and not one that reflects just what *you* feel comfortable doing.

- Bring in outside resources. When working with a group of children for some time, it is easy to become biased after a while—to not see the forest for the trees. Requesting an outside person to come in and evaluate your room, curriculum, methods of observation, and routines introduces a new perspective and offers opportunities to re-evaluate the program.

- Maintain motivation and accountability. One of the challenges to observing children's behaviour is the belief that nothing is ever done with the information anyway, so why bother? If staff members feel an ever-dwindling interest on the part of administrators to conduct observations, the staff's motivation to do so may also lessen. Accountability usually involves standards and a desire to achieve what is best. Having the support of administrators—valuing the process of observation and supporting this effort—is critical. Remember, however, that it is ultimately your responsibility to be accountable for the children in your care. Saying "Oh, we don't do observation in this centre" means that you have agreed not to do it either. You can see how teachers may slide down the slippery slope from enthusiasm and commitment to doing the bare minimum.

- Be aware of your own biases. Your personality, attitudes, and philosophy regarding children will influence your evaluation of their behaviour. If you believe that children should have free choice to do whatever they like, then your appraisal of certain behaviours will be quite different from that of a teacher who runs a highly structured program. Again, consider the purposes of observation and remind yourself of these purposes regularly.

Forms of Bias

Being aware of our *biases* or judgmental errors is the first step in addressing them. There are several.

Leniency, the most common form of judgmental error or bias, means being overly generous in rating children's behaviour. One type of **leniency error** we have all experienced is that of the "teacher's pet." It is interesting to note that almost every teacher or student-teacher expresses the intent to work very hard not to have favourites or at least not to show that they do. Most student-teachers can remember their own school experience of being the teacher's pet or knowing classmates who were favoured. They can also remember the feelings associated with this bias.

For every teacher who has a favourite, there is a teacher who has a least-liked child. Perhaps the child's appearance, habits, or mannerisms bother the teacher, leading to severity toward that child. Often, a child who is disruptive or displays unacceptable behaviour (like constant fighting) is labelled "trouble maker" or "problem child." Sometimes, there is no obvious or conscious reason to dislike a child, but the bias against him or her exists, and the child's behaviour is consequently rated with a **severity bias.**

A **central tendency error** is often committed by new teachers in the field of early childhood education. They evaluate all children the same way, regardless of the children's individual characteristics. Central tendency may result from a lack of confidence in expressing personal views on the part of the teacher or simply a lack of experience in drawing conclusions about age-appropriate behaviours.

Expectancy or logical error refers to assumptions made about two seemingly related behaviours. This type of error is made when the observer makes assumptions or has certain expectations that are not based on direct observation. For example, if Miguel is the first one to put on his coat for outside play, waits first in line at the door, and dashes outside the second the door is opened, we conclude quite logically that he loves to be outside. Knowing how active Miguel is and watching him run around or ride a bike, we might assume he has excellent gross motor skills. However, if we were to observe his gross motor skills closely, what we might find is that Miguel runs and rides a bike but has yet to throw or catch a ball or to walk a balance beam. As a result of systematic observation, we may find that he needs to develop many of the gross motor skills demonstrated by other children of his age. The logical error is made when we relate Miguel's active nature outside to his enthusiasm for outdoor play, and from this derive a faulty conclusion. We were expecting that because he did *that,* he was good at *this.* Without systematically observing and recording the behaviour of young children, even experienced teachers can make expectancy errors.

Observational drift is another common error in defining what to observe. For example, when teachers are asked to observe and record "children sharing," each may begin

observing with a firm idea of the target behaviour. Teacher A may record examples of children sharing only materials, while teacher B may record examples of children sharing space, ideas, and so on. When the teachers compare their observations, they find that they have "drifted" with their own interpretations of what constitutes sharing.

Does it matter if children are rated on different criteria? Yes, it does: **inter-rater reliability** means the extent to which two or more people rating the same behaviour will yield the same results. The teachers need to agree on what exactly to observe, the type of record to be used, and how to obtain the data. This systematic approach does not guarantee objectivity, but it does tend to eliminate much subjectivity and increase the reliability of the information.

Do We Believe What We See or See What We Believe?

Unfortunately, a common practice in child-care settings is to conduct observations only if staff perceive a problem. Often, it is the child who is identified as having "the problem." If you are confronted with the notion that observations are to be done only where there is a problem, diplomatically query that notion. The idea that you pay attention only when a problem arises is very limiting; even worse, it can lead to a focus on the child being the problem, rather than a focus on discovery, which includes the teachers, environment, and curriculum. Bias or preconceived ideas can lead to erroneous assumptions about a child. If the child has already been identified as "a problem," then the likelihood of that perception remaining is quite high. One of the perceptual errors of human nature is to see what we believe, rather than believe what we see. Being proactive, rather than reactive, in observing children and their environment expands the early childhood educator's attention to all behaviours and not just those that are problematic. Keep this in mind.

Becoming aware of personal bias and judgmental errors is an important step in identifying and dealing with attitudes that influence the children and other adults with whom you work. This process is essential if we are to become early childhood educators who demonstrate sensitivity, awareness, and professionalism.

Organizing Observations around Areas of Child Development

When you first begin to observe children, you may not have a specific purpose in mind. You may not be sure of your focus. The following ideas could represent a beginning for you:

- In a group of children, think about what makes a particular child interesting. Is the child shy and timid? What would you like to observe? When you decide, include clusters of these traits, such as the ways in which Sarah communicates with others in the playroom. What would you observe? You could begin by noting who Sarah talks to (both adults and peers), if she talks to herself, the ways she uses language, for example, to direct others, as well as her facial expressions and body language.

- If you watch a video, write down the behaviours of a child that catches your interest. If you are interested in aspects of social development, then record how a child plays with others. If you are observing an infant, you might write down all the body motions an infant makes while sitting in one place.

In the examples just cited, chunks of information are being organized into similar groupings of behaviours. These grouping of similar behaviours can be described as areas of child development. Supposing your observation does not focus on similar clusters of behaviours, but loosely records the activity of a child. When the observation is finished, it may then be possible to read through the observation and organize all the examples and decide your focus for subsequent documentation.

Children's behaviour and areas of child development are defined in many different ways. Some developmental psychology texts classify development into such units as personality and social learning, language, cognition and perception, and physical growth and development. Different developmental psychology texts will not all be the same as there are variations in terminology. These variations have evolved from historical and philosophical models, and the choice of which one to use as a guide depends on your philosophy or where you received your education.

Observation texts have often focused on developing observation skills around a particular age group (ages three to five years). Other authors have chosen to highlight general growth patterns (ages two to five years) and development of young children in several chapters before introducing the observation methods. This text makes references to and discusses areas of child development from infancy to school age but makes the assumption that readers are taking related courses in child psychology and child development. Understanding how children develop and grow is one of the most important and fundamental studies in an early childhood education program. Your child development studies combined with your observation skills will provide you with a basis for understanding each individual child in the group. With that knowledge you will be able to develop a responsive curriculum, making age-appropriate adaptations to meet the needs of the group.

Areas of Child Development: Which Are More Easily Observed?

Most early childhood educators would agree that some areas of development are more readily observed than others. For example, the developmental areas easiest to observe and record are fine motor, gross motor, or self-help skills. These behaviours

EXHIBIT 3.7 EASILY OBSERVED AND INTERPRETED AREAS OF DEVELOPMENT

Area of Development	Examples of Behaviour
Gross motor	Hopping on one foot for 1 metre
	Throwing a ball overhand
	Climbing up a playground ladder
Fine motor	Twisting lids on and off
	Using pincer grasp to pick up pom-poms
	Picking up puzzle pieces
Self-help	Putting on shoes independently
	Drinking from a cup with one hand
	Choosing creative materials from shelf

can be observed as discrete units: they tend to have a beginning, a middle, and an end. They are observable behaviours that can be readily identified with a minimum of contradictory interpretation. Look at the examples in Exhibit 3.7. This list of behaviours in the three developmental areas can be readily observed.

The areas of social and emotional development, and speech and language skills, are more complex to observe and/or interpret. The cognitive, which concerns itself with learning, is another area of development when documenting behaviours. **Cognition,** or the capacity for knowledge, is an internal process; we can observe only the behaviours that tell us that learning is taking place. A child matching colours is providing a clear example of cognitive activity: "This blue bear looks just like that one." Cognitive activities such as matching, labelling, comparing, ordering, and classifying are often what first comes to mind when giving examples of thought process and learning. Social problem solving is also a cognitive activity. On the playground, this cognitive function might be represented by "Who's going first?" or "Let's pretend we're camping!" These behaviours are tangible evidence that the children are learning social problem solving in their environment. Yet these play-based examples are usually not the first thing we think about when we examine the cognitive skills of young children. Look at the examples of behaviour in these developmental areas in Exhibit 3.8. Remember from Chapter 2 that a behaviour is something you can see, count, or measure. In Exhibit 3.8, "remembering" is an internal process. What would you need to observe in order to conclude that a child has "remembered"? She or he would have to demonstrate a behaviour, such as telling you what everyone ate at snacktime yesterday. "Enjoying" is another internal process. Actually, many of the examples are not behaviours at all but examples of internal processes. These examples also leave

EXHIBIT 3.8	LESS EASILY RECORDED/INTERPRETED AREAS OF DEVELOPMENT
Cognitive	Discussing rules to social games
	Remembering yesterday's snack
	Deciding which toy to select from the shelf
Socioemotional	Demonstrating a reasonable attention span
	Engaging in pretend play
	Enjoying playing with older children
Speech and language	Imitating sounds of peers
	Pointing to something
	Talking to no one in particular

room for personal inferences about what is a reasonable attention span or what a child's thoughts are when "talking to no one in particular."

When discussing behaviour, internal processes, characteristics, and inferences, we have to be careful to clarify the distinctions as we did in Chapter 2. This clarification will help us to separate the behaviour we observe from the interpretations we make.

Establishing Baseline Information

Collecting observations on a child over a period of a few days or weeks will furnish you with numerous samples of behaviour representing all the developmental areas. When this information is gathered within a time span of two to three weeks, during different times of the day, in various settings, with diverse people (peers and adults), a **baseline of information** is established. This collection of representative behaviours will include the child's strengths, interests, areas to improve, and characteristics: a child's **current level of functioning.** Many centres have procedures stating the number of observations to be conducted during the first weeks after the child is enrolled. Why establish this baseline of information? This information helps the teachers and parents monitor how the child is settling in, who are his or her friends, the activities that interest him or her, and any fears or concerns. This baseline of information is helpful to everyone. For the family members, the information will help them to form an idea of how their child is settling in. This information aids the early childhood educators in assisting the child to feel comfortable and secure in the new environment. The educators find out what calms the child when the parent leaves in the morning and what engages the child throughout the day. The shared observations of parents and teachers help make the transition into group care easier for the child.

Determining Time Periods and Strategies for Observation

Observations are of particular importance to centre staff. Some centres establish a timeline or monthly planner that predetermines months that will be critical for observations (see Exhibit 3.9). These observations will be used as a basis for reports to parents and professionals. Other centres may designate certain days of the week or parts of the day when staff will work together to carry out their observations. How these decisions are reached depends on those most directly involved: the supervisor or director, staff in the playroom, resource teachers, and parents. Staff meetings are a useful forum for how, when, where, and why observations will be conducted.

The frequency and duration of the observations may also be determined, in part, by the type of child-care setting and the reasons why the child is enrolled in the centre. For example, if a child with special needs is integrated into a daycare centre, a number of other professionals may be involved, such as an occupational therapist, a physiotherapist, and a speech therapist. Each of these professionals may have a particular need for information from the daycare staff. If self-help skills are the focus of the occupational therapist, then certain feeding or toileting programs would need to be monitored by careful observation. The therapist may want to know daily how independent the child was during mealtime, or the child's reactions to the new, adapted cutlery. The physiotherapist may want information on the child's gross motor skills, such as stability while walking and balance while on uneven ground outside. The speech therapist may have suggestions for a child who requires staff

EXHIBIT 3.9	TIMELINE FOR OBSERVATIONS

This timeline sample is a guideline for a child starting in a program in the fall.

September	• Entry to program (Parent accompanies on first day)
	• First two weeks—observations
End of September/	• Initial entry report
Beginning of October	• Regular updates to observations
January/February	• Parent conference and/or report
	• Regular updates to observations
End of April/	• Parent conference and/or report for children
Beginning of May	• Leaving program or continuing into summer program

to encourage verbalization and keep a record of the child's sounds and words. Time periods and strategies ensure that particular observations are completed. These specific observations may be unique to a particular child or group of children. Do not get the impression that the only time observations are done is when data is monitored or collected for another professional. As an early childhood educator, you will complete many and varied kinds of observations. Specific observations could be those of a child who is experiencing upheaval at home, a child newly immigrated to Canada, or a child whose behaviour has caught your interest. Teachers also observe for changes in the curriculum, environment, and teaching strategies. Still, the most important observations are those recorded events that uncover the thoughts and feelings of a child—the child who talks while drawing his grandpa's house, who asks "What colour are the holes in the clouds?" or just plays in the dramatic centre with wild abandon.

During the child's enrollment, observations will be ongoing to determine whether the child's skills, interests, or abilities have changed and, if so, to comment on those changes. Not only our observations but also our interpretations should be constantly reassessed. For example, after two weeks, Nicholas has stopped crying during the morning and is following routines with fewer prompts and reminders. We could now conclude that "Nicholas seems to be growing more independent. He now appears to understand the routines and is settling in." This revision in our observations provides an excellent opportunity for parent–teacher communication.

What Do We See?

Early childhood educators recognize the all-important link between individual children's learning and curriculum (See Exhibit 3.10). They understand that planning appropriately for all the children involves more than just hunches or good guesses. Quality programming depends largely upon developed skills as an observer. The influence of current theorists, such as Howard Gardner and his theory of multiple intelligence, Daniel Goldman's theory of emotional intelligence, and Jerome Kagan's research on personality types, has made professionals in the field more aware of the need to pay particular attention to children's learning styles. Theories such as these

---

EXHIBIT 3.10   FRAMING THE ASSESSMENT DISCUSSION

Achieving an understanding of young children's learning is deeply rooted in teachers' powers of observation. Up-close, ongoing observation and recording of what children say and do can yield valuable information about children's interests and emerging understandings. Teachers can use this information to create rich learning environments and to implement effective instructional programs.

SOURCE: Jacqueline Jones, "Framing the Assessment Discussion". *Young Children*. January 2004, p.14.

influence teachers' philosophies, the curriculum they develop, and their teaching and documentation methods. Most crucial, however, is the teacher's willingness to learn from the children. This willingness requires a commitment to observe on a daily basis. What is *your* image of a child? How do children learn and develop? Do you think that will influence what you see in the playroom?

Summary

Chapter 3 has been about getting started with the actual process of observing and recording the activity of young children. While documenting your observations you will be discovering not only what you uncover about a child, but also your own thoughts and beliefs! Writing clear, descriptive, objective observations is a skill that takes a great deal of practice. If you are unaccustomed to writing, a significant degree of practice and determination on your part will be required. You will need to carefully observe children following the guidelines of preparedness. Your communication style will change as you adapt your language to the new role of teacher–observer. You will be required to simultaneously observe and document a child's behaviour while maintaining vigilance in wording your descriptions so that what you record is positive, professional, and accurate. Use all opportunities to practise your own style of observing and recording.

Developing specialized observation skills is crucial to the role of the early childhood educator. We have learned that observing and recording children's behaviour is a complex process. Conducting observations involves defining the purpose, choosing the type of record that best suits the purpose, recording the observation, reflecting on the documentation, the process, and its relevance, and evaluating the information while consulting with others.

PROFESSIONAL REFLECTIONS

I believe that observing young children is like being a detective. The observer needs to develop skills that enable her to look at all aspects of the child's development. She needs to be able to watch how the child being observed acts and interacts with his environment, his peers, other children and adults. A good observer catches the special way a child expresses himself verbally and non-verbally; how capable he is of following verbal and non-verbal directions; how he responds to different stimuli in his environment—the expected and unexpected occurrences.

In order to observe and interpret one's observations effectively, the observer must have a solid understanding of child development and the usual pattern of developmental sequences. Recognizing when a child is developing in an atypical way helps the early childhood educator know how to program more effectively for the child.

I recall a situation when I was working with 3&½ year olds and realized that there was one child with whom no one wished to play. Mike seemed like an actively involved and happy child. He always had playmates before. I put a pad of paper on top of the cubbies and whenever I had a free moment, I would observe Mike and jot notes. What I saw completely surprised me. Whenever Mike walked through an area of the room, he would, while looking straight ahead, unobtrusively hit or kick another child as he passed by. In talking with his Mom, we learned that he was angry that his cute younger brother had begun the same school, and that he was hitting his brother at home, too. We worked with the parents to spend more special time with Mike, and accenting the things he was able to do because he was their "big boy." At school, we gave him special jobs and attention. We continued to observe, and soon discovered the inappropriate behaviour had disappeared.

I urge you to be a constant observer, to watch a child's posture, how he moves into the room when he first arrives, and does he seek out other children. Be the detective who uses observation as a means of better understanding children and then being able to respond supportively to meet their needs.

—Carol L. Paasche,
Seneca College

Note: I was a student in Carol Paasche's ECE Continuing Education course over 20-plus years ago and that is when I realized how much I loved the process of observation. She was my mentor then, and we still share the same passion for observation after all these years.

KEY TERMS

baseline of information	expectancy or logical error	paraphrasing
central tendency error	inter-rater reliability	pragmatics
cognition	leniency error	semantics
current level of functioning	observational drift	severity bias

DISCUSSION QUESTIONS

1. How does the discussion of language assist you in writing clear, descriptive, reader-friendly observations?
2. Why is writing a physical description of a child good practice for writing observations?
3. Are objective observations harder to write than subjective interpretations? Why, or why not?

4. When interpreting observations, why is a solid knowledge of child development so important?

5. How does increased awareness of the kinds of judgmental errors teachers can make help you with writing objective observations?

6. Why is writing observations of a child different than taking lecture notes in class?

ADDITIONAL READINGS

Gordon, Ann Miles, and Kathryn Williams Browne. *Beginning Essentials in Early Childhood Education.* Clifton Park, NY: Thomson Nelson, 2007.

This American-based text demonstrates developmentally appropriate practice (DAP) in theory and practice. A multicultural approach is embedded within each chapter, helping teachers increase their sensitivity to other cultural practices and values.

Klein, M. Diane, and Deborah Chen. *Working with Children from Culturally Diverse Backgrounds.* Albany, NY: Delmar Learning, 2001.

Several chapters in particular complement this text, such as "Cultural Influences on Communication Skills and Styles." The aim of the text is to increase the educator's understanding of the ways culture can influence child-rearing practices as well as the behaviour of children.

Weiss, Amy L. *Preschool Language Disorders: Resource Guide.* San Diego, CA: Singular 2001.

A comprehensive book on the topic of language development, this text was written for "clinicians in the field." Yet, it yields many good ideas, suggestions for rating scales and checklists, and gathering information about a child's language competencies.

Part 2

HOW IS OBSERVED BEHAVIOUR RECORDED?

The act of observing has been likened to being a detective hunting for clues, and/or a fishnet being cast out to sea. These are good analogies for the process of observing children's behaviour: a detective searches for clues to discover truths, and a fishnet when thrown open into the sea will capture many surprises!

In Part Two, we will look at the planning involved in conducting observations: defining the purpose, selecting the type of record that best suits the purpose, conducting the observation, and separating the objective observations from the subjective interpretations. This systematic process includes all the children in the group and ensures that all have a file or **portfolio.** Portfolios consist of documentation about a child taken from different days, during different times, in different settings and situations, with teachers and other observers.

TWO MAJOR CATEGORIES OF RECORDS

One of the purposes of this text is to present the practical methods used to record observations in the field of early childhood education. These key methods can be grouped into two major categories:

- The records used for unanticipated behaviours
- The records used for targeted behaviours

Chapter 4 features those methods best suited to recording unanticipated behaviours. Chapter 5 examines the observational tools that are purposely selected to record targeted behaviours. Chapter 6 introduces alternatives to print-dependent documentation, as well as the media-assisted means to complete observations, such as photographs, tape recordings, and videotapes.

4

OBSERVING AND RECORDING UNANTICIPATED BEHAVIOURS

PHOTO: Courtesy of Michael Vieira.

Three-year-old Maria is standing in front of Mohammed, who is riding on an inflatable bouncing car. Maria stares for about 30 seconds, then all of a sudden lunges toward Mohammed and the car, grabs hold of the steering wheel with both her hands, and starts to scream. Still holding onto the wheel, she swings her right leg up to get herself onto the car and, in the process, nearly pushes Mohammed off.

He, in turn, gives her a push and she falls on her back. Maria starts to cry. A teacher arrives and comforts Maria as she rubs her eyes and continues crying while pointing to the car with her right arm extended. The teacher tells Maria that she has to wait for Mohammed to finish his turn. While the teacher is talking, Mohammed gets off the car and runs to another area of the room. Maria's eyes widen as she watches him leave. All of a sudden, she stops crying, pushes herself up, and grabs onto the car. She swings her right leg over the seat in one swift movement. As she begins to bounce up and down, Maria smiles broadly and squeezes the steering wheel tightly with both hands.

Overview

Recording methods that capture behaviours like those of Maria are like fish nets cast out to sea—you never know what you may catch. This open method of recording spontaneous behaviour is flexible and unstructured. It suits the catch of the day: unanticipated behaviours.

In this chapter, the featured types of records are

- anecdotal records,
- running records, and
- event sampling/ABC analysis.

These records represent some of the many variations that are used in early childhood education.

Unanticipated behaviour means the unexpected, unpredictable, or unknown behaviour. Part of the excitement of unanticipated events is the element of discovery, and part of the excitement of discovery is doing something new, uncovering something unknown, or having to respond unexpectedly. Educators will tell you that unanticipated behaviour in the playroom is a daily occurrence. Children, by their very nature, are spontaneous and their behaviours unpredictable.

This chapter is the first of three chapters that describe various observational tools that are used to collect objective information about young children. Each type of record in this chapter will demonstrate the practice of separating objective information from your subjective interpretations of that information. All observational tools provide the possibility of some interpretation. If the interpretations are not a specific part of the record, then they may be inferred from the collected information.

After reading this chapter, you should be able to:

- Describe three observational tools for recording unanticipated behaviour.
- State the main purpose for using each of the three tools and its unique feature(s).
- Identify the format used for each of these types of records.
- List the advantages and disadvantages of each tool.
- Explain the importance of interpretation when using these types of records.
- Suggest some possible applications for each of the three types of records.

Anecdotal Records

Purpose and Unique Feature

One of the most popular recording methods in early childhood education is the anecdotal record.

An anecdotal record is written in narrative form; it is a description of what the observer saw and heard (see Exhibit 4.1).

Some have described an anecdotal record as a word picture, a description so clearly written that when read, the image of the child's activity immediately comes to mind. An anecdotal record could consist of a paragraph or a page or more, depending on the purpose of the observer. Anecdotal records capture spontaneous behaviour as it occurs. When the teacher documents a child's activity, she or he is telling a story—an anecdote. The story, however, is not fiction—it is real. Anecdotal records of children's behaviours should be as objective and accurate as possible because they reveal important information. Anecdotal observations are shared with parents, used for curriculum development, or may become the basis for many other decisions made by the team (including parents) in future planning.

The key feature of anecdotal records is their flexibility; they can be used to record the behaviour of children in any setting, within any philosophy or set of practices and under any conditions. All you need is paper and a pen or pencil.

Using anecdotal observations in informal settings captures behaviours that are unanticipated. In the examples of Maria and the car, and Shazi's active enthusiasm (see Exhibit 4.2), the observer wrote what actually occurred. With even such brief episodes, we can learn a lot about Maria and Shazi. The familiar setting combined with the open-ended style of the anecdotal observation means the teacher could take advantage of free playtime to record their behaviours. Teachers can be prepared to take advantage of any opportunities to record their observations using stick-on notes, loose-leaf paper on a clipboard, or a notebook.

EXHIBIT 4.1   ANECDOTAL RECORDS

ANECDOTAL RECORDS:

- document unanticipated behaviours
- record contextual information
- consist of objective observations and subjective interpretations
- are used in informal settings to document behaviour that is natural and spontaneous
- are setting-independent (can be used in child-care setting)

EXHIBIT 4.2   TEN-MINUTE OBSERVATION

Child's Name: Shazi   **DOB:** February 4   **Age:** 4

Observer(s): Jessica   **Date(s):** April 17   **Time:** 10:15–10:25

Activity: Free playtime—at the easel

Shazi is standing squarely in front of the easel with her left arm at her side. She is painting using her right hand, making short, purposeful strokes. "It's rain!" she yells out to no one in particular. "Laa-lalalalaladeebeedeebeedeebee," she chants as she continues dipping her brush into the purple paint and dabbing it onto the uppermost part of the newsprint. She stops to pick up the purple paint container with her left hand, tucks it up close to her body, and grinds the brush around the bottom. With her brush laden with paint, she carefully lifts it to the paper and firmly drags it down to the bottom. She picks up the brush, tongue sticking out between her teeth, and repeats the same gesture. She looks down at the other colours and selects green by dipping the brush into the green paint, and then slowly makes a green stroke parallel to the purple. Then, she stops and carefully raises her brush and begins another slow, green vertical line. Halfway down the page, Shazi begins to swish the paintbrush quickly back and forth across the purple and green vertical lines in a rapid, frenzied manner.

"I'm done now!" says Shazi. She pulls her painting smock up over her head with one efficient swoop, turns, and stuffs it on the chain that attaches the two sides of the easel. She runs toward the dramatic centre, wiping her hands as she runs. A voice calls out, "Walking feet, Shazi," but Shazi has already reached the dramatic centre. "I'm here!" she yells out to the three children. In a flurry of conversation, Shazi sits at the table and puts both her arms on the table, looking straight ahead. One of the children puts a plate in front of her on the table. "It's hot," Naomi says. Shazi looks down and blows on the plate, making huffing and puffing sounds. She picks up the plate and puts it over her face, making more sounds. "I'm done," she shouts, "gimme some more." She bangs the plate on the table. A ladle appears and is banged on the plate. "It's hot," Paul says. Shazi repeats the blowing on the plate. This time she calls out, "I'm done, I'm done. See, Mummy, I'm done." Shazi shoves her chair backward with her legs as she gets up. The chair falls over. Shazi walks around the table to the dress closet. She drops to her knees and crawls into the closet, then backs up holding onto a black shoe with her right hand. She pulls off her right shoe with both hands, grabs the black shoe, and again with both hands tries to get her foot into the point of the shoe. She looks up at the children around her. As she sits watching them, the teachers begin to sing the tidy-up song. Shazi quickly grabs the black shoe, pulls it off her foot, and throws it in front of her. In one movement, she reaches forward to get her own shoe, rolls onto her knees, and pushes herself up to stand, calling out, "Wait! Wait!" She pushes her way past two children, steps over another, and bangs into the stove and table as she crashes out of the doll centre holding her shoe high.

These notes should be transcribed at the earliest available time. After Maria's and Shazi's teacher wrote her initial rough notes, she transcribed them soon after noting key words such as verbs, adverbs, adjectives. As we learned in Chapter 3, systematic recording of children's behaviour involves investigating strategies for efficient ways to document observations. The open-ended style of an anecdotal observation in a familiar environment also allows for reference to **contextual information.** What was some of the contextual information in the example of Maria and the car? What happened in the environment that influenced Shazi's behaviour? Did the teacher play a pivotal role in both observations? When you record your observations of children, make sure to include references to other children, adults, and the environment.

This observation represents the first part of the anecdotal observation: the factual account of a child's activity. The actual observation could stand alone; it could serve to provide others with a written account of this event. Typically, however, an observation is accompanied by an interpretation. What are interpretations?

Interpretations are personal and professional judgments or beliefs. After writing our observations, we add the interpretations: our appraisal about what we just observed. Interpretations relate directly back to the observation using such words as "seems," "perhaps," "as if," and "appears." Using such words tells us that interpretations are speculative and subject to personal bias. These and similar words convey the tentative nature of interpretations. They are not the truth—they represent only our best efforts to explain what is meaningful about the observations. Barbara Ann Nilsen's text, *Week by Week: Documenting the Development of Young Children,* states: "The Anecdotal Recording recounts the event, telling the reader when, where, who and what. It does not answer the question *why* in the body of the recording. That conclusion or inference is separated from the recording. An inference is an informed judgement or conclusion based on observation" (Nilsen 49). While reading over the brief anecdotal observation in Exhibit 4.3, ask yourself the following questions:

- What is the relevance of the information in this brief observation?
- Does this anecdotal give you insight into Kate's personality?
- What inference can you make about the way Kate utilized the props in the centre?

EXHIBIT 4.3   IN THE DRAMATIC PLAY CENTRE

Kate runs quickly over to the dramatic play centre where she confronts Holly standing at the play sink pretending to wash dishes. "Those are mine," says Kate to Holly. She grabs two of the red dishes and rushes over to the table where she picks up the cordless phone. "Hello Nana," she says, "I'm ready to come over now," while she pushes the buttons randomly and puts the phone to her ear. "Goo-by, goo-by," she then says and drops the phone on the table, twirls around, and looks around the room.

When reading and interpreting observations, we generally have more information than what is presented in Exhibit 4.3. Yet, the exercise is instructive as it illustrates the fact that good quality observations will provide enough information to make interpretations.

Understanding and Interpreting Observations

In our daily lives, we are inundated with information; we constantly make observations of people and events around us and spontaneously assign a value to these observations. We have all developed strategies to navigate our way through our busy lives based on our observations. Let's say you are sitting on the bus when a scruffy-looking person gets on. You look up. Immediately you form an impression. Do you want that person to sit next to you? We have become experts at making spontaneous judgments about people, places, or things as we observe them.

Whether we realize it at the time or not, we respond to our environment with a personal judgment: like/dislike, trust/distrust, accept/reject. We may **accommodate** new information or reorganize it to align with other experiences. This process happens spontaneously and quickly. For example, if you are introduced to someone who strongly reminds you of another person you do not like, what is your initial judgment of the new person? Is it fair? Probably not. We have learned to form quick impressions and make hasty interpretations of events or people, partly to compensate for the sheer volume of information in our environment. In our personal lives, we order and classify many experiences, events, and people based on values that are uniquely ours: good or bad, right or wrong, important or trivial. While we filter and buffer ourselves against what we encounter, we build our own eclectic views, incorporating new experiences into our existing beliefs.

When observing and recording children's behaviour, however, we must observe first and then interpret. We will need to begin to separate those two processes. Separating what we see from how we think or feel about the person/event is exactly the opposite process of what we've spent a lifetime learning to do. No wonder our initial observations of children will include words or phrases that refer to our thoughts or feelings.

Instead of saying, "Independently, Sarah spent over 10 minutes putting together the multiple piece puzzle" (*observation*), or "It seems Sarah is good at solving complex puzzles" (*interpretation*), a novice observer may say, "Sarah was so smart because she put the multiple piece puzzle together by herself." The interpretation ("so smart") is imbedded in the observation.

We share our personal observations with friends and family, freely expressing our observations and judgments. However, as teachers of young children we have to pause and reflect, asking the question: "How will my views impact others?" We need to communicate professionally with colleagues and families/caregivers to share our perspectives, not dictate them. This means accommodating the viewpoints of others and discovering what *they* find relevant and why. What is their interpretation? What aspects of the observations were meaningful? Sharing your observations with

EXHIBIT 4.4   POOR EXAMPLE OF AN ANECDOTAL OBSERVATION

Child's Name: Lacey Borders   **DOB:** January 5   **Date of Observation:** March 10

Physical Description: Dirty blonde hair, brown eyes, average weight

Activity: Playdoo table

Observation

Lacey was playing with the pink playdoo. She and Crystal played together. She communicated to her that she wanted the wooden roller. The teacher walked by. She was bored so she got up and left the table. She went to the drama centre and started to play. She was there for quite a while.

Interpretation

Lacey loves to do all the creative activities in the room. She gets bored easy. She didn't really want to play with Crystal because she went to the drama center. Lacey is so easygoing. She likes to play in the drama centre because she's always in there.

other educators and families is really about good communication and developing responsive relationships.

Let's critique this observation. First, in the essential information section at the beginning of the observation, the last name of the child was included. Second, the description of the child was hardly flattering or even descriptive. See Chapter 2 for a more in-depth examination of these two errors commonly made when providing the essential information of an observation.

What about the observation itself? Did you find the interpretation within the observation? If the child was "bored," that interpretation should go in the interpretation section. The word "went" was used, which is neither detailed nor descriptive. Saying the child "was playing" gives very little information and could be expanded. How did the child "communicate"? To whom does "she" refer in that sentence? How long was "quite a while"? Are there spelling mistakes? Correct spelling is important in order to discern the meaning of the word and its use in a sentence. It appears from this observation that the teacher had no interaction or any real effect on the children's behaviour.

Was the teacher walking by worth adding to the observation? What about the interpretation? Interpretations must reflect the observation. Should the observer comment that Lacey "enjoys all the activities in the room" when there was no evidence of that in the observation? Did Lacey walk to the dramatic centre because she didn't want to play with Crystal? How can an interpretation like that be made when there is no evidence to support it? Saying Lacey was "always" in the dramatic centre is erroneous; the observer should comment only on the actual content of the observation and not on what she may generally know about the child. There are other errors in the observation and interpretation that could be highlighted for discussion. Can you find them?

Format of Anecdotal Records

The format of the anecdotal observation is flexible and open-ended. Various adaptations to the format can be made, such as the one shown in Exhibit 4.5. You will note that the observer can check off whether or not the observation was remembered or live, as well as whether it was a *natural* or a *contrived observation*. **Contrived observations** refer to those that are staged by the teacher, researcher, or **play therapist.** The majority of references to observations made in this text are about **natural observations;** that is, events that happen spontaneously in familiar surroundings. Can you think of an example of when a teacher would want to stage a contrived observation?

EXHIBIT 4.5 RESPONSIVE ENVIRONMENT DAILY OBSERVATION FORM

Child's Name: _____

Date: _____

Observer(s): _____

_____

_____

Check one:
- ❏ Remembered observation
- ❏ Specimen (live) observation

Also check one:
- ❏ Natural observation
- ❏ Contrived observation

Observations	Interpretations	Decisions
This column should simply answer when, what, where, how, to whom, from whom, and with whom. Use descriptive verbs.	This column should answer why and in what way with what reason or motive. Guess, speculate, discuss, evaluate. Use "seems" or "appears" when making judgments.	This column should deal with actions based on observations and inter-pretations.

SOURCE: Courtesy of David Lockwood, Humber Institute of Technology & Advanced Learning.

EXHIBIT 4.6   ANECDOTAL FORMAT

Child's Name: _____   DOB: _____   Age: _____

Observer(s): _____   Date(s): _____

OBSERVATIONS

- objective
- factual
- a word picture
- a description of what happened

INTERPRETATIONS

- subjective
- speculative
- how we respond to an event
- spontaneous assessment drawn from personal experiences and understanding

Having the observations and related interpretations in column form, side-by-side, displays the objective information and the subjective information in left-to-right sequence. This format has the advantage of making connections between the two columns relatively easy. Others would suggest that the anecdotal record format in Exhibit 4.6 is easier to write, as observations are generally written first and the interpretations are added afterward in a before–after sequence.

Adapting Anecdotal Records

Anecdotal observations can become part of another type of record, such as a participation chart. A participation chart (see Chapter 5) targets particular behaviours and does not include a narrative or anecdotal record. Yet, teachers often like to include a comments section in the chart for contextual information or information about the child that doesn't "fit" in the chart, but that is still highly relevant. Combining or adapting certain records to include the narrative of the anecdotal record is common practice. The types of records we will be examining in Chapter 5 and 6 can easily be adapted to include an anecdotal section.

Records may be adapted to include anecdotal observations or a comments section for other reasons. These adaptations may reflect a specific request for information

ORIGINAL DRAFT OF FARAH'S OBSERVATION

Observation No:- 2

Date:- 29.1.02

Observer :- Farah
Child's Name :- Tiffany
Child's Age:- 4 yrs old
Setting:- Manipulative corner
Aim:- To observe cognitive and social/emotional behavior
Objective:- To observe/record child's cognitive ability and interaction.

Time Commenced:- 9:45 am

Time Ended:- 9:51 am

Anecdotal Record:-

Tiffany sat beside Xu Yin facing the box of unifix cubes which was directly in front of the shelf filled with manipulative materials. Tiffany looked into the box and smiled. She turned to Xu Yin and said, "I play with you ok?" Xu Yin nodded. Tiffany used her right hand to pick red colored cubes and placed it on the floor next to her. She said softly, pointing to the cubes, "one, two, three, four, five." She then picked the cubes one after another to join them using both her hands. She turned again to look at Xu Yin for a few seconds. She tapped Xu Yin's left shoulder and said, "See, I make bed for godilocks."

Conclusion:-   (Interpretation)

- It seemed that Tiffany is a courteous girl because she asked permission from her friend to join in or rather play with 'e cubes.

- Her language acquisition is not bad for a 4 year old. (Pro-social behavior - interact well with peer.)

- Well, perhaps she was happy, fascinated with 'e cubes. or that was what she was expecting cause she smiled as soon as she saw the cubes.

- seemed that she is acquiring math concept such as classification and counting.

- find that she's quite imaginative.

- seemed relax and happy as she takes her own time exploring 'e materials. (did not rush)

What are the similarities/differences between the format of this anecdotal taught in Singapore and yours?

from parents or professionals working with a child. Suppose teachers kept an ongoing checklist from September to November on the developing language skills of the toddler group, and in this group, there is a child with special needs. The resource teacher and the child's family may want specific language samples used by the child with peers and adults. The early childhood educators may be requested to record contextual comments, such as the one in Exhibit 4.7.

Similar adaptations can be made when the teachers provide topics and activities for the children and the resource teacher/consultant has specific objectives for a child with special needs. Observing the group and the individual child supports team teaching and a planning process that benefits all of the children.

Not having a preconceived idea of what to look for keeps the windows of perception open to numerous discoveries. If we want to observe Seth because it has been a long time since we have done so, then we will probably be open to whatever it is Seth says or does. Recording information only to learn more about the child reduces bias on the part of the observer, and that is an advantage for everyone.

EXHIBIT 4.7   CHECKLIST WITH ANECDOTAL SECTION

Child's Name: _____   DOB: _____   Age: _____

Observer(s): _____   Date(s): _____

Time: _____   Activity: _____

BEHAVIOUR	YES	NO

- Repeats key words such as: me, no, mine, go
- Imitates sounds of others during play
- Engages in play, making sounds and using gestures to communicate with peers
- Imitates actions of others during play

**Please include anecdotal comments about the activity of Child A as well as the conditions in the environment when the checklist was completed.

ADVANTAGES OF ANECDOTAL RECORDS

There are many advantages of anecdotal records. Some of them are that they

- require little preparation (paper and pen/laptop);
- contain a rich reserve of specific behaviour samples from a variety of play settings, and peer and adult interactions;
- provide the teacher with patterns of behaviour that are not significant by themselves, but together form a pattern, such as a child who tends to play alone, always sits on the right-hand side of the teacher, and/or seems to ignore any adult directions. It may lead the teacher to question: Could this child have a hearing impairment? Documentation can provide a revealing pattern that catches the teacher's eye and prompts him or her to pay special attention to that child;
- are setting independent: observations can be used in any school or centre, regardless of the particular philosophy or practices;
- can be conducted at almost any time; different times of the day reveal different kinds of behaviours from young children;
- allow the observer to record the observations of two children at the same time, giving a two-for-one advantage; noting relationships between children and making it possible to observe more than one child at a time for the same purpose, i.e., cooperative play.

- deal with children in a familiar environment where they feel comfortable and their play displays a full range of behaviours. Here is where you will find what you were not expecting;
- are taken in context. Contextual information is critical when observing children as certain things, such as the height of the self-help shelf or poor lighting, can affect their behaviour.
- will cause you to rethink how you see the world. You will be fortunate to watch young children build self-confidence, make new friends, overcome fears, learn new skills, and share with others.

Paradoxically, the anecdotal observation has also been seen as one of the most biased types of records because of the strong role given to personal interpretation. Is that an advantage as well as a disadvantage?

Imbalance of Perceptions

Before we look at the obvious disadvantages of anecdotal records, let us examine the question of subjective influences in anecdotal observation. Although we try to be as objective as possible, some subjectivity is bound to influence our observations. Is a "sly smile" different from a "winning smile"? An "awkward-looking walk" is laden with perception as well, isn't it? A few words placed here and there can make a difference between a child being perceived as assertive and confident and being perceived as aggressive and bossy. Reading too much into an observation that may be based on inexperience or misunderstanding can bias our observation and potentially present that child inaccurately. Reading too little into our observations can also mean we have clear, factual observations, but we will not be able to use them to their full advantage by providing insight and perception into the child's behaviour, thereby losing the potential for better understanding. This mbalance of **perception** could be seen as a disadvantage to using the anecdotal observations.

Overlooking the obvious can be just as calamitous as reading too much into observations. Inaccurate perceptions can be the result of lack of experience or confidence or lack of knowledge about a particular age group. For example, suppose the observer was watching an infant who was seated and making babbling noises. After writing down the child's actions and recording the babbling as "Mamamama, lalalalalalabbbbbbbbb," the observer surmises that the infant is trying to tell the teacher something about her mother. After discussing this interpretation with the infant's teacher, however, the observer may learn that he or she is probably playing with sounds or practising making sounds, rather than attempting to communicate in words. Perhaps the teacher will explain that the infant's cognitive processes have yet to be developed enough to know what words represent, and where the beginning of some sounds end and other sounds begin in order to make actual words.

DISADVANTAGES OF ANECDOTAL OBSERVATIONS

There are many disadvantages of anecdotal records. Some of them are that they

- require a great deal of time. Even though the initial set-up is easy, the teacher still has to write the observations, interpret them, rewrite them so they are meaningful to others, and keep track of these observations for each child in the room. When teachers say, "I haven't got time," they are probably referring to this entire process, not the initial observations themselves. In reality, rewriting, editing, and interpreting *is* time-consuming.

- not only take time, but take another mindset: going from active participant in the room to a reflective person sitting, writing/typing, and analyzing the anecdotal information.

- increase the possibility of bias if there is a time delay between the observing and the recording of the events. Reading significance into behaviour may be more likely when you are trying to remember what actually occurred, and isolated incidents may be taken out of context and misinterpreted;

- require time for observation, which has to come from somewhere. This means that a team member may have to cover certain areas of the room or activities going on to free up a person to conduct observations. If not all the ECEs in the room value observation in much the same ways, then taking time out for this practice may be problematic for the team.

Interpretations

Let's examine interpretation and the critical role it plays in the recording of unanticipated behaviour. This knowledge will be relevant to your understanding of every type of record in this chapter. Anecdotal records, running records, and event sampling methods rely on factual descriptions of events and behaviours; however, to make these records useful, we need to ascribe some meaning to our observations. *Remember that your interpretations rest on your observations, and your observations achieve significance with your interpretations.*

Observations will probably contain some bias or subjectivity, but the aim of the teacher is to remain as objective as possible. As discussed in Chapter3, being aware of your own biases is a good starting point to writing clear, factual observations.

Terminology and Levels of Interpretation

Some observation texts refer to interpretations as comments, conclusions, **inferences,** perceptions, judgments, opinions, insights, or **evaluations.** Many of these terms and others could be used interchangeably with the word *interpretation* since they all are essentially talking about the same thing. The important issue here is separating the objective (observation) from the subjective (interpretation). From the following levels of interpretations, you can see the gradual increase in complexity when writing interpretations.

First Level—Interpretations from Only Brief Observations

A brief observation (five minutes or less) relies on the descriptive skills of the observer. When it is written with detail, action verbs, and descriptors, such as adverbs and adjectives, even a short observation can yield enough information to form some basic interpretations. Look at this example of an observation:

> Jeremy put the telephone receiver to his ear, turned sharply to the two children in the dramatic centre, and said, "Shhhh!" His eyes were cast down. The children were talking noisily. Jeremy said loudly, "I'm on the phone!" and tapped his right foot rapidly on the floor.

From this brief observation, you can make inferences about Jeremy's behaviour. For example, the observer used words such as "sharply," "noisily," and "rapidly" to describe the action, and these words help form impressions about how Jeremy might be feeling. From the observation, we can comment on how Jeremy communicated, which tells us a little more about Jeremy:

> Jeremy appeared to be bothered by the loud voices. He used both verbal and nonverbal means to communicate his feelings.

Perhaps we could even comment on Jeremy's ability to role-play or know the functions of familiar objects, such as a telephone. These interpretations are based on very little information and are, therefore, quite sparse. You can make *inferences* only if you have sufficient, quality observations. However, even brief examples are invaluable when they are added to what we already know about the child and are included in the child's portfolio. See if you can form interpretations on the basis of the following:

> Daria is standing in front of a table. She is holding a puzzle. Both of her thumbs are on top of the puzzle and all of her fingers are on the bottom of the puzzle. She raises her arms and puts the puzzle on the table. Her eyes are directed at what she is doing.

Daria's behaviour is described in detail, but did you get a real sense of Daria? The behaviours in this example seem to be almost robotic. Why is it hard to form interpretations from this example? What do you need in order to be able to form them? Remember that anecdotal observations should tell a story. Part of good storytelling is knowing what to include. How could you change the writing of the observation of Daria?

Whether or not an observer can make valid interpretations on the basis of one observation sample is debatable. However, as you can see from the two preceding

examples, if observations describe the *quality* of the behaviour, then you can probably make reasonable inferences from them.

Second Level—Interpretations from Expanded Observations

Interpretations from one set of expanded observations will include many more examples of behaviour. By sheer quantity alone, you would be able to net some meaningful samples of behaviour that would offer opportunities for ample interpretation. Although quantity is no substitute for quality, having an expanded anecdotal record will allow you to see more behaviours that are similar or related and to see patterns that are characteristic of a child. See Exhibit 4.8 for an example of an expanded observation and the accompanying interpretations.

Third Level—Summary Statements: A Collection of Observations over Time

The third level of interpretation is made from observations taken over several days/ weeks. When compiling all the information from various observations, a more complex set of skills is needed. Interpretations compiled from multiple observations involve reflection, analysis, synthesis, and making references and comparisons. What

EXHIBIT 4.8 EXPANDED OBSERVATION AND INTERPRETATION

Child's Name: Emmanuel   DOB: December 12   Age: 3

Observer(s): Lisa   Date(s): May 20

Time: 2:15–2:25   Activity: Free playtime—cognitive table

PHYSICAL DESCRIPTION

Emmanuel is a three-year-old boy with thick, brown hair cut in a bowl shape. He has clear olive skin with no marks or blemishes, long eyelashes, and a round face. He is of average height for his age and is a stocky, healthy boy.

OBSERVATIONS

Emmanuel is sitting on a chair at the table. His left leg is hooked around the front chair leg. He is slowly thumping his right leg rhythmically against the right front chair leg. An animal puzzle is in front of him on the table. He gently traces the outline of the animal pieces with his forefinger. He yawns and looks around the room, then looks back down at the puzzle. With both hands, he brings the puzzle up toward him while bending his head down toward it. He kisses the puzzle and puts it back down on the table. With his right hand, he neatly picks up the top left-hand piece by its red knob with a pincer grasp. He places it directly along the top edge of the puzzleboard. He hangs onto the puzzle with his left hand. He is humming to himself. He picks out each of the six puzzle pieces and lines them up in a horizontal line, one after the other, along the top of the puzzleboard. He does not look around. He hums the whole time. When all the pieces are out, he puts both hands on either side of the puzzleboard and pushes it away from him until his arms are stretched out and his upper body is resting on the table. His feet and legs come together under the table. He lays his head down on the table. His arms are stretched out in front still holding onto the puzzle. He remains like this for a few moments. He has stopped humming. Then, suddenly, he sits upright in his chair and yells, "Me no do dis!" With a sweep of his right arm, he pushes all the pieces, as well as the puzzleboard, off the table onto the floor. He quickly looks around the room, briefly glances at the puzzle pieces on the floor, then jumps out of his chair. Emmanuel runs across the room, his arms curled close to his body, his elbows swinging back and forth, to the dramatic centre.

Melissa calls out to Emmanuel, "Do you want to play baby with us? Okay? Play baby?" Emmanuel stops in his tracks and jumps up and down in one spot several times, flapping his arms up and down. "Me wanna pway, me wanna pway," he chants while jumping. At that moment, the teacher approaches Emmanuel, reminding him to go back and pick up the puzzle pieces. Emmanuel

(continued)

whirls around to face the teacher and shouts loudly, "No, no, no!" and throws himself on the floor, covering his ears with his hands and kicking his feet against the floor.

INTERPRETATIONS

Emmanuel appears content, yet sleepy. Perhaps he has just woken up from his nap. He wraps his leg around the chair leg as if to help anchor himself securely. It seems he likes the animal puzzle. Although he appears tired, he is still able to coordinate his efforts to take out the puzzle pieces and line them up. His sudden burst of activity in jumping out of his chair, running, and jumping suggests good gross motor coordination. Emmanuel appears immature in his speech and language development. He seems very excited about being asked to play and then very upset about being directed elsewhere by the teacher. Covering his ears seems to send the nonverbal message that he does not want to hear the teacher.

makes these kinds of interpretations different from the two previously mentioned is that the interpretations usually take on an evaluative function. The topic of writing summaries will be covered in Chapter 7.

Running Records

Purpose and Unique Feature

The **narrative,** or **running record,** is rarely in dispute as the oldest and longest-serving recording method we still use today. A running record documents a child's activity in the narrative and, as such, is similar to the anecdotal observation. The main purpose for using a running record is to focus on a child and record the child's activity over time. There are many reasons why an observer would wish to conduct a running record, such as documenting the social interactions of a child with peers, logging the verbal exchanges of one child with adults and other children, or noting the physical efforts of a child with special needs to maintain safe mobility within a busy room.

The unique feature of the running record is that it is chronological in nature; a series of observations in a sequence: minutes, hours, days, or weeks. This open-ended approach to collecting information on a child over time requires dedicated observation time and considerable commitment. A running record generally focuses on a child throughout the day, recording samples of behaviour from morning until the child leaves the centre, perhaps every day for weeks, even months. Ideally, the observer should be a nonparticipant in the playroom. As teachers rarely have the opportunity to devote hours of time solely to observe one child, outside resources could be enlisted to conduct this function. Centres that have access to a resource teacher/consultant are fortunate that they can call upon this professional for assistance in this process.

Format of Running Records

This method records behaviour as it occurs. The narrative may be recorded in detail or captured as a sketch of events to be filled in with more description after the events. The reason for the documentation will, in effect, determine the number of entries and their detail. 糨糊 建易.

What should be the length of a running record? No set number of days or number of entries per day is recommended, as it depends on the purpose of keeping the record and many other variables.

What else could be included in the running record? When formatting the running record, an observer could include the activities frequented or a description of the setting, or the adults and children involved. The actual formatting of the running record would include the variables that are relevant to the purpose. John, in Exhibit 4.9, was referred from a behaviour clinic to a community program. To report on his progress during this transition from one program to another, a running record was required. The running record appears to be appropriate in the short term. Most child-care settings, however, simply do not have the capacity to conduct these intensive kinds of observations regularly; therefore, running records are the exception, rather than the rule.

The example in Exhibit 4.9 illustrates briefly the sequence of time, the behaviour that was documented, and the comments. The comments show that the observer makes brief notes that are open-ended and speculative. The pages and pages of similarly recorded observations that must be presumed to continue would yield a wealth of information. Perhaps then, after days or weeks, patterns could be identified, strategies developed, and resources identified for John during this transition to the community program.

Diaries: A Type of Record Similar to Running Records

Diaries are similar to running records. Historically, diaries are one of the oldest methods of recording children's development (remember Piaget's diaries of his children's cognitive development?). The diary typically documents a child's development over an extended period of time and includes logged specimens of that child's behaviour. In that traditional sense, diaries are rarely carried out in early childhood settings. What many people refer to as diaries today in early childhood settings are daily **at-a-glance records,** feedback books, logs, or **specimen records.** What is important and universal to them all is that they collect daily information that is objective, meaningful, and useful.

EXHIBIT 4.9 **EXAMPLE OF RUNNING RECORD**

Child's Name: John **DOB:** February 3 **Age:** 3

Observer(s): Aline **Date(s):** March 15

The setting: Free play time indoors in the morning (8:40-11:45)

Time	Observations	Comments
8:40	Runs around corner into room. Yells "Hi, guys!" Stops, looks, runs over to water play, dashes both hands in water (still has winter clothes on), splashes until teacher removes him.	Loves program. Mom seems unable or unwilling to direct him to cubby upon entry to room. Second week in program.
9:10	Runs to easel and stops, grabs brush, smacks brush on paper, laughs, runs to dramatic centre.	Appears eager to try things.
9:30	Pulls truck out of B.'s hands, J. yells, B. laughs, J. pulls harder at truck, glances at teacher, drops truck.	Perhaps still enthusiastic about everything new— sharing.
9:55	J. is screaming. Teacher is holding onto him. Children lining up at the door.	Work on transitions?
10:10	Volunteer walks with J. in the hall. J. is doing the talking.	Seems to calm him. Appears happy.
10:30	Cloakroom. Chatting to K. about TV program. Animated. Listening to K.	Knowledge. Communication skills good.
11:45	Runs to other end of playground when parent arrives, refuses to leave, cries and screams, throws self on ground. Teacher intervenes. Parent watches.	Second time for this occurrence. Yesterday was OK.

ADVANTAGES

- Running records are comprehensive and rich with detail and contextual information. The sheer volume of information that can be gathered on one child includes environmental influences.
- A detailed running record provides examples of all areas of development. Educators would be able to see how the areas of child development are interrelated. For example, a child's non-verbal communication style would have an influence on her social development.
- The greatest advantage of running records is that they allow observers to see patterns of behaviour over time. Instead of focusing on one incident as with anecdotal records, running records profile a child's behaviour over days, weeks, and even months and years.

DISADVANTAGES

- The main disadvantage of the running record is in how much time it requires. To maintain a running record, such as the example in Exhibit 4.10, during the entire day, each day for possibly days or weeks, is extremely time-consuming.
- This type of record demands a high level of commitment from teachers in the room. Early childhood educators state that keeping a running record on even one child in the group on a daily basis is unrealistic.
- If a sustained observation over time is required, then it may be necessary to enlist the support of an outside person, such as a resource teacher/consultant, which may be difficult to arrange and/or cost-prohibitive in some areas of the province/territory.

Longitudinal Studies

Longitudinal studies, or research conducted over an extended period of time, are used extensively to confirm the relevance of a particular theory, explore the merits of specific teacher practices, or explore contemporary issues. This type of research could involve behavioural observations involving groups of children. For example, in her article "Teachers Observe to Learn: Differences in Social Behaviour of Toddlers and Preschoolers in Same-Age and Multiage Groupings," Mary Ellin Logue investigates the benefits of same-age grouping versus multiage grouping of young children. The article cites examples of longitudinal studies, including cross-cultural studies, conducted by others to illustrate the discussion. Investigating methods such as running records and research-based observations lay the groundwork for future studies.

PHOTO: Humber Institute of Technology & Advanced Learning

Event Sampling/ABC Analysis

Purpose and Unique Feature

The types of records known in early childhood education as **event sampling** (Billman and Sherman) or **ABC analysis** (Beaty) have been around for a long time. The informal, familiar environment is ideal for this method of recording children's behaviour because it is here that the day unfolds naturally. Indeed, observing behaviour in the context of a familiar setting is essential to understanding what took place, what preceded the behaviour, and what followed. Contextual information offers clues as to why certain behaviours may occur.

This type of record targets certain behaviours; for example, biting or hitting. What concerns the teacher is not only the behaviour, but the circumstances leading up to the behaviour and the responses to that behaviour. The information that "sets the scene" or gives the context of the behaviour is often as important as the behaviour that was initially targeted for attention.

Event sampling/ABC analysis records a sequence of related events. First, what happened prior to a particular behaviour or event that occurred simultaneously to influence a behaviour is recorded (the stimulus or **antecedent**). Next, the *behaviour* itself is recorded. Then, the **consequences** of the behaviour are recorded. Knowing the consequences helps, in turn, to understand how future behaviours may be influenced.

> Because event sampling is a cause-and-effect type of observation, the observer is looking for clues that will assist in solving the problem. Bell and Low (1973) used ABC analysis with the observed incident to understand the cause of the behaviour. A is the antecedent event, B is the target behaviour and C is the consequent event. (Wortham 93)

Format of Event Sampling/ABC Analysis

The antecedent is the catalyst that triggers a certain behaviour. What the child says and/or does is obviously the child's behaviour. But we also want to find out what happens because of or as a result of that child's behaviour. What happens to the consequences if the antecedent or the behaviour changes? How do the consequences become the antecedent for future behaviours?

To see how event sampling/ABC analysis is part of our everyday life, let us take a look at Exhibit 4.10. Can you think of other examples?

Event sampling can be used in an open-ended way to observe and record situations as they occur. These samples of events note the child's behaviour, interactions with other adults or children, materials, equipment, and the setting. This type of recording can also be used to gather information on events that have caught the teachers' attention. Perhaps the teachers are unclear about what is causing certain behaviours or how the behaviours affect others in the room. Event sampling can also be used to examine teacher–child interactions or to assess how children are interacting with each other or coping with various transitions of the day (see Exhibit 4.11).

By using an event-sampling observational tool, the teacher is able to analyze what seemed to cause the behaviour as well as to examine the consequences of

EXHIBIT 4.10	EXAMPLE OF EVENT SAMPLING/ABC ANALYSIS	
Antecedent	**Behaviour**	**Consequence**
Alarm clock rings	Wake up; shut it off	Get up
Let us change the antecedent in the example:		
Forgot to set the alarm clock	Sleep in	Miss exam
Let us change the behaviour in the example:		
Forgot to set the alarm clock	Dad wakes you up	GET UP!!!

EXHIBIT 4.11   EVENT SAMPLING: GILLIAN

Child's Name: <u>Gillian</u>   DOB: <u>August 26</u>   Age: <u>3</u>

Observer(s): <u>Vince</u>   Date(s): <u>September 14</u>

Time	Antecedent	Behaviour	Consequence
8:45	After sitting with Gillian for 10 min., Mom gets up to leave for work.	Gillian, who had been lying on the floor next to Mom, starts crying.	Teacher intervenes, picks up Gillian, waves bye to Mom.
9:30	Gillian sits quietly on teacher's lap. Tidy-up song is sung and everyone goes to cloakroom.	Gillian clings to teacher and begins to cry.	Teacher takes Gillian, still crying, with him to the cloakroom.
10:00	Gillian sits on edge of sandbox alone and cries (peers and teachers have left area).	Teachers encourage Gillian to play with peers.	Gillian continues to cry, not moving from sandbox.

that behaviour. The primary reason for using this type of record is to document behaviours that may be unacceptable, unusual, or atypical. These behaviours could be aggressive behaviours such as hitting, pushing, biting, or swearing; episodes of mild/severe seizures; bullying behaviours, or destructive group dynamics. Rarely do teachers use event sampling to record, unravel, or analyze positive, prosocial behaviours, such as helping, sharing, or taking turns, or to delve into causes of happiness or contentment.

Embedded in the purpose of using ABC analysis are expectations: expectations of age-appropriate, acceptable behaviour; cultural and familial expectations; or, given our knowledge of a particular child, expectations of what is typical behaviour for this child. So, before we start to use event sampling/ABC analysis, we need to examine our reasons for using this method.

Event Sampling and the Behaviourists

Event sampling/ABC analysis bears a resemblance to the studies of such behaviourists as Pavlov, Skinner, and Watson. These theorists centred on animal learning as an **analogue,** or model, for human learning, and focused on external stimuli in the learning environment, rather than on internal states or conditions of the learner to explain learning behaviours. The application of their theories is still seen in education settings today. B.F. Skinner's concepts of **operant conditioning** and **reinforcement** are commonplace in modern social learning theories, and educators are familiar with the statement that often typifies his theory: "Behaviour that is rewarded is likely to be repeated." The use of rewards, such as stickers for completed work or candy for sitting during circle can find its roots in behaviourist theories. Behaviourists tend to maximize the importance of reinforcers, such as rewards (consequences), and minimize the importance of the internal cognitive states.

Theories that examine *antecedents* or *consequences* are looking for explanations for certain actions or behaviours. The behaviourists applied their theories to learning situations that either centred on enhancing the learning process or reduced or redirected unacceptable behaviour or inefficient learning. Using ABC analysis to uncover reasons for certain behaviours or to unravel complicated behaviours reflects a reliance on the scientific principles of these theories of learning.

Often, parents ask teachers for advice on what to do at home about certain behaviours, such as acting out at mealtime, sibling rivalry, or temper tantrums. Most home-based problematic behaviours are highly complex, personal, and certainly not solvable by a quick conversation. It is wise to listen carefully and to ask pertinent questions before giving suggestions. The child's behaviours are usually only one part of the equation. The ABC analysis model can be effective in uncovering the concerns or expectations of the parents. Assisting the parent to see what caused the behaviour and/or identify how the consequences may be adding to the problem is a positive outcome. How the parent feels is also important. Talking through this process may assist the parent in unravelling and, therefore, understanding the complex nature of the situation.

Adapting Event Sampling/ABC Analysis

Although this type of recording is used mainly with individual children, event sampling can be used to analyze a group of children or specific group relationships, or to evaluate the environment. For example, perhaps the teachers have noticed that the transition time between free play and outdoor activity seems to include children pushing, shoving, or crying, and the teachers having to remind, remove, and reproach. Usually, no one has the luxury of objectively observing this transition because everyone is caught up in it! Yet, if we could arrange to take time out to observe, we would find something like the following:

> The transition time from indoor free play to outdoor activity begins at 9:30. The teachers give warning of the transition by singing songs, reminding children, assisting the children in getting started by tidying up with them, and establishing a presence in the cloakroom.

As in most centres, some children run immediately to get dressed to go outside, others dawdle, and still others move their chairs even closer to the tables, sending a clear message that they intend to stay inside.

Anyone who has been in a playroom at a time like this can predict quite accurately what types of behaviours will occur. Transitions can be difficult for young children; having to stop playing is like asking a theatre full of moviegoers to stop watching the movie, tidy up the area around them, and leave the theatre! Scheduled time is relevant only to older children and adults. Teachers are well aware of this fact, and yet, the point of the event sampling would be to examine the behaviours in the context of the morning transition. The children are telling us something—we need to listen. Once the observations are completed over a number of days, analyzing the data may indicate what acts as an antecedent to the behaviours at morning transition time. Perhaps the behaviours of some children are inconsistent, and the only pattern is that there is none. That too is always a possibility. However, other interpretations may indicate how the noisy routine evolves or who may be the major players in the complex set of events. Observing and recording behaviour in a meaningful way can and does make a difference. Perhaps moving the schedule around to allow more playtime or putting playtime earlier or later in the schedule may be the answer. If, after making these observations, the teachers conclude that only a few children seem to be having a difficult time during this transition, then they can try to find the best solution for each child. Perhaps the obvious answer is simply to change the amount of time needed in the cloakroom, but to avoid not seeing the forest for the trees, a step back to observe is necessary.

Event Sampling and Curriculum Evaluation

Event sampling can be effective if you want to evaluate a process. For example, if the playroom is set up with the theme of "On the Beach" and, as part of the main activities, you have a sandbox in the room, you will want to focus on how each child responded to and learned from the activities. You may also want to observe how the materials were used each day. Setting up the sandbox activity in an event sampling format, such as in Exhibit 4.12, you will be able to see how materials influence behaviour, and how the way in which the children utilized the materials had its own outcomes or consequences.

From the example in Exhibit 4.12, you can see how different materials affect the behaviour of the children, for example, the choice to participate. In this example, the activity was basically the same every day, but the materials changed. If you were to analyze several days' observations more thoroughly, you would see how the consequences of further play exploration affected the use of materials, which in turn affected later behaviours. It confirms our assumption: curriculum affects behaviour.

EXHIBIT 4.12   EVENT SAMPLING: SANDBOX

Antecedents	Behaviours	Consequences
Monday Introduced activity. Added cars, trucks, small blocks. Limit of four children.	Four children (boys) dove into box. Some disagreements, much verbal and physical pushing for space.	Reminders about noise level and sharing materials. Eventual sharing of space around sandbox.
Tuesday Reintroduced activity. Added pieces of cardboard. Role-modelled making a city with streets.	Three girls and one boy sifted through the box, watched, and participated in getting more cardboard, space and materials.	Quiet shuffling of cardboard in the box. Children took up spots around the box. Children played together sharing.
Wednesday Reintroduced activity. Added pinecones, popsicle sticks, odd bits of wood, trucks, toy people.	Two girls and two boys rustled through variety of materials.	Quickly set up city and named what things are and what they are used for. Added people. Children played co-operatively sharing ideas.
Thursday Reintroduced activity. Added cars, train tracks, animals. Provided large mural paper on wall next to box and markers to draw.	Four boys pile materials in arms. Two girls take markers and watch and draw cities.	Major discussion of who does what. Three boys and a girl begin to set up a city. One boy and one girl draw set-up of the city on mural paper.

ADVANTAGES

- Being able to break down complex behaviours to get an idea of what causes the behaviours or maintains them is a major advantage of ABC analysis. Discovering the reason for certain behaviours goes a long way in explaining and helping to resolve the issues that may be involved. Chunking information into what precipitated the behaviour, what types of behaviour resulted, and the outcomes of the behaviour may clearly identify what intervention is necessary.
- Another major advantage is the inclusion of contextual information. It is very helpful to know the conditions under which the behaviour occurred. These events or persons may be the catalyst or contributor to the behaviour.
- As with anecdotal records, event sampling provides the teacher with a collection of behaviours that can be used as a reference point. These examples can then be compared with future behaviours when different strategies have been applied. By comparing the antecedents or consequences, the teacher can evaluate what changes have been effective, if any, or decide what new ideas to try.
- Similar to anecdotal records, setting up or organizing event sampling is quite simple. In this case, it just requires that you divide your paper into three columns for antecedent, behaviour, and consequence. Alternatively, you could indicate these categories in your observations as you write or when you complete your observations.
- Using this method also yields information about programs, other children, or relationships that can be useful in other ways. Using methods like event sampling can help teachers cross-reference topics, such as teaching strategies or guiding techniques for certain children.

DISADVANTAGES

The disadvantages of event sampling/ABC analysis are similar to those of anecdotal records.

- This method requires time to observe, record, and analyze. It records complex behaviours, such as emotions or social interactions between individuals. The process requires time for analysis and insight to occur. If teachers are looking for a fast, check-off-the-item method, event sampling/ABC analysis would not be their choice. Checking off items is the job of other observational tools we will examine in Chapter 5.
- In a busy playroom, a teacher will need to divide her attention between a particular child or event and the ongoing supervision of the environment. To compile enough information to begin to examine the relationships and events, and to formulate ideas about who, what, and why, will involve many observations. This method demands a substantial commitment during a busy day.

- This task requires team members in the playroom to support and assist, and as a result, roles/ schedules must be adjusted for this process to occur. Unless this process is supported by the administration, the coordination of staff could be disorganized and roles misunderstood. The disadvantage is the coordination it requires between staff; some may find it too taxing and therefore lack the will to begin or continue.

Further Applications of Open-ended, Narrative Records: Anecdotal Records, Running Records, and Event Sampling/ABC Analysis

Each observation tool discussed so far is designed to catch the unanticipated behaviours of children. Educators also use these open-ended narrative records to focus on the contextual information found in the observations. For example, through a careful reading of your observations you may find that the children are telling you through their behaviour that the puzzles are too challenging or the books have been on the shelf too long! Consider their behaviour and make adjustments accordingly. Alternatively, perhaps you have observed the children playing inappropriately with the props in the dramatic play area. Based on these observations, you could then indirectly change their behaviour by altering the set-up and props, or by role-modelling the behaviour you wish to see as you are interacting with them.

Another example would be to motivate play in an unused area of the room by sitting there.

Because of your presence (antecedent), the children would investigate the activity (behaviour), and the unfrequented area would be utilized (consequence). Observations are of no use if we do not act on them.

Adaptations based on observations can represent small changes that affect one child or influence significant changes within the group. If the special needs of a child are accommodated by making adaptations, it is quite possible other children may also benefit. For example, suppose a child with a visual impairment joined a preschool group. A resource teacher may make suggestions for successfully including the child in the group. Two of these might be as follows:

- When you address the child, always use the child's name first, and then say what you intend. That way, you have the child's attention first, so she is ready to listen to what you have to say. Children with visual impairments may not have the visual acuity to pick up on nonverbal communication, so they rely on the auditory message. Use the child's name first, and then deliver the message.
- Explain the sounds in the environment. Children are sensitive to sounds and are startled by sounds that are unexpected or unknown to them. Whether you are outside or in the playroom, describe the sounds. Tell the child what they are and even what they do: a furnace, a truck backing up with its beeping sound, or sounds certain toys make.

The slight changes in the teacher's communication patterns will probably influence the behaviour of all the children in that group. Both these suggestions would benefit the entire group, and these changes would have resulted from the observations of one child.

Perhaps you have a group of young toddlers who are beginning to refine their fine motor skills and are working on the ability to control objects and to make things. After observing their struggles with crayons rolling off the table or putting objects back into a container, you may want to make some changes to facilitate their efforts and give them more opportunities to be successful. For example, you could put modelling clay and accessories in a shallow cafeteria-style plastic tray. The low, curved edge helps to confine rolling and sliding objects, yet still allows the toddler to be independent. This independence is the consequence of the adaptation, but the antecedent was the teacher's observation.

Planning the curriculum is a joy for early childhood educators. Planning what kind of materials, toys, and equipment to use or how to arrange the environment and set up areas for activities involves creativity, exploring ideas, problem solving, and exciting communication with team members. Chapter 7 and 8 will be devoted to the decisions that are made on the basis of the teachers' knowledge of the group. Planning that is based on observations and adaptations made to the curriculum as a result creates a responsive climate in the playroom.

Other Usages of the Narrative

Narratives such as the anecdotal record can be shared verbally with parents. A brief anecdote at the end of the day may be just what a parent needs to hear. It is a non-threatening way to communicate, and parents like to hear stories about their child that are pleasant, revealing, or encouraging. Too often, teachers communicate with parents only around directives ("We need more diapers.") or ordinary events ("He ate all his lunch today.") or unpleasant messages ("Anthony bit another child today."). Anecdotal records are brief accounts of what happened. What parent would not smile at the following anecdote?

> Today Sophie was painting at the easel. She stayed at the easel at least 10 minutes and carefully used all the pastel colours available (see attached!). I went over to her and told her what a beautiful job she was doing and how much I liked her painting. You know what she said? "Don't worry, Miss Sandy, someday you can paint like this too."

Summary

This chapter featured three main types of records—anecdotal records, running records, and event sampling/ABC analysis. These observation tools record unanticipated behaviour. They each have unique features, allowing teachers to choose the most appropriate type of record for a specific purpose. The types of records used for unanticipated behaviours are flexible and open-ended, allowing for a diverse range of uses. These observation tools form one of the major groupings that should be represented in the child's portfolio. Interpretations play a prominent role in these tools. Since the behaviours are recorded as they occur, reflective, personal interpretation is necessary to give meaning to those behaviours.

PROFESSIONAL REFLECTIONS

Much of what we know about children's interests and phase of development we learn from the observation process. The unique function of observation in early childhood education settings is to gain an understanding of the children's developmental milestones, needs, and interests so that the environment is designed to offer children experiences that support their interests and phase of development.

Developmentally appropriate practice requires early childhood practitioners to design and implement a curriculum that is reflective of each child's phase of development, their identified interests and needs, combined with their cultural and family values. By observing children's interactions on a continual basis and observing how the play environment influences children's behaviours, practitioners have the data needed to inform their practice. The information collected through observations is used in discussion with parents to further explore the needs and interests of the child, provide developmental information about the child to the parent, and explore potential program direction with the program team.

The process of observation is one of the key skills necessary for early childhood practitioners to develop and refine throughout their career. These skills are developed over time and can best be achieved through practice, discussion, evaluation, and reflection. When practitioners observe children they weave together their knowledge of child development, teaching/learning methods, philosophies, current trends, and professional practices. This process provides practitioners with the opportunity to analyze and reflect on what they are seeing and experiencing.

Observations made of children's interests, environmental factors, and personal practice provide information to practitioners in their quest to assess and reflect on their own performance. When practitioners engage in effective observation and reflective practice, they role model this skill to children. This facilitates children in gaining the foundation skills of observation and reflection by encouraging them to examine, revisit, represent, discuss, and demonstrate areas of inquiry. This, in turn, sets the stage for problem solving, critical thinking, abstract thought, and lifelong learning for both children and the practitioner.

–Beverlie Dietz,
M.Ad.Ed., B.Ed, Loyalist College

KEY TERMS

accommodate

analogue

antecedent

at-a-glance records

consequences

contextual information

contrived observation

evaluation

event sampling/ABC analysis

inference

interpretations

longitudinal study

narrative/running record

natural observation

operant conditioning

perception

play therapist

reinforcement

specimen record

DISCUSSION QUESTIONS

1. What are the three open-ended observational tools for recording unanticipated behaviour discussed in this chapter?
2. What is the main purpose for choosing each of the three types of records?
3. What are the advantages and disadvantages of each tool?
4. Why is interpretation a vital component of these open-ended types of records?
5. How could these three types of records be used in child-care settings?

ADDITIONAL READINGS

Hendrick, Joanne, and Patricia Weissman. *The Whole Child*. 8th ed. New Jersey: Pearson Education, Inc., 2006.

The Whole Child, when used in conjunction with this text, provides students with topics to explore such as developing social competence and fostering emotional health in young children. The text offers theory and examples that assist students in discovering what are, for example, the hallmarks of an emotional healthy child. Learning about social competence helps students in understanding what behaviours they would need to observe to conclude a child is developing in a socially healthy manner.

Logue, Mary Ellin. "Teachers Observe to Learn: Differences in Social Behavior of Toddlers and Preschoolers in Same-Age and Multiage Groupings." *Young Children* 61.3 (2006): 70–73.

In a multiage study involving 31 children ranging in age from two through five and one-half years, this teachers' action research project found that dominance behaviours (hitting, kicking, spitting, taking or demanding objects, etc.) were significantly less prevalent in multiage groupings than in classrooms of same-age peers.

Nilsen, Barbara Ann. *Week by Week: Plans for Documenting Children's Development.* 4th ed. Clifton Park, NY: Delmar Learning, 2008.

Week by Week presents a manageable plan that will help students gather documentation on all the children in all developmental areas while developing an extensive portfolio. Along with the weekly plans are tips on sharing observations with families. The chapter "Using Anecdotal Recordings to Look at Self-Care" is insightful.

Pimento, Barbara, and Deborah Kernested. *Healthy Foundations in Early Childhood Settings*. 3rd ed. Toronto: Thomson Nelson, 2004.

Although this is not a text with an observation focus, several vital topics such as child abuse and health and wellness are linked directly to observation. These topics are thoroughly investigated and contribute to students' knowledge of the crucial role observation plays in child care. Separating objective observation from subjective interpretation is of paramount importance in writing accident/wellness reports or documenting an incident of child abuse.

Wortham, Sue C. *Assessment in Early Childhood Education*. 3rd ed. Columbus, OH: Merrill, 2001.

The author suggests that entering the new century means that educators must realize that the times are changing and so are the means of assessing young children. Many of the chapters in this text are useful in further exploring such topics as informal evaluation measures, types of observation, and assessments. Wortham encourages students to produce knowledge, rather than reproduce knowledge, in keeping with Piaget's position of the constructivist.

Chapter

5

OBSERVING AND RECORDING TARGETED BEHAVIOURS

PHOTO: Courtesy of Janet Blaxell

Three-year-old Sonja always comes to school neatly dressed. Her tidy physical appearance is complemented by her sweet, pleasant personality. She always complies with the teachers and, rarely, if ever, makes a fuss. It seems she usually engages in solitary play. When you stop to think about Sonja at the end of the day, it is hard to recall what she did the entire day!

Children like Sonja are not always noticed because they are independent and self-reliant and may drift from activity to activity without the teachers taking notice of their interactions or choice of activities.

138

NEL

Specific, purposeful observations ensure no child is overlooked. If a teacher had collected information on all the children in her group, she would have included Sonja, and learned more about this quiet child. Perhaps the teacher would have learned from this chart where Sonja spent most of her time each day by using a participation chart such as the one displayed below.

Activity	Monday	Tuesday	Wednesday	Thursday	Friday
Dramatic play	✓✓✓	✓✓✓✓	✓✓	✓✓✓	✓✓
Listening centre	✓✓✓	✓✓✓✓	✓	✓✓	✓
Creative (messy)	✓	✓	✓✓✓✓✓	✓✓✓	✓✓✓
Puzzles	✓	✓✓	✓✓	✓	✓✓
Block area	✓	✓			
Sensory bins	✓✓	✓✓✓	✓✓	✓✓✓	✓✓

This chart gives you a quick, at-a-glance visual of Sonja's activities. This type of record captures specific information, such as the participation of a child in the various play areas in the room. What are her favourite activities? Which is her least favourite activity? Does her participation at certain activities change from day to day? How would this information be helpful in discussing with her family what she seems to enjoy in the playroom? These questions plus many more can be answered by using the participation chart and other observational tools described in this chapter.

Overview

Chapter 4 explained how anecdotal records, running records, and event sampling/ABC analysis are used to record *unanticipated* behaviours. This chapter groups together a second broad category of observation tools that record targeted behaviours. **Targeted behaviours** are those that are preselected by the observer.

The featured types of records discussed in this chapter are

- checklists,
- rating scales,
- participation charts,
- profiles, and
- behaviour tallying and charting.

These are **closed methods** used to record preselected behaviour. Closed methods are not open to recording whatever behaviour the observer witnesses but, rather, target specific behaviour to be observed. In Chapter 4, we became familiar with the concept of *open methods*. Using the analogy of the fish net cast out to sea, narrative or **open methods** are "open-weave" and represent an open-ended, loosely constructed way of collecting information—"catching" whatever is there.

Not surprisingly, closed methods are designed to catch specific, preselected behaviours. These observations do not have the storytelling characteristics of the narrative but, rather, are precise, brief descriptions that are easily recorded as single words, marks, codes, or point-form notes. When educators are focused on the neutral dimensions of checkmarks or codes and preselected behaviours, they are more likely to observe in an objective manner, thus decreasing subjectivity.

Each of the observational tools is designed for a purpose:

- Checklists allow you to check off instances of particular behaviours.
- Rating scales rate behaviour against specific criteria.
- Participation charts record participation in various activities.
- Profiles focus on areas of development.
- Behaviour tallying counts the frequency of behaviours.

The types of records in Chapter 5 are different from those presented in Chapter 4 in yet another way. The narrative record forms in Chapter 4 were quickly set up, and the "real" work began after the observation—rewriting the observations and reflecting upon and writing the interpretations. The record forms in this chapter require the majority of the work to be done before the observation begins. Using the methods of documentation in Chapter 5 means organizing and conceptualizing the format, essentially designing it to fit the purpose; the "real" work takes place before the observation itself.

After reading this chapter, you should be able to:

- Describe the observational tools that record targeted behaviours.
- State the main purpose and unique feature of each method.
- Identify the format used for each of these types of records.
- List the advantages and disadvantages of each method.
- Explain how information can be interpreted using these methods.
- Indicate some possible applications for each type of record.

Preparing to Record Targeted Behaviours

Once the purpose for the observation has been established, there are many other decisions to be made. When you design and develop your own method of recording observations, you will have to

- determine the behaviours you wish to observe;
- define those behaviours clearly and in such a way that anyone using the form will have the same understanding of what those behaviours are;
- ensure that the targeted behaviours are norm-referenced with typical behaviours demonstrated by children in the same age group; and
- decide, if applicable, which symbols to use: numbers, check marks, or specific descriptors.

Making choices about which descriptors to use or how to ascribe certain symbols to represent some kind of evaluation is a complex task. Even defining the behaviour to be targeted and monitored may be difficult. For example, if "sharing" is the targeted behaviour, teachers may interpret sharing in a variety of ways. Some educators may refer to sharing in relation to toys, while others consider the sharing of space, ideas, or friends to be more relevant. If the teachers have different ideas about what kinds of sharing are important to observe and record, then the information they collect will not be consistent. When defining what behaviour is to be observed, other factors enter into the decision-making process as well.

Frequency versus Duration

Recording **frequency,** or the number of times something happens, relies on behaviour that is stated in well-defined terms. The preselected behaviour must be a discrete unit and sharply defined to minimize subjective interpretations. Some examples of behaviours that are easily observed are "kicks ball," "folds paper," "draws a circle," and "removes shoes." Each of these samples is a distinct behaviour and is straightforward enough that its frequency of occurrence can be recorded with ease. See Exhibit 5.1 for examples.

Duration refers to how long the behaviour occurred. Duration refers to how long it took a child to put away his toys during a transition period, complete a puzzle, or eat lunch with a spoon. The purpose of observing and recording duration may be quite different from the purpose of observing frequency. See Exhibit 5.1 for examples.

Recording duration is effective for the types of behaviours that do not appear to have definite boundaries. These behaviours occur over a varying amount of time and are complex, encompassing other behaviours. For example, while Joseph is painting, he is watching other children, scratching his nose, and wriggling; during circle time, even though Muriel is sitting, she is talking, tickling her neighbour, pulling her hair, and leaning from side to side.

Frequency behaviours are those discrete, self-contained behaviours with a beginning, middle, and end. When they are observed, they can be checked off. Duration

EXHIBIT 5.1	EXAMPLES: FREQUENCY AND DURATION
Examples of Frequency Behaviours	**Examples of Duration Behaviours**
throwing ball	wandering
printing name	crying
pointing to nose	gazing
zipping up jacket	painting

behaviours are complex, occur over a period of time from minutes to hours, and include subsets of behaviours. The following are examples of an observed behaviour with subsets:

- "wanders around the room at the end of playroom time,"
- "plays cooperatively with peers," and
- "communicates with her peers."

For ease of observing and recording, these broad statements of behaviours could be separated into more distinct, targeted behaviours. For example, "communicates with her peers" could be subdivided in any number of ways: nonverbal communication, listening skills, expressive language. Examining the concepts of frequency and duration assists us in selecting the type of record that most effectively suits our purpose for observing.

Considering the complexity of designing types of records to document targeted behaviour, it is not hard to understand why commercially produced observation tools such as checklists or rating scales are popular.

Developing any observation tool is a lengthy process involving

- a defined purpose and vision of outcomes,
- research,
- clear strategies of information gathering,
- knowledge of child development, and
- good communication among team members.

This process, although complex and perhaps tedious, provides opportunities to enhance the professionalism of early childhood educators. Making decisions based on research and the data they have compiled encourages and empowers teachers and parents, builds self-confidence, and develops trust in their ability to construct their own work together.

Checklists

Purpose and Unique Feature

The checklist is the most basic of the recording methods discussed in this chapter, and a good place to start. The **checklist** is used to record the presence (yes) or absence (no) of a behaviour. The response is usually recorded in the form of a check mark or some **coding scheme.**

Checklists are used so routinely to gather information in our everyday lives that they are already very familiar to us. We are often asked to respond to a questionnaire, as anyone who has strolled through a mall or been interrupted by a telephone survey will attest. Does this sound familiar? "Hi, I'm calling on behalf of the XYZ Association. Would you mind taking a few minutes of your time to answer yes or no to the following questions?" Organizations that use checklists are aware that people are busy, and they use this method in order to gather as much information as possible in the least amount of time.

For our purposes, the behaviours chosen for the checklist need to

- be readily observable,
- occur frequently,
- be observable unobtrusively during certain routines of the day,
- be easily elicited from the child, such as the clapping of hands,
- be consistent in construction (using same word order and verb tense), and
- be stated positively.

Given these criteria for an item appropriate in a checklist, take a look at Exhibit 5.2. Do the items in that brief, homemade checklist meet the criteria? For example, are the items readily observable, stated positively, or observable during routines of the day?

When constructing any checklist, make the form user-friendly. For example, including a *comments section* gives the observer space to write down examples

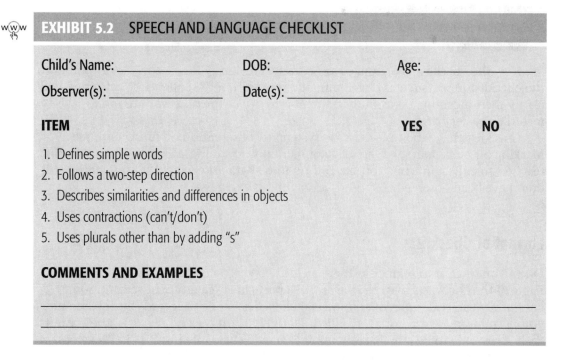

EXHIBIT 5.2   SPEECH AND LANGUAGE CHECKLIST

Child's Name: _____   DOB: _____   Age: _____

Observer(s): _____   Date(s): _____

ITEM	YES	NO
1. Defines simple words		
2. Follows a two-step direction		
3. Describes similarities and differences in objects		
4. Uses contractions (can't/don't)		
5. Uses plurals other than by adding "s"		

COMMENTS AND EXAMPLES

_____

_____

of the child's responses. The observer may also include important information, such as "not very talkative today" or "Celine has been away for two days and just returned today." These notes may have an impact on the information recorded that day and may cue the observer to re-evaluate the information on the checklist.

Checklists are an efficient means of recording discrete units of behaviour that are known in advance. For example, if we wish to record examples of a child's fine motor skills, we would look for the following items on our checklist:

- transfer a toy from one hand to another,
- use the pincer grasp,
- play pat-a-cake, and
- put objects into a container

All these examples gives the teacher information about the child's fine motor skills. Targeting behaviours that are likely to be repeated during the day gives the teacher many opportunities to observe and record. The teacher can adopt a spectator role or a participant role, whichever is the best way to observe at that time.

Checklists are effective for recording activities that can be sequenced. For example, in the cloakroom during winter, the teacher of a group of three-year-olds may not find "can dress self" as accurate as a breakdown of that skill:

- cooperates in dressing
- puts on jacket independently
- puts on jacket and zips up/closes fasteners
- puts on boots

How the checklist is organized affects how efficiently it is used. A logical order to the checklist items, such as developmental progression or sequence of activities, will clarify their meaning, contribute to the objectivity of the observations, and make recording easier.

Checklists have their place in the systematic observation of young children. Marking off behaviours that are developmentally appropriate is an efficient way for teachers to collect information. Recording these data for each child until all the children have been observed ensures that no child is excluded.

Format of Checklists

On the Internet or in textbooks there are dozens of good examples of checklists. Some of the checklists may be relevant to a particular age group or setting. Some commonly used examples of commercial checklists made to record the behaviours of young children are the Portage Guide to Early Education (see Table 5.1), the Hawaii Early Learning Profile (HELP; see Exhibit 5.3), and the Nipissing District Developmental Screen (see Chapter 8, page 278, 279, 280).

TABLE 5.1 CHILD DEVELOPMENT TOOL FOR OBSERVATION AND PLANNING (TOP)

Communication/Language/Literacy

Code:

Always or consistently (✓)

Occasionally (O)

Cannot do/not observed (N)

Mark date and code

4 to 5 years

Strands		Things to Consider	OBSERVATION	
			Dates	Code
Early Reading	6 Recites songs, rhymes from memory or makes them up	A predictor of later reading success is found in a child's ability to recognize matching sounds and rhymes in word games and songs.	1	
			2	
			3	
			4	
	7 Retells a story, but may confuse some of the facts	Children understand and remember a sequence of what comes first, next and last. Reads book from memory.	1	
			2	
			3	
			4	
	8 Identifies at least 10 letters of the alphabet, especially those in their own name (record letters below).	Talk to children about the letters of the alphabet by name and sound. Point out letters and words in the alphabet.	1	
			2	
			3	
			4	
	9 Recognizes a word as a unit of print	Child realizes that print, rather than pictures, carries the meaning of the story and that print corresponds to the oral version.	1	
			2	
			3	
			4	

Comment:

SOURCE: Reproduced with permission of Portage Project.

ADVANTAGES

- The main advantage of a checklist is that it is quick and easy to use. The checklist, whether commercially produced or tailor-made by the centre staff, means less time documenting.
- When the same form is used by teachers in the same way, observer bias or judgment error is reduced, leading to a more objective report of the child.
- If the same form is used for all the children, then the likelihood that all children will be given equal attention is maximized.
- Specific items of behaviour on a checklist provide a focus for observing. When behaviours are highlighted for observation, they are less likely to be overlooked.
- A completed checklist presents an overall impression of the child's skills (items checked off as accomplished) and areas to improve (indicated by a dash or other symbol as having yet to be completed).

DISADVANTAGES

- Checklists generally do not provide information on the quality or proficiency of the behavioural item, only that it has occurred. The yes/no response does indicate whether this skill is an emerging skill (just beginning to be demonstrated) or if this skill has been mastered (able to be performed anywhere, any place, or with anyone).
- Checklists typically do not provide contextual information that may be critical in determining the level of difficulty of the item. If an item states "hops on left foot," does it refer to one to three times or across the room? Depending on the location or certain materials, a child may demonstrate very different kinds of skills or give different responses.
- If the child is not well or is having a bad day, the results of a one-time checklist may not be an accurate indicator of his or her typical behaviour.

Adaptations of Checklists

Checklists can be adapted to meet the needs of the group. For example, a checklist designed by centre staff could be adapted to consider unique linguistic needs. If the checklist item is "Responds appropriately to social words," "Hi" and "Bye" could be included as examples as well as the corresponding words in the child's first language.

This is a good opportunity to exhibit the social and cultural uniqueness of the centre's population. Adding items to include or illustrate linguistic and social skills or providing comment areas after each developmental area to record examples of first language or cultural nuances is a way to identify or monitor the strength and needs of all children.

EXHIBIT 5.3 CHECKLIST ITEMS FROM HELP

2-8 Sign Language Skills

2.184	2–3	Watches face and body of speaker to get clues as to meaning of signed communication
2.186	2.6–3.2	Responds to single signs pertaining to own wants or needs when signed by another
2.190	3.0–3.4	Imitates single signs expressing own wants or needs when signed by another
2.191	3.0–3.6	Produces single signs expressing own wants without a model
2.194	3.0–3.8	Uses one sign for own name when signed by another
2.195	3.0–4.0	Uses face and body to give clues to meaning of signs
2.196	3.0–4.0	Smiles/frowns for clue to meaning of signed communication
2.197	3.0–4.2	Uses hands, arms, feet, shoulders to add expression signs
2.198	3.2–3.6	Imitates sign for own name when signed by another
2.202	3.4–4.2	Uses speed and vigour of signing to express hate, fear, anger

3-9 Wheelchair Skills

3.208	3.0–6.0	Stops wheelchair in any manner
3.209	3.0–6.0	Moves wheelchair forward using one push forward and release
3.210	3.0–6.0	Moves wheelchair backward using one pull back and release
3.211	3.0–6.0	Turns wheelchair in a circle to the right
3.212	3.0–6.0	Turns wheelchair in a circle to the left
3.213	3.0–6.0	Sets brake on wheelchair to stop or remain stationary
3.214	3.0–6.0	Releases brake on wheelchair to resume movement
3.215	3.0–6.0	Travels forward 10 feet in wheelchair
3.216	3.0–6.0	Travels backward 10 feet in wheelchair
3.217	3.0–6.0	Travels length of classroom in wheelchair

Another way to adapt a checklist to a specific population could be by using a commercial checklist, such as the HELP (Hawaii Early Learning Profile; see Exhibit 5.3). This developmental checklist includes specific competency items for children who use sign language or for those needing assistance with their mobility (i.e., standers, walkers, or wheelchairs).

Rating Scales

Purpose and Unique Feature

Rating scales are similar to checklists: they record behaviours that have been targeted in advance. However, the unique feature of rating scales is that they provide a broader range of possibilities for evaluating behaviour.

In early childhood education settings, rating scales are used for evaluating staff, children, curriculum, and the environment. Perhaps you are being evaluated on a rating scale during your practice teaching. In this chapter, several uses of rating scales will be explored.

Format of Rating Scales

Choosing the items for the rating scale is similar to choosing items for a checklist: the behaviours are decided on prior to the observations. However, unlike the checklist, rating scales will provide one more unique feature: a scale against which the behavioural items are rated. The rating scale is used to judge an item of behaviour by the degree or frequency with which the behaviour occurs along a chosen **continuum.** The rating scale is, therefore, a kind of checklist that includes judgments about the behaviour. Exhibit 5.4 shows a rating scale that describes how the children use the books in the centre. In this example, the teachers wanted to get an idea of not only whether the children were using the books, but, more importantly, how they were using the books. The quality or range of judgment is determined by the **descriptors,** or qualifiers: not descriptive or true, moderately descriptive or true, and

---

EXHIBIT 5.4   RATING SCALE FOR BOOK CENTRE

Child's Name: _____   DOB: _____   Age: _____

Observer(s): _____   Date(s): _____

	Not Descriptive or True			Moderately Descriptive or True			Very Descriptive or True	
1. Turns book right side up	1	2	3	4	5	6	7
2. Hands book to adult to read	1	2	3	4	5	6	7
3. Points to and names pictures	1	2	3	4	5	6	7
4. Turns pages one at a time	1	2	3	4	5	6	7

---

very descriptive or true. These descriptors are then given a value on a numerical continuum. If a researcher or consultant evaluates these behaviours along the continuum by adding up the numbers, he or she would derive a summative evaluation. Clinical research, observations, and assessment tools use these measurements for their reliability and validity. Computing the scores provides the researcher with data to compare and **correlate** with other scores. However, in early childhood settings, the information from rating scales is generally used for making decisions about individual or group development, the environment, or planning for future curriculum.

The Judgment Factor

You would think that any form that has a built-in judgment factor would be the most biased of all the observational tools. However, this is not necessarily true. If the behaviours to be observed and the scales to rate those behaviours are devised by the teachers and all dimensions are agreed upon, then that process goes a long way in decreasing subjectivity.

Subjectivity enters when the dimensions of the behaviour are unclear or ambiguous. When the teacher is not sure how to interpret the item, she or he will rate it differently from other teachers. Agreeing on the meaning of the scales is also critical: if a scale uses such terms as "often" or "sometimes," the door to subjective interpretation is left wide open. Since "always" or "never" rarely exists in a real world, how valid is the following scale?

Always   Often   Sometimes   Never

When judgment is involved in a rating scale, it should be an informed, realistic, and controlled judgment.

ADVANTAGES/DISADVANTAGES: RATING SCALES

ADVANTAGES

- Once you have an appropriate rating scale, it can be used very efficiently. Recording observations on a rating scale evaluates along a dimension that in itself provides further information. The scale provides a common ground for comparison; it can be used to compare the skills of a group of children. From this data, a variety of educational decisions can be made and translated into the individualization of curriculum.
- Rating scales, as we will see with the Harms and Clifford scales in Chapter 8, are used effectively to rate the environment. The resulting information, in turn, can form the basis of discussions that can contribute to quality care decisions in the centre.

(continued)

DISADVANTAGES

- Sometimes the rating scale descriptors do not adequately judge the dimensions of behaviour they were designed to judge. A rating scale should, therefore, be field tested to determine its usefulness for the job prior to administering it "for real."
- Although the amount and degree of information that can be obtained from rating scales can be rewarding, this method takes time to construct. Since judgment is clearly indicated in rating scales, the team has to devise not only the items of behaviour they wish to observe but the levels of expectancy as well. If values from "mastery" to "inexperience" are used as criteria, setting those values along a continuum is straightforward. However, the team still needs to agree on what constitutes mastery and what is meant by inexperience. You would think that that is easy to do, but many seasoned teachers and researchers suggest that it is not.
- Even if commercial rating scales are used, some basic training is required to interpret the items of behaviour and the rating scale itself. Unless the teachers have had some training in the design and use of rating scales, they may use inappropriate methods and derive invalid results.
- Recall from Chapter 3 the various errors of judgment, one of them being the error of central tendency. Unless the items and the rating scale are chosen very carefully, teachers may avoid extremes in rating children's behaviour, scoring the children's performance as a 3 out of 5 rather than rate lower or higher and, consequently, end up with a central tendency error.

Adaptations for Special Populations

Early childhood educators rarely design and develop rating scales to evaluate children; rather, they rely on rating scales already on the market and available from educational institutions and publishers. Professionals contributing years of empirical research have developed commercial rating scales for children and many good examples exist for special populations. These assessment tools can usually be ordered as a package containing a manual, scoring sheets, and other materials. The Childhood Autism Rating Scale (CARS) is suitable for use with any child over two years of age and uses observation as well as parent reports and other information to rate each child. The child is rated along a seven-point continuum, indicating the degree to which the child's behaviour deviates from that of a normal child of the same age. Another example of a rating scale used for special populations is the Children's Depression Rating Scale for children aged from six to twelve. This rating scale is based on a semi-structured interview with the child. The interview approach is different than the CARS, which is based on observation and parent reports. Unlike the CARS, which can be utilized by a variety of professionals, the Children's Depression Rating Scale is available only to registered test users.

Rating Scales in Early Childhood Education

Valid rating scales are complex to construct. Their design requires a good deal of research, not only in terms of the behaviours to be rated, but also in terms of the rating system itself. The possibilities for judgmental error can exist at several levels:

- The components of behaviour
- The order in which these components are listed along the continuum
- How the teacher is allowed to rate the behaviour along the continuum
- The possibility of multiple inferences from each behavioural component
- The type of scale used
- The appropriateness of the scale in relation to the behaviour being rated
- The weighting of each behavioural component
- The appropriateness of the wording of the rating scale

Long as this list is, it represents a limited view of the entire process. The purpose of identifying these variables here is to explain them, rather than to dissuade you from developing your own. By understanding some of the complexities involved, we can appreciate the efforts of those who have already devised successful rating scales, such as Thelma Harms, Richard M. Clifford, and Debby Cryer (see scales displayed in Table 8.1, Chapter 8). Rating scales are a major form of evaluation; their value has been proven.

Participation Charts

Purpose and Unique Feature

The *participation chart* targets behaviour, and logically, what is recorded in the chart is participation. A child's participation at various activities can be recorded easily by creating a list of curriculum items or behavioural descriptions and then checking them off. Participation charts can be organized to record the participation of each child in the group taking part in a specific activity, or they can be organized to include all the possible activities and areas available in the playroom. If desired, a number of variables can be presented on the chart:

- a column for frequency: how many times the child visited the activity
- a column for duration: how long the child stayed at each activity
- a comments section: an area to comment on the child's playmates, their interactions, types of play, or specific information relevant to the teachers

The unique feature of the participation chart is that it can record the participation of one child, a small group, or the entire group of children. This versatility allows the observer more possibilities to collect information than some of the other methods. The observer may also vary the depth of information sought. For example, he or she may collect basic information on all the children (their participation during outdoor play) but may also choose to focus on one child during this activity and include some quality indicators (what types of play the child is engaged in).

Format of Participation Charts

The organization of the participation chart will depend on your initial decision: do you want to include all the children, some of the children, or only one child? If the chart is set up for one child, then the initial organization will be similar to those charts we have already seen, similar to Exhibit 5.5.

However, if the participation chart is to be organized to include a group or all of the children, your set-up may be quite different. For example, if you wanted to observe the group during morning free playtime, you could set up your chart as in Exhibit 5.6. The information provided by this chart is significant. With just a brief look, you can immediately see who played where that morning. Are there any

| **EXHIBIT 5.5** PARTICIPATION CHART FOR ONE CHILD |||||

Child's Name: _____ DOB: _____ Age: _____

Observer(s): _____ Date(s): _____

Activity	Monday	Tuesday	Wednesday	Thursday	Friday
Sand play					
Science table					
Listening centre					
Book corner					
Block area					
Dramatic area					
Creative (messy)					
Creative (dry)					
Interest table					
Computer area					
Self-help shelf					
Floor toys					
Puzzle shelf					

EXHIBIT 5.6	PARTICIPATION CHART FOR MORE THAN ONE CHILD

Observer: Heather   **Date(s):** Week of October 10 (Mon.–Fri.)

Setting: Indoor play activities   **Time:** 9:45–10:30 a.m.

Name	Creatives	Dramatic	Blocks	Bookshelf	Sand Play
Lakesha	✓✓✓✓	✓✓		✓	✓
Devon	✓		✓✓✓✓	✓	✓✓✓
Tiffany	✓✓✓	✓✓			
Ahmed	✓✓✓	✓✓			✓✓

particular activities or areas that were seldom used or not used at all? Judging from the number of children who used particular areas, which were the most popular areas? Does this information give you any ideas about the curriculum? Does the chart confirm your hunches about who usually plays with whom?

Let us assume that the participation chart in Exhibit 5.6 was implemented on Friday after four straight days of rain and no outdoor play. If you arranged the same or similar activities on Monday after a weekend of beautiful weather, and implemented another participation chart, would you find the same clustering of children at the same activity areas? What changes might you expect?

Using a participation chart to record the behaviour of all the children in the group several times over a three-month period presents a rudimentary pattern of group activity. From that information, you can make a variety of educational decisions. You may want to pay particular attention to the group dynamics. Perhaps these charts have indicated a few children whose time spent in solitary activities is of concern to you. The simplicity or complexity of participation charts provides teachers with many possible educational and managerial decisions.

Interpreting Participation Chart Information

Before you begin writing your interpretations, organize the information you collected from your participation charts in rough draft form.

- Use headings such as frequency, duration, and the developmental areas.
- Lay your charts out and systematically go through them, compiling the behaviour you observed under each appropriate heading.
- If you made interpretations in your comment section, make sure to record them using *seems, appears, as if,* and *perhaps* to indicate your opinions.
- Begin to analyze the information, summarizing it in a meaningful way as the basis for staff discussions on curriculum, individual children, or the group as a

whole. This information can also be shared with parents and included in the children's records or portfolios.

The number of times a child engages in an activity over a period of two weeks should indicate a number of possible conclusions: the child likes this activity, he or she is good at it, he or she likes the other children who frequent the activity as well, he or she has a good attention span, or he or she is attracted to the physical environment of that space. These suggestions are not an exhaustive list, but provide examples of the information that can be generated by one segment of the participation chart. Check your interpretations of the child's behaviour with those of other teachers. Did they come to the same conclusions you did?

Similarly, how would you interpret the information in the duration column? What are some reasons for a child staying at an activity for a short time? For a long time? Is the child's behaviour reflective of the age group. What can be said about the interest in the activities? What can be learned about the child's interests, learning style, personal characteristics, or peer relationships? These are some of

PHOTO: Courtesy of Paul Till

ADVANTAGES/DISADVANTAGES: PARTICIPATION CHARTS

ADVANTAGES

- Participation charts can be used for one child, a small group, or the entire group of children. Few other observation tools allow the teacher the flexibility to record such a wide variety of variables, such as likes, dislikes, frequency, duration, brief anecdotal notes, areas of curriculum, comparisons of a.m./p.m. curriculum, to name only a few.
- Participation charts complement many other types of records. Combining participation charts with anecdotal records provides an overview of the children's activities as well as highly descriptive detail for five- or ten-minute segments.
- The environment can be evaluated while observing the children. Based on the participation of the children, most popular and least used activity areas can be quickly noted.
- Participation charts are user-friendly for parents. Sharing information about what a child did during the day is a refreshing and exciting way to communicate with the parents. The charts give the parents information about where their child spent most of her or his time. The charts also show what activities their child did not attempt. This information is of interest and often a surprise to the parents. Participation charts are a nonthreatening point of reference from which teachers and parents can begin to develop discussions.

DISADVANTAGES

- Some teachers report that completing the participation chart in a busy playroom is unrealistic, particularly when more than one dimension is being observed and recorded during the same time frame. They also say that focusing on several variables on a chart at the same time is too complicated to do for any sustained period of time. If participation is the only variable being observed, a chart for one child or even a group of children is easily managed. However, if other variables such as duration are added to a group chart, then the work involved is also compounded.

the questions to be asked when analyzing and interpreting information from the participation charts.

Adaptations of Participation Charts

If you wanted to focus on social skills or specifically comment on the social skills of the child as he played, you could set up a participation chart such as the one in Exhibit 5.7.

| EXHIBIT 5.7 | PARTICIPATION CHART FOR SOCIAL SKILLS |

Child's Name: _____ DOB: _____ Age: _____

Observer(s): _____ Date(s): _____

Activity	Frequency	Duration	Comments on Social Skills
Block area			
Bookshelf			
Sand/Water play			
Puzzles			
Creative (messy)			
Creative (dry)			
Dramatic centre			

Adding an open-ended comments section targeting social skills is one way to further adapt a participation chart. Another way to adapt the chart could be by adding other columns or dimensions. Instead of the open-ended comments, you could include the types of play and arrange them so that each item need only be checked off as in Exhibit 5.8.

If you observed and recorded over a two-week period, you would collect 10 days of interesting behaviour! What types of play would you expect to find in the dramatic play area? What types of play would be most documented in the puzzle area?

If you choose to have a comments section, it is a good place to jot down any observations you deem interesting or relevant. Recording behaviours that reflect the socioemotional area might be your focus. What evidence could you find for the following?

- Accepts/rejects direction
- Is a leader/follower
- Is independent/dependent
- Is active/passive
- Initiates/responds

When you are looking for patterns over time, using indicators such as these will help focus your search and classify similar behaviours that are representative of the socioemotional area.

Examine the Participation Chart for Outdoor Play (Exhibit 5.9). The set-up is similar to the charts organized for indoor play. However, the content of

EXHIBIT 5.8   PARTICIPATION CHART WITH TYPES OF PLAY

Child's Name: _____   DOB: _____   Age: _____

Observer: _____   Date(s): _____

Activity	Unoccupied	Onlooker	Solitary	Parallel	Associative	Cooperative
Block area						
Bookshelf						
Sand/Water play						
Puzzles						
Creative (messy)						
Dramatic centre						

EXHIBIT 5.9   PARTICIPATION CHART FOR OUTDOOR PLAY

Child's Name: Jules   DOB: April 20, 1995   Age: 4

Observer(s): Jeff   Date(s): May 6, 1999

Time: 2:15   Activity: Outdoor play

Items	Frequency	Duration	Comments
Climber	✓✓✓✓	Total: 20 min.	First time: 5 min. alone Second time: 10 min. with two friends Third and fourth times: five min. with one friend
Tricycle	✓	10 min.	Rode around in circles on the path quietly
Sandbox	✓✓	5 min.	Both times stood and watched, then sat down and watched

Note: Jules spent about five minutes wandering around between activities. He did not appear to talk to peers during this time.

PHOTO: Humber Institute of Technology & Advanced Learning

observations taken outdoors is usually highly interesting. Observations taken during outdoor play may reveal very different information about children at play. Compare their play choices outdoors with what children choose indoors. What might you find?

Profiles

Purpose and Unique Feature

Profiles do not target specific behaviours, but, rather, focus on specific areas of child development, such as fine motor or communication. This targeted developmental area is somewhat broad, yet it does help to focus the observer on specific behaviours typically demonstrated within that developmental area. This narrowing of focus typifies the closed methods of conducting and recording observations.

The positive outcome of using this type of documentation is that it allows the observer the flexibility of selecting examples of behaviour that are meaningful in terms of the child's environment, family, and cultural influences. This contextual or **ecological approach** offers a broader perspective of a child than the narrow confines of preselected skills.

Format of Profiles

The format for recording profiles can be structured easily by listing the developmental areas and allowing space between each area for examples of behaviour to be recorded. In Exhibit 5.10, Haseena has organized examples of Nadia's behaviour under Cognitive Development. There are some typical examples of cognitive development, such as "matching primary and secondary colours," but there is also an example that obviously takes place in the child-care setting (contextual information).

Profiles can be used for a variety of reasons. The purpose for developing a profile will influence what information is gathered and in what ways. For example, if parents ask for feedback about their child's ability to take care of his or her personal needs, a teacher will collect information concerning toileting, dressing and undressing in the cloakroom, and mealtime behaviours. The teacher would make point-form notes throughout the day for several days or until a number of representative behaviours were collected. The completed profile would provide the parents with examples of how their child manages his or her personal needs. An additional benefit perhaps could be the sense of confidence it would give the parents, not only in the child's abilities, but also in their parenting skills. The behavioural examples would confirm for them that what is being taught at home is being transferred to the child-care setting. This information may be quite significant for families who have been working on these skills at home, or for families who have recently immigrated and wish to gain insight into different methods of learning basic life skills.

 EXHIBIT 5.10   PROFILE OF COGNITIVE DEVELOPMENT

Child's Name: Nadia   **DOB:** December 1   **Age:** 3 years

Observer(s): Haseena   **Date(s):** October 17–22

Developmental Area: Cognitive

EXAMPLES OF RECORDED BEHAVIOUR

- Matches all primary and secondary colours.
- Can sort and classify animals, toys, food, and pets, but mixes up fruits and vegetables.
- Tells her playmates how to take paintings off easel and put them on the drying rack without getting paint on anything.

ADVANTAGES

- The use of profiles allows early childhood educators to record information about a child in the context of the group/environment. If a child eagerly shows you a ladybug found in the playground and says, "We got some like this at home!" he is demonstrating his association, recall, and matching skills, which may be missed if you recorded only his knowledge of matching colours and shapes. The fact that the child is excited about insects can also lead to extensions in curriculum.
- Centres whose philosophy is similar to the High/Scope **key experiences approach** build their curriculum on the interests of the individual children. Profiles can be an effective recording tool for child-centred curriculum planning. Profiles respond to the variations among and within children, yet provide the structure of developmental areas in which to record the data. This child-centred approach differs in focus from a curriculum-based, thematic approach.
- Student-teachers were asked if learning how to develop profiles was helpful in enhancing their knowledge of children. Their feedback, in Exhibit 5.11, suggests some advantages of using profiles.

DISADVANTAGE

- One of the confusing aspects of profiles to an inexperienced teacher is the idea that a certain behaviour can fit into several broad areas. For example, when a child recalls the favourite part of her story, is that behaviour related to cognition or to speech and language? If a child bangs his hands on a toy piano to make sounds, should that behaviour be put under the cognitive area or the gross motor area? How is that cross-referencing decided? By going back to your purpose: if you are looking only for examples of cognition, then "remembering" in the first example and "associating sounds with objects" in the second example belong in the profile.

Adaptations of Profiles

Profiles are used in the elementary school system, ECE settings, and inclusive settings with children who have special needs. Imagine the difference in items of behaviour that you would observe in the following environments:

- An infant room
- A drop-in centre in a multicultural/multilinguistic community
- An integrated or inclusive centre with children with a variety of special needs
- A family grouping in private home daycare
- A junior kindergarten room
- A parent cooperative preschool

EXHIBIT 5.11   STUDENT-TEACHER FEEDBACK ON PROFILES

- It strengthened my ability to observe children.
- I found out information my teacher did not know about Meika (the child speaks English).
- They give a focus to my observations.
- I made more of a conscious effort to observe specific areas of development.
- It helps my planning for the children.
- Getting information from the profiles allows me to seek out appropriate activities for each child.
- I like to do profiles on infants because it helps me understand what they can do.
- Collecting examples of behaviour over a period of days allows you to see the good days and the bad days.
- I thought this one child was dependent on the others, but I found out he's not!
- I like the point form because I'm not a very good writer.
- Grouping the behaviours under developmental areas ensures that a more holistic approach is taken: seeing the child first as a child, rather than as the child's problems. Profiles do not guarantee a holistic approach, but the format and procedures are in place that go a long way in encouraging such an approach.
- When early childhood educators gather examples of behaviour for children's profiles, they will probably record examples that have some contextual reference. These examples provide parents with evidence of the child's real, everyday experiences. Using profiles thus encourages trust and confidence between parents and teachers.

In ECE settings, profiles are developed and used in a variety of ways. In an infant-care setting, parents will want to know how much food their baby ate, how many bowel movements he or she had, and how long he or she slept. A brief list of point-form notes could be given to the parents on "What Christopher did today." Dramatic changes in development occur during infancy weekly, if not daily. I remember a student-teacher who had her field placement in an infant room. She was struggling at first with this new age group, and we decided that in the back of her binder she would keep a profile on one child. The purpose of the profile was for the student-teacher to become acquainted with what infants can do,

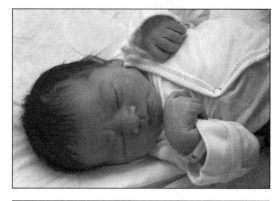

PHOTO: Courtesy of Glenda M. Powers/Shutterstock

and then from that knowledge of one infant in particular, plan an activity based on the infant's interests and skills (see Exhibit 5.13). The results were not only successful but also very rewarding. When the teacher and the student-teacher told the baby's mother about the special activity that had been designed just for her son, she was overwhelmed! The mother expressed great pleasure, as well, in learning more about what her infant son could do!

Even in a hospital setting, where children may be kept over a period of weeks or months, it is possible to record relevant information, such as appears in Exhibit 5.12. In this setting, commercial or more traditional checklists are not always helpful. No preformatted list of anticipated behaviours could ever take into consideration the unique behaviours that occur in a hospital. The relevance of kicking a ball or walking a balance beam would be seriously in question. In the example from Exhibit 5.12, what was relevant was Child A's small steps while pulling her intravenous (IV) pole down the hall. Devising a profile list of relevant behaviours in point form allows the observer more flexibility in delivering such information.

The details that this brief hospital profile reveals are mighty, indeed. Lifting heavy things is not only a demonstration of gross motor skills but also an indication of confidence. Confidence and self-esteem are important when a child is hospitalized. The information gathered on this child will form the basis for communication with parents and others. Be ready so that you do not miss any noteworthy behaviours.

For each of these settings and many other examples, educators need an observation tool with some flexibility to allow for the variety of possible ways to record

---

EXHIBIT 5.12 PROFILE OF CHILD IN HOSPITAL

Child's Name: Child A   DOB: March 23, 1996   Age: 2

Observer(s): David   Date(s): September 12 and 13, 1998

Relevant Medical Information: Acute myelocytic leukemia

GROSS MOTOR SKILLS

- Sits in rocking chair on her own
- Uses both hands to lift objects that are heavy (e.g., tape recorder)
- Demonstrates good upper torso flexibility (stretches to reach for objects)
- Walks in very small steps (due to IV unit)
- Good sense of balance (bends over, picks up objects from the floor)

SOURCE: Courtesy of David J. Fenech.

EXHIBIT 5.13   PROFILE IMPLEMENTATION

Child's Name: Christopher   **Age:** 18 mos.

Profile of Areas of Development (Observations from April 27–May 15)

Gross Motor:

Climbs onto low mat/in and out of low chair

Crawls easily from one area to another

Balances upper torso while sitting and playing with toy

Squats to pick up objects on the floor

Walks sideways and forward

Fine Motor:

Uses palmar grasp to hold toys and release

Has good eye–hand coordination, that is, moves object from one hand to another

Exhibits good pincer grasp, that is, picks up small objects

Self-Help:

Uses spoon to pick up food and place in mouth

Pulls off own shoes

Holds cup with both hands when drinking

Seeks out adult for comfort

Communication: (Nonverbal)

Listens and responds appropriately to basic directions or greetings

Smiles

Pushes other child when child is too close

Approaches new activity readily

Waves "bye-bye"

Gives kisses upon request

Communication: (Verbal)

Cries when upset

Babbles and "la-la"s to himself (sings)

Says a dozen words besides "mama" and "dada"

Laughs aloud

Uses key words to express needs and wants

(continued)

Socioemotional:	Plays by himself (solitary play)
	Affectionate to caregivers and peers
	Is cooperative throughout routines, that is, sleep time/mealtime/change time
	Appears interested in exploring and manipulating his environment
	Separates easily from parents
Cognitive:	Can find object if only a part of the object is in view
	Displays understanding of cause and effect, that is, presses pop-up top
	Points to simple objects upon request
	Imitates adults and peers, that is, plays peek-a-boo and other social games

Once teachers have documented the child's skills and interests in all developmental areas, planning activities for the child is just a further extension of engaging the child. The child plays, the teacher observes and plays with the child, and more is discovered about how the child learns and develops.

Activity: Based on Information from Profile (Observations from April 27–May 15)

Purpose of Activity:	To increase Christopher's gross motor skills
Materials:	Balls of different sizes
	Balls that have bells inside them
	Push-pull toys that make sounds
My Role (as a Teacher):	To role model by engaging Christopher's attention and demonstrating enthusiasm for the toys
	To role model pushing and pulling the toy
	To label my actions, "See, Christopher, I'm pulling the toy!"
	To label Christopher's actions, "You're rolling the ball!"
	To repeat key words, that is, *push, pull, ball, roll*
	To recognize and encourage all of Christopher's efforts

a child's habits, needs, abilities, interests, and characteristics. The profile records behaviours sensitive to the subtle influences of the home culture, the playroom environment, and even media influences. Profiles can include all developmental areas or only one or two. The observer may record periodically throughout a two-week cycle. How do you know what is worth writing down? When you first observe a child, almost any data are relevant. Later, after the child has been observed for several weeks, new or noteworthy behaviours become evident when they do not fit into the established repertoire. Some of your notes may reveal significant milestones in the child's life. Others will be more subtle but represent, for example, a shift from one area of interest to another.

Behaviour Tallying and Charting

For **behaviour tallying,** as with checklists and rating scales, the observer must determine the purpose and predetermine the targeted behaviour to be observed.

Purpose and Unique Feature

Behaviour tallying counts the frequency of behaviours: how many times does it happen? Behaviour tallying tends to record unacceptable behaviours, such as hitting, biting, or swearing, or behaviours that are worrisome because of their frequency, such as the number of times a preschooler falls while playing outside in the playground, or daily living behaviours, such as monitoring the progress of toilet training.

Behaviour Tallying: The Middle Man

Behaviour tallying almost always takes the middle-man position in the observation process. Some type of observational tool lays the groundwork for behaviour tallying, and it is then followed by further observation. Let's use the behavioural example of hitting to illustrate this process. Firstly the hitting behaviour may be uncovered by an observation tool, such as an anecdotal record. The behaviour to be tallied or counted is then identified: hitting. Once the question is answered (How many times?) by using behaviour tallying to record the frequency, then further observations (ABC analysis/event sampling) will need to be carried out to determine if the teacher intervention strategies have been successful in decreasing the number of times the child hits others.

One of the most common uses of behaviour tallying is to support the notion that a certain behaviour is significant enough to warrant further observations. Behaviour tallying works in tandem with other observations as it generates substantial data rather quickly, demonstrating that a behaviour has occurred, and how many times.

A Use for Behaviour Tallying and Charting

Let's use the example of two teachers on the playground on Friday afternoon, talking and watching the children. Teacher A mentions that it seems Daniel has been regressing in his toilet training lately; he has soiled his clothes during the week. Teacher A asks Teacher B if she thinks this is an area of concern. Taking the initiative, Teacher B suggests that they observe Daniel. They decide to record how many times Daniel soils his pants in the coming week. Their toileting chart is similar to the one in Exhibit 5.14.

Teachers A and B discuss their observations and ideas with Daniel's parents. Since their new baby's arrival, the parents have also noticed that Daniel seems to be regressing. The teachers and the parents agree that the teachers will monitor Daniel at the daycare to see if, indeed, accidents are increasing. See the chart they set up for this in Exhibit 5.14.

A two-week timespan for behaviour tallying is most commonly used in early childhood settings, as it is often adequate for patterns to emerge. On the basis of those patterns, the team can make interpretations and form conclusions. However, after two weeks, a pattern may not seem apparent. The question often asked is: What do we do if there is no pattern? Depending on the child, the context, and the purpose for using this observational tool, a variety of possibilities exist. The observation may be continued for another one or two weeks. There may have been extenuating circumstances that prevented a real pattern from emerging. Another option is to stop recording and analyze the information that has already been collected. Perhaps it is time to re-evaluate the purpose and the type of form being used. There are no easy answers, no magic wands, and no one right way. The important key is communication: sharing of information, ideas, and strategies.

Format of Behaviour Tallying

Another unique feature of behaviour tallying is the format in which the collected data is displayed. The collected information can be displayed in various ways, but we will look at the two formats most commonly used.

The first format is a simple tally of the number of times a child demonstrated a particular behaviour. The behaviours to be observed are defined, the times they occurred are checked off on a chart, and then conclusions are drawn on the basis of the completed data. Alternatively, you could choose a list of behaviours, check off how many times they occur, and then display your information in chart or graph form. The chart or graph will give you a visual picture of a certain set of behaviours from which you can draw some quick conclusions; for example, from Monday to Friday, the number of unacceptable behaviours decreased substantially from 10 instances on Monday to 5 on Friday.

EXHIBIT 5.14   **TOILETING CHART**

Child's Name: _____   DOB: _____   Age: _____

Observer(s): _____   Date(s): _____

	Monday	Tuesday	Wednesday	Thursday	Friday
8:00–8:30					
8:30–9:00					
9:00–9:30					
9:30–10:00					
10:00–10:30					
10:30–11:00					
11:00–11:30					
11:30–12:00					
12:00–12:30					
12:30–1:00					
1:00–1:30					
1:30–2:00					
2:00–2:30					
2:30–3:00					
3:00–3:30					
3:30–4:00					
4:00–4:30					

Legend	D = Dry pants W = Wet pants B = Bowel movement – pants
	X = On potty – nothing P = On potty – urination
	BP = On potty – bowel movement

Comments	

A coding system displayed as a legend provides a quick visual reference. The toilet training chart (see Exhibit 5.14) includes a legend with a relevant coding system. The teacher can quickly see that "W" = wet pants and use that, rather than writing out the words. The use of symbols or letters to represent a particular concept makes recording behaviour quick and easy.

Using a Conventional Graph

Making a conventional graph (see Exhibit 5.15) to display data is straightforward. The standard graph has a vertical axis on which you plot **ordinates,** or vertical coordinates (the levels of behaviour). The horizontal axis, where you plot the **abscissas,** or horizontal coordinates, is where you indicate the dimension of time (hours, days, weeks), quality, or another indicator.

With the assistance of a computer program, graphs can present your data in visually elaborate and impressive ways. Using computer programs, all you need to do

EXHIBIT 5.15 STANDARD GRAPH

A standard graph consists of
◄— Vertical axis (ordinate)
   Horizontal axis (abscissas) ↓

The horizontal axis represents time, quality, or another indicator.
The vertical axis represents the performance level or range of behaviour.

Graph with categories: paint, sand, blocks, dramatic, water

Legend: ■ week 1 ■ week 2 ■ week 3 ■ week 4

is enter your raw data into a spreadsheet format and convert that information into graph form; it is quite straightforward. Behaviour can be charted on a graph. Graphs chart visually the increase, decrease, or sameness of behaviours. For example, graphs can show the popularity of curriculum areas based on the number of times the children attend an area at any given time. From this at-a-glance perspective, teachers can form conclusions and make recommendations.

Interpreting Observations, Charts, and Graphs

Counting how many times a particular behaviour occurs requires a very different kind of interpretation than narrative observations. If your purpose is to observe how many times a particular behaviour occurs or how many children can accomplish a particular skill, then few interpretations need to be made. Perhaps you need to ask why the behaviour is occurring or what the result of these occurrences is. You would also likely evaluate the information in terms of curriculum: if 10 out of 15 children can label the secondary colours, do you need to continue reinforcing this concept? Who in the group has yet to accomplish this task? You would also likely evaluate each child's performance in terms of whether your expectations are age appropriate.

A few cautions might be considered when constructing a chart or graph to display or support your findings:

- Was enough time allowed to clearly indicate a pattern or a true rate of progress?
- Did the observation period represent an anomaly, or was it a good representation of typical behaviours for a child?
- Have you traded comprehension for simplicity?

ADVANTAGES/DISADVANTAGES: BEHAVIOUR TALLYING

ADVANTAGES

- One of the major advantages of recording behaviour tallying is that it is quick and easy to use. Recording the frequency of a preselected behaviour can easily be done on forms attached to a clipboard or on stick-on notes.
- Counting the number of times a child successfully used the potty or how long a child was able to stay on task at a puzzle are indicators that tend to give an unbiased account of what happened. This information can then be used as a basis for decreasing or increasing intervention strategies or setting up a conference with the parents.

(continued)

- Using a graph or chart to record the behaviour on a daily basis encourages monitoring and tracking. Recording data on a chart gives a visual account of progress or lack thereof and thereby quickly gives visual feedback without a lot of writing. The standard graph is also a neutral way to present clear information to parents. If presented in a narrative, the information might be less well received.

DISADVANTAGES

- The major disadvantage of "information bytes" is that they usually do not include the interactive factors of setting, people involved, mood of the child, home culture, or any other conditions that may have influenced the behaviour being recorded.
- Behaviour tallying does not give qualitative information, such as intent, degree, or other conditions of the behaviour itself.

Adaptations of Behaviour Tallying

In the adaptation of behaviour tallying in Exhibit 5.16, the behaviour "cutting with scissors" was chosen in order to obtain information about each child's skills in the morning and afternoon kindergarten groups. The targeted behaviour was further divided into more precise behaviours and counted to determine how many children could complete each developmental progression of the task. Study Exhibit 5.16 for the progression of the cutting skills program.

EXHIBIT 5.16   CUTTING PROGRAM

The purpose of this program was to determine the range of cutting skills in both the a.m. and p.m. kindergarten classes. Many activities in early grades assume the skill of cutting with scissors. I wanted to find out which of the children knew how to hold the scissors properly, cut a variety of textures, or cut along a straight line.

I chose to implement this program in a task-analysis approach. The children started off with simple things to cut and ended up cutting specific, small objects from magazines. The skills I monitored and subsequently graphed were cutting along a straight line, cutting along a zigzag, diagonal line, and cutting along a wavy or curved line.

After providing many opportunities for cutting in the classroom, I tallied up the results of the a.m. cutting program. The results were as follows:

A.M. Cutting Program	Straight Line	Diagonal Line	Curved Line
David	X	O	O
Kenaul	X	X	X
Leah	X	X	X
Matt	O	O	O
Jonathan	X	X	X
Chantel	O	O	O
Sukhjit	X	X	X
Vincent	O	O	O
Michael	X	X	X
Andre	X	X	X
Yulika	X	X	X
Yves	X	O	O
Francis	X	X	O

x = Successful
o = Unsuccessful

From the list of children, you can see at a glance that some children had yet to develop the skills necessary to cut along a straight line. I will keep working with these children to ensure they are able to hold scissors properly and cut basic thin strips of paper before we move on to cutting along a straight line.

The graph shows that more children in the morning group could cut along a straight line than a diagonal or curved line.

I conducted the same cutting program with the afternoon group, which was presented in the same way. I discovered that the children in the afternoon group could cut along a straight line better than a diagonal or curved line.

Originally, I had predicted that the afternoon children had a lot more skills in this area than the morning group. I was shocked when the charts showed the opposite! I honestly thought the afternoon children showed more fine motor skills, yet when I really thought about it, the a.m. children tended to be more involved in all the creative activities. The afternoon group had a lot of

(continued)

boys who usually played in the block area or with the train set. Some of the children are from different cultures, and they do not seem to be familiar with things like scissors. With my charts, my data, and my observations, I discovered that the a.m. children appeared to demonstrate better cutting skills as a group than did the p.m. group.

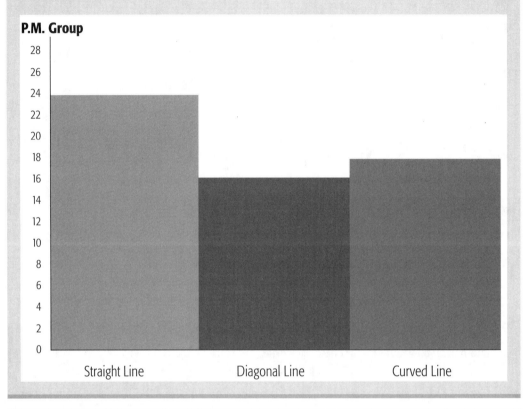

P.M. Group

SOURCE: Kim McCrindle

Summary

In this chapter, five main types of records have been featured that represent practical, commonly used observational tools for recording targeted behaviours in early childhood settings. These types of records are used when the behaviours to be observed have been targeted in advance. Each of these closed methods has its own unique features and uses, which allows educators to choose the most appropriate one. These observational tools can be self-designed or commercially made. They can stand alone or be adapted by adding an open-ended record component. Combining the specific preselected items of a closed method with open-ended documentation provides a contrasting cross section of knowledge: a concentration of exact information with examples and/or contextual references.

PROFESSIONAL REFLECTIONS

Observation of young children's skills, behaviour, interest, and learning is one of the cornerstones of best practices in early childhood settings. The process of observing ensures that learning experiences developed for children are relevant and developmentally appropriate.

It is critical to gather information about individual children in order to plan appropriate learning experiences for them. Knowledge about the skills children have will help the early childhood educator provide appropriate materials, equipment, arrangement of learning spaces, and learning experiences. Observing children's behaviours provides information that will help you to understand the reasons behind the behaviours. A child who withdraws from situations periodically may be withdrawing because he or she is afraid of certain situations, is tired, needs some time alone, is overwhelmed by certain situations, may dislike certain aspects of learning situations, or may not want to interact with certain individuals. It is only when observation and recording over time and in different settings occurs that accurate interpretations can be made.

Children learn through active interactions with the materials and individuals within their learning environments. Children also learn best when they can solve their own problems and make their own choices. Careful observations will guide the early childhood educator to provide for children's interest to determine what choices should be provided and what problems are possible for children to solve. Additionally, learning opportunities may be provided through experiences that encourage practice or enhancement of skills.

When learning opportunities are developed without observations of children's skills, behaviours, interests, and learning, children are deprived of learning opportunities that are based on individual skills and interests or based on the individual's right to learn through active exploration and experimentation.

—Dr. Ingrid Crowther
Athabasca University

KEY TERMS

abscissas	checklist	coding scheme
behaviour tallying	closed methods	continuum

correlate   frequency   profiles
descriptor   key experiences approach   rating scales
duration   open methods   targeted behaviours
ecological approach   ordinates

DISCUSSION QUESTIONS

1. What are the observational tools that record targeted behaviours?
2. What is the main purpose for using each of these observational tools?
3. How does the format of each of these observational tools reflect the purpose?
4. What are some of the advantages and disadvantages of each method?
5. How can information be interpreted using these methods?
6. What are some possible applications of each of these types of records?

ADDITIONAL READINGS

Examples of observational tools presented in this chapter, such as checklists and rating scales, can easily be found on the Internet. Here is just a sample of what can be found:

www.brightfutures.org — An Early Childhood Checklist

www.hanen.org — Focus on Language and Parents: Understanding Language Delays and Disorders.

www.ericdigests.org — A Young Children's Social Development Checklist

www.ncbi.nlm.nih.gov — The National Library of Medicine and the National Institutes of Health's website is a useful resource when looking for more information on behaviour tallying. The article entitled "'The latent variable structure of the Compulsive Behaviour Checklist in people with Prader-Willi syndrome' is a great article on the subject matter" (Feurer et al.).

Beaty, Janice J. *Skills for Preschool Teachers*. 8th ed. New Jersey: Prentice-Hall, Inc., Pearson Education, 2008.

The text is exactly as the title suggests—a text to be used by college or university students who are taking academic courses concurrently with internships or field practicums. The observation tools used to evaluate curriculum are primarily checklists that are designed for a specific purpose, such as Self-Concept Checklist or a Classroom Safety Checklist.

Bentzen, Warren R., and Martha B. Frost. *Seeing Child Care: A Guide for Assessing the Effectiveness of Child Care Programs*. Clifton Park, NY: Delmar Learning, 2003.

The authors state that their goal is to provide the reader with the knowledge and practical skills needed to determine the effectiveness of early childhood programs. The chapters provide many practical examples of rating scales used with infant, toddler, and preschool-age groups. The observation objective is to determine the degree to which the infant's, toddler's, and preschooler's needs are met in the child-care environment.

Capone, Angela, Tom Oren, and John T. Neisworth. *Childmate: A Guide to Appraising Quality in Child Care.* Clifton Park, NY: Delmar Learning, 2004.

Childmate is a text responding to the challenge of providing quality care for children ranging in age from two months to sixty months. The text looks at three factors that influence a child's interactions with his/her environment: caregiver behaviours, toys and materials, and physical attributes of the environment. A checklist is provided for each age range (infant, toddler, and preschool) for each of these factors, providing detailed information about the quality of care. This text is a good reference resource for students of early childhood studies.

ALTERNATIVE DOCUMENTATION OF CHILDREN'S ACTIVITY

Our Baby

Name _____

Born at _____

On _____

Time _____

Weight _____

Parents _____

_____

PHOTO: Courtesy of Sally Wylie

Beginning in infancy, children's growth and development are documented more now than ever before. Photographs, taken soon after birth, begin the child's pictorial history. The first photos are a source of joy and pride for family and friends. In addition to the Baby Book, where hand-documented entries are inscribed, are the photo albums and videotapes, the CDs, websites, and blogs. The sights and sounds of childhood can now be captured in such a variety of ways. These recorded memories represent the personal history of a family's milestones and meaningful events.

Overview

This chapter offers students examples of some of the more visual means of documentation. Chapter 6 explores alternative, less print-dependent methods that can be used to record children's behaviour. Examples of these visual, graphic representations are

- pictorial representations,
- sociograms, and
- mapping activities.

Examples of media-assisted methods discussed in this chapter are

- the camera,
- tape recorder, and
- video camera.

Observation rooms or observation areas will also be included in this chapter, as they represent an alternative way to observe children. These specially designed observation areas often feature headsets connected to microphones in each room, which allow the observer to hear as well as see the activity of the children.

Toward the end of the chapter, we will look at the role of computer technology in early childhood education and how this technology assists teachers in the observation process.

After reading this chapter, you should be able to:

- Discuss ways graphic or pictorial representations and media-assisted observations can be used to document the activities of young children.
- Identify the types of media used to assist observation.
- Discuss the benefits of specially designed observation areas for parents and teachers.
- Examine the possibilities for recording individual children's behaviour using a combination of methods.
- Describe how technology is influencing the role of the teacher-observer.

Alternatives to Print-Dependent Documentation

There are many ways to document a child's activity other than writing anecdotal observations or setting up participation charts. In this chapter, three types of records represent this category of documentation: (1) pictorial representation, (2) sociograms, and (3) mapping. Each of these methods is unique in its purpose, but their pictorial or graphic commonality is what makes these types of records interesting. Later in the chapter, how a graph can be generated from spreadsheet data will also be explored as yet another way data from observations can be converted into a visual presentation.

Pictorial Representations

Pictorial representations are, as the term suggests, pictures, images, or graphic drawings that represent persons/objects. Maybe you remember the first type of pictorial representations you created in kindergarten. First, you painted or drew a picture, and then the teacher had you tell the story while he or she transcribed it and wrote it beneath the picture. In this example, the text supported the picture, that is, the text clarified the visual image. Sketches, drawings, and similar pictorial representations can also be useful to illustrate an idea. These representations illustrate or give visual appeal to a text-laden publication. But how can they be used to assist in documenting children's behaviour?

Educators with seasoned skills in working with children who may not have achieved a high degree of writing skill may find pictorial representation a welcome alternative to print-dependent documentation. Writing observations and interpretations requires a level of skill that not every person is able to attain. Not being able to communicate effectively in writing does not mean, however, that a particular individual is not a good observer. It just means that his or her ability to communicate clearly in writing has not yet been adequately developed. How unfortunate it would be not to utilize the skills of a good observer! What are some ways to put those skills to use? Using less print-dependent, more visual ways of recording information is a way to make use of the teacher's observations. Using pictures to document information is one way an educator can combine pictures of a child with key words, phrases, or sentences. These pictures could represent a key developmental milestone, such as walking or sitting independently. The pictures could represent a type of grasp, such as **palmar grasp** or **pincer grasp.** For example, in Exhibit 6.1, the age group is infants.

The pictorial examples are accompanied by phrases or sentences depicting the action that is portrayed. The person who observed the infant demonstrating these skills could merely circle the picture or copy the description into the infant's record book. A team member or supervisory personnel could then assist in compiling, writing, or interpreting the information.

This method could be used with people who are culturally unaccustomed to developing documentation on children, yet possess an observant, reflective manner with children. Finding ways to accommodate their skills within a team approach is a positive and innovative way to utilize the many ways of documenting children's behaviour.

Pictorial Combinations: Photographs and Anecdotal Records

The combined use of photographs with a brief anecdotal record is highlighted in several areas of this text; it is an exciting way to document the *process* of learning. Digital technology has given us the ability to economically use photographs with greater flexibility than before. Several good pictures out of many can be chosen for their strong visual images that capture a particular behaviour or event. These photographs

EXHIBIT 6.1   DEVELOPMENTAL PROFILES

Focuses and reaches for objects.

Recognizes inverted but familiar objects.

Responds to own name.

Still friendly with strangers.

SOURCE: E. Allen and L. Marotz, *Developmental Profiles: Pre-birth Through Twelve,* Fourth Edition (2003). Reprinted with permission of Delmar Learning, a division of Thomson Learning

can then be further enriched with brief anecdotal comments, such as those found in Exhibit 6.2.

What did these photographs and anecdotal comments tell us about Emma? Bushra, who provided the material in Exhibit 6.2, wrote that "she can create many things when given the materials. She seemed very patient, and focused on her work. She likes to be independent." Visual imagery can be complemented by teachers and/or

During a community workshop in Singapore attended by early childhood supervisory personnel, considerable time was spent finding ways to document children's activities with which everyone felt comfortable. In Singapore, as in Canada and other countries, teachers who work in the ECE field may have immigrated from other countries where child-care practices differ. Often, some of these teachers may not have the language/writing skills necessary to complete essential records. During the workshops, we brainstormed ways to include *all* staff in the process of documenting children's behaviour. Pictorial representation was one of the methods determined to be successful in achieving this purpose. Including all staff in the process of documentation is important, acknowledging that any group of teachers will demonstrate a wide variety of skills and knowledge in recording children's behaviour. Not all of them are writers. Finding ways to include their observations is critical in establishing a positive climate of collaboration.

EXHIBIT 6.2   EMMA MAKING BREAD

Emma is able to pour the flour with stable hands without the teacher's help. She looks focused on what she is doing.

Emma is enjoying playing with the flour and maybe that's because it's soft. She pretends to make dough by mixing the flour. She looks like she is imitating her mother, because in her culture, the mom used to make the dough all the time to make bread. Her facial expression reflects her hard work to mix the dough.

SOURCE: Photos and text by Bushra Qasim.

parents adding significant written commentary, as in the example of Emma and in the next example in Exhibit 6.3.

The use of photographs will be discussed in further detail below under the heading "Media-Assisted Observation."

EXHIBIT 6.3 **CURTIS AND GRACE DEMONSTRATE THEIR UNDERSTANDING**

Curtis and Grace demonstrate their understanding of "instant" photography. Their method consists of drawing the subject they are about to shoot and placing the "frame" in the slot at the front of the Polaroid camera, simulating the real thing.

How is a photograph made inside the camera?
Curtis: "It's just pretend!"
Really. How does a Polaroid camera work?
Curtis: "It's a better camera because you get pictures right away. I know how to do cameras."

SOURCE: Photo and text courtesy of Jason Avery, Artists at the Centre.

ADVANTAGES/DISADVANTAGES: PICTORIAL REPRESENTATION

ADVANTAGES

- Documentation is achieved without requiring a high level of writing skill
- Easy to record key skills or brief descriptions

DISADVANTAGES

- Reliance on availability of pictorial templates or camera
- Limited information to form interpretations

Sociograms

A sociogram is one of the types of social maps used to examine the social context of a child. What is a social map? Social maps are graphic or pictorial representations of how or where a person fits into a group. The most common example of a social map is the *family tree;* it is a familiar type of social map. In this chapter, however, the main type of social map that is most useful for our purposes is the sociogram. The reason for this focus is simple; sociograms are used in the field of early childhood to document a child's social relationships. Teachers can use sociograms to track social acceptance and relationships. For example, in September, children in a group may be relatively new to each other, and a teacher may want to monitor who plays with whom, how often, or how long. Instead of using pages of written observations, the teacher could construct a sociogram. Using this format, he or she could indicate by a picture or simple graphic representation children's social connections, using arrows going from and to individual children. A few months later, the teacher could, using the same graphic representation, track the relationships to see if the same patterns still hold.

Sociograms have also been used extensively as a research technique. They can be used effectively to monitor the social relationships of children. Are some children more popular than others? Do some children consistently seek out others in play? Sociograms, such as in Exhibit 6.4, could be used to demonstrate the dependence or independence of certain children using a simple visual overview.

EXHIBIT 6.4   CHILD/PEER INTERACTIONS

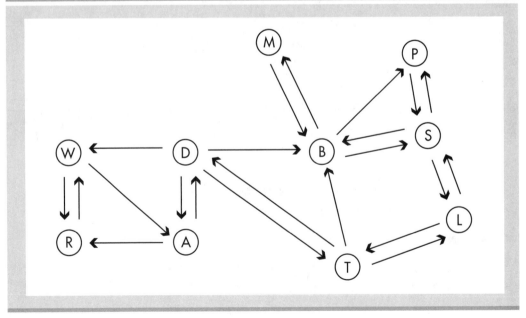

Sociograms are useful in collecting information on social behaviours. They can be used to obtain information on a particular child, a child within a group, or group dynamics. A sociogram could be created with input from the children. However, this variation would most likely be used with older children. For the construction of a sociogram on "who is the most liked child in the group," a child would have to have the understanding and maturity to define the parameters of the teacher's questions.

Sociogram Variations: Ecomaps

Sociograms can also be created to visually communicate the social influence of others in the life of a child. How many adults are in a child's life? How many groups of children does a child socialize with on a regular basis? How can the groupings of family, friends, child care, and other extracurricular events be represented? Using the two ecomaps represented in Exhibit 6.5, examine the social differences between Sarah and Joel. What is similar? What is different? How would this knowledge of Sarah and Joel assist the teacher in his or her interactions with them?

EXHIBIT 6.5   ECOMAPS OF SARAH AND JOEL

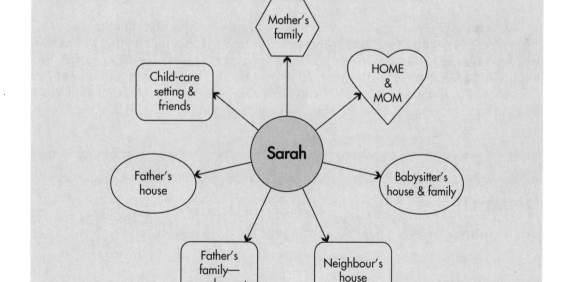

Sociogram/Ecomap of Sarah

(continued)

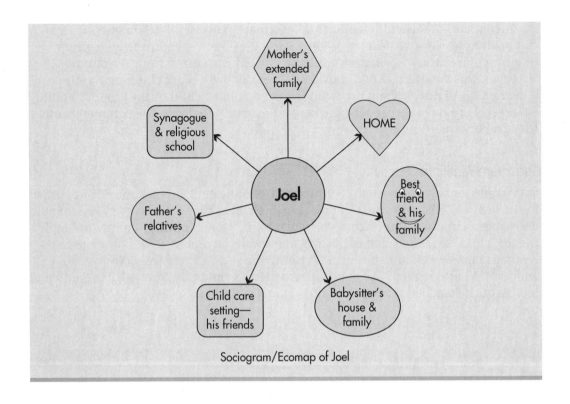

Sociogram/Ecomap of Joel

As discussed in other chapters, the family is not the only social influence in a child's life. Discovering the social influences in a child's life is enlightening. Moyra constructed a type of sociogram or ecomap to get a sense of the diversity of people in Child M's life and a sense of her socioemotional development. The sociogram was constructed from an audio taping during several **interview** sessions with Child M. In Exhibit 6.6, you can, at a glance, get a sense of who and what is important in Child M's life.

ADVANTAGES/DISADVANTAGES: SOCIOGRAMS

ADVANTAGES

- A visual representation of social relationships or other social dimensions
- Offers opportunities to monitor changes in a child's daily life without intensive writing

DISADVANTAGES

- May oversimplify complex relationships
- A multistage process is needed to construct a sociogram or variant

EXHIBIT 6.6   SOCIOGRAM VARIATIONS: MOYRA'S EXAMPLES

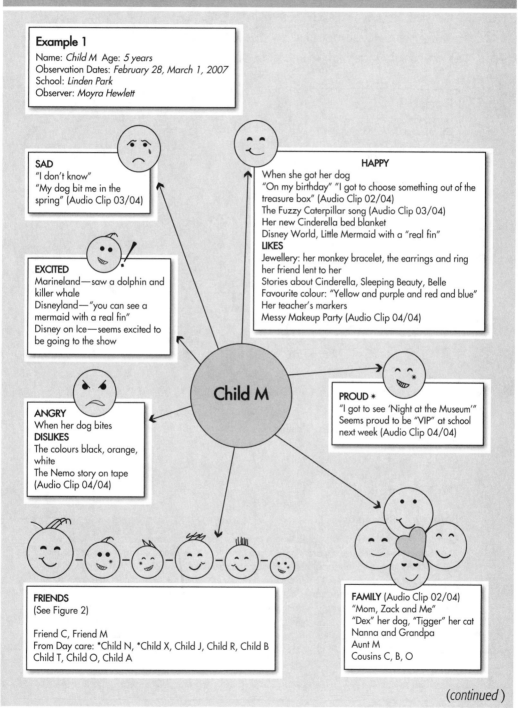

Example 1
Name: *Child M* Age: *5 years*
Observation Dates: *February 28, March 1, 2007*
School: *Linden Park*
Observer: *Moyra Hewlett*

SAD
"I don't know"
"My dog bit me in the spring" (Audio Clip 03/04)

HAPPY
When she got her dog
"On my birthday" "I got to choose something out of the treasure box" (Audio Clip 02/04)
The Fuzzy Caterpillar song (Audio Clip 03/04)
Her new Cinderella bed blanket
Disney World, Little Mermaid with a "real fin"
LIKES
Jewellery: her monkey bracelet, the earrings and ring her friend lent to her
Stories about Cinderella, Sleeping Beauty, Belle
Favourite colour: "Yellow and purple and red and blue"
Her teacher's markers
Messy Makeup Party (Audio Clip 04/04)

EXCITED
Marineland—saw a dolphin and killer whale
Disneyland—"you can see a mermaid with a real fin"
Disney on Ice—seems excited to be going to the show

Child M

PROUD *
"I got to see 'Night at the Museum'"
Seems proud to be "VIP" at school next week (Audio Clip 04/04)

ANGRY
When her dog bites
DISLIKES
The colours black, orange, white
The Nemo story on tape (Audio Clip 04/04)

FRIENDS
(See Figure 2)

Friend C, Friend M
From Day care: *Child N, *Child X, Child J, Child R, Child B
Child T, Child O, Child A

FAMILY (Audio Clip 02/04)
"Mom, Zack and Me"
"Dex" her dog, "Tigger" her cat
Nanna and Grandpa
Aunt M
Cousins C, B, O

(continued)

The first example shown in Exhibit 6.6 details information obtained by a media-assisted (tape recording) interview. The recorded interview provided the information for the creation an interesting variation of a sociogram. The other example, another set of observations of the same child, provided still another variation of a sociogram: a sociogram with inferences.

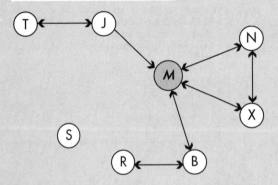

Example 2
Name: *Child M* Age: *5 years*
Observation Date: *March 1, 2007*
School: *Linden Park*
Time: *2:20–3:20 p.m.*
Observer: *Moyra Hewlett*

Child T: 3 years, male
Child J: 4 years, male
Child S: Age unknown (3 years?), female
Child R: 3 years, female
Child B: 3 years, female
Child X: 2 years, female
Child N: 4 years, female

Inferences of Sociogram

Child M seems to be a popular child with a dominant personality and a strong self-identity. She seems to include other children in her dramatic play while being cheerful and talkative. She appears to exhibit prosocial behaviour by sharing, taking turns, and showing genuine affection for her classmates. Her language skills seem to allow her to communicate her intentions and feelings to her peers. She seems to enjoy the company of children and seems capable of forming meaningful attachments to others. Child M rarely plays alone. She seems to prefer sociodramatic, cooperative, or parallel play. Child M seems to assume adult roles and express feelings during her dramatic play. In her day care she appears to be a ringleader, adopting the role of teacher/caregiver with many of her peers.

SOURCE: Moyra Hewlett

Mapping

Mappings are some of the more visually interesting ways to monitor children's behaviour. Mapping includes the contextual information of the environment and, therefore, adds another dimension to the documentation. Like the observation methods examined in Chapter 5, mapping requires the observer to organize and set up the observation record before the observations begin. A map or terrain of the environment must first be drawn before the actual mapping or monitoring of a child's activities can be done. A basic mapping chart of a toddler room is shown in Exhibit 6.7.

In Chapter 5, you learned to tally behaviours. This method is effective when tracking or monitoring discreet behaviours that have a beginning, middle, and end, such as kicking a ball or pulling on boots. Behaviours like *wandering* are not captured by that type of record. Mapping is ideal to record a behaviour such as wandering. Mappings are familiar if you think about it. Newspaper comics use mapping to illustrate how a character roams the neighbourhood, such as the little boy in "Family Circus."

Using mapping requires preplanning. If teachers wish to monitor the wanderings of a child, then they would have to create a diagram of the room with all essential areas and items noted, such as curriculum area, equipment, furniture, supplies, and space appropriately indicated. The playroom diagram would have to be relatively accurate, portraying effectively, for example, the distance between areas in the room

EXHIBIT 6.7 MAPPING CHART

Child's name: Julie   **DOB:** July 10   **Age:** 27 months

Date: October 20   **Time:** 8:55 – 9:30

1 Sits on edge of trampoline and watches child
2 Sits in tunnel and watches a child
3 Sits on trampoline
4 Tosses ball with two hands, runs to pick up ball, and returns
5 Stands and looks around
6 Crawls in tunnel following peers; sits at end, and crawls back
7 Climbs up on top of soft blocks
8 Sits on mat to put on shoes
9 Lines up at door with peers

(continued)

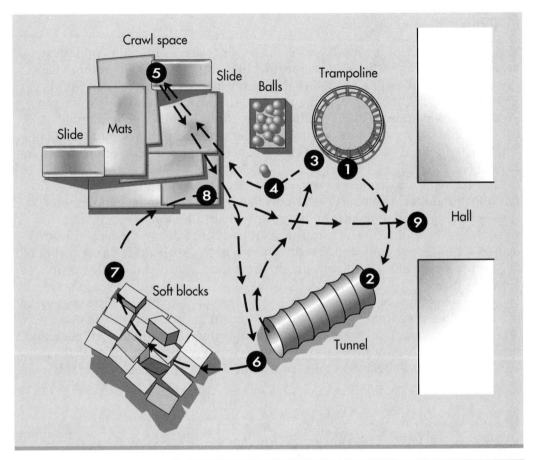

SOURCE: Adapted from Julia Graham.

and spaces between pieces of furniture. In Exhibit 6.8, Jacqueline has constructed a classroom layout of the J.K./S.K. room. She noted with a dotted line where Child A.C. started out, and where he went within an approximately 45-minute time frame. With just a quick glance, you can get a sense of his activities from one end of the room to other areas, ending up at the rug area for Circle Time, Storytelling, Calendar, and a Mini Lesson. For each area (1–12), Jacqueline also noted in point form how long he stayed and a brief description of what he did there. For example, at destination 8 and 9, A.C. spent mere seconds grabbing a Kleenex (8) and standing briefly with the teacher (9). He stayed most of the time on the carpet next to the toy shelves (10) playing Lego with his friends.

From the mapping diagram, it is quite impossible to gauge time and/or activity, but with brief notes, the mapping takes on further significance. From the mapping and brief notes, it is possible to gather inferences of the child's behaviour and ascribe

EXHIBIT 6.8 **J.K./S/K. CLASSROOM LAYOUT (FOR MAPPING A.C.)**

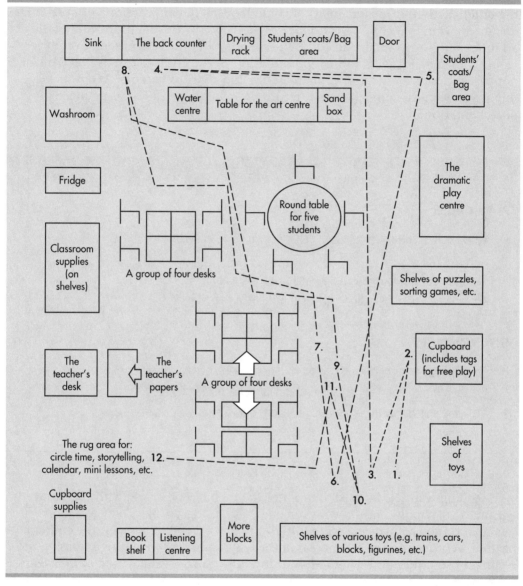

SOURCE: Jacqueline Salvador

meaning. Mapping can be used to monitor the individual wanderings of a toddler or how clusters of preschoolers utilize the curriculum areas in a room.

Mapping adds a new dimension to documentation. This type of record allows the observer/recorder to see where the child goes throughout the room, indicating areas of interest and non-interest. Point-form notes can accompany the mapping chart to assist the reader in understanding the significance of the child's activity. This information could be used in conjunction with other documentation in a child's portfolio. Collectively, the information would tell an interesting story about the child. Presented with other documentation, it would provide another graphic representation of the child to discuss with his or her parents. How would you explain a mapping chart to parents? What message might you want to convey when offering the mapping as a revealing piece of documentation?

ADVANTAGES/DISADVANTAGES: MAPPINGS

ADVANTAGES

- Offers staff opportunities to record behaviours in new ways without intensive writing
- Used to track individual children as well as a small group
- Offers contextual information, such as curriculum area preferences

DISADVANTAGES

- Templates or maps of playrooms have to be reasonably accurate in terms of distances between curriculum areas, equipment, and furniture; made to scale
- Data are limited and, therefore, interpretations drawn from the data may be inaccurate

---

Mappings can also be used to monitor the mobility of a child with special needs within the playroom. A child with cerebral palsy, using a walker, may feel more secure in certain areas of the room initially. However, as time goes by, the child may begin to venture into the other areas of the playroom, demonstrating initiative and feelings of security in the room. Monitoring this change over a period of time using a mapping chart can show not only areas of preference over time, but also provide a measure for self-confidence.

Mapping a cluster of preschoolers who tend to travel around the play area in a small herd could pose a challenge! Using a different coloured pen or marker would be a logical way of tracking the various routes of each of the children. If coloured markers are used, a legend could be created. Mapping the behaviours of children in the group could be designated for staff who feel comfortable with this method and less comfortable with print-dependent documentation.

Media-Assisted Observation

Photographs

Photographs are generally found everywhere in a playroom. Photos of family, pets at home, pictures of familiar toys and objects are used frequently and in various ways in early childhood (see Exhibits 6.9 and 6.10). These photos often find their way to the Birthday Bulletin Board, to the child's cubby or portfolios, or mounted low enough on the wall for the kisses and smiles of infants and toddlers. Photos of family members help ease children's stress at being away from family for the first time. Together,

---

EXHIBIT 6.9   USING PHOTOGRAPHY IN EARLY CHILDHOOD

Teachers of young children can use digital photography to build, almost instantly, a sense of community and belonging, promote feelings of security, build children's self-esteem, aid in classroom management, communicate with parents, document children's growth, promote language and literacy, and enhance other areas of the curriculum.

Pictures of parents picking up children can be displayed on a bulletin board to help young children feel secure and to serve as a reminder that moms and dads will be returning. An interactive family bulletin board allows children to match their pictures to those of their parents; this is another way of demonstrating attachment when parents and children are separated.

SOURCE: Good, Linda. "Snap it Up", *Childhood Education: Infancy Through Early Adolescence,* 82.2 Winter 2005/2006, pages 79–85.

EXHIBIT 6.10   USING PHOTOS TO PROMOTE LANGUAGE

Photos beg children to talk about them. What better way to promote language and literacy? A teacher might post a "photo of the day" to discuss at group time. One child might be selected daily, on the class "job chart" to report to the class about what the photo depicts. In this way, the selected child learns to examine the photo and to think about what s/he would like to say about it. This practice gives children rehearsal time prior to performance time. Children who are English language learners may be very motivated to talk about photos of themselves doing something at school!

SOURCE: Wellhousen, Karen, and Rebecca M. Giles. "Building Literacy Opportunities Into Children's Block Play: What every teacher should know." *Childhood Education,* 82.2 Winter 2005/06, (p. 75)

teachers and parents make up photo albums of the child's family, pets, toys, and home for the child to have at the centre. Teachers often keep the camera ready at the parents' request. Taking a picture of a young child standing on his or her own for the first time is a celebration for teachers and parents alike and provides a worthy photo of the milestone in the child's development.

Many child-care centres maintain their own photo albums, which are kept in a special place in the playroom. Here, the children can sit and look at pictures of themselves, school trips, special holidays, birthdays, family members, and their friends. These albums are a rich source of learning—of developing memory for past events and sequence of time, and of becoming aware of a shared past with people other than family members.

Visual communication with pictures embraces the concept of **total communication.** Photos are used to assist children with special needs in their communication. Photos can be pointed to, looked at, named, and used as a visual means of communication. Children with special needs use pictures of materials or toys in a personal photo album to show what they would like to play with. Their photos can also represent meal choices, functional items they need, or activities in which they wish to engage. The pictures are supplied and organized by family members, teachers, and professionals. To provide this kind of pictorial aid, the people must be aware of the child's interests, likes and dislikes, needs, and skills. Carefully observing the child will give the teacher clues about what pictorial aides would be most useful and appropriate. Ongoing monitoring will also be necessary to make sure the choices are significant, relevant, and helpful to the child.

As you will see again in Chapter 7, the possible uses of photographs to document children's behaviour and activities are endless. Photos can reveal specific behaviours while a child plays in the dramatic centre or block area, constructs a house of blocks, or plays outdoors. Some of the most significant photographs to parents and teachers concern peer relationships in the process of an activity or special achievements. I have many such photos of my child in daycare: being pulled in the wagon, being hugged by his favourite teacher, and posing for Halloween pictures. Interestingly, he looks back at these now, some 20 years later, and remembers exactly what happened on those days. So, photos can be memory-makers for families of a particular time in their lives that can be rediscovered again through this medium.

The text accompanying photos can be written in the narrative by the parent/ teacher as in the example of Ivy stacking the blocks (Exhibit 6.11). This approach is most familiar as it speaks to the play process as viewed and interpreted by an adult. However, as we can see in the example of Ivy in the next photograph, the text narration takes a new, creative approach, describing the process from the viewpoint of the child as written by the adult.

Photographs can complement, supplement, or illustrate records of children's development and behaviour. Even though photos are quick stills of life and, therefore, are limited in their role as observational tools, they can be a powerful, visual tool in sharing information with families when accompanied by documentation.

EXHIBIT 6.11   IVY: TWO EXAMPLES

It has taken a bit of work and time for Ivy to gather up blocks one at a time, to dash across the classroom with them held in her arms, and to hide them under the coat bench. And all this was

done without being noticed by Toby, who is madly using blocks to make a wall in dramatic play. Once she has squirreled away what she deems to be an adequate amount, the construction begins. Ivy pulls one block at a time from its hiding place and slowly, painstakingly places it on its end. Again the process is repeated but this time with a tongue poking out, and both hands so slowly, so carefully coming away from the new tower after the block is placed.

The third block comes just as slowly, with Ivy oblivious to the distractions to the room, and smiling in anticipation of another job well done.

Ah, here I am as I begin the long day ahead of me with a little light reading. I picked the choicest cushion from the library centre and plopped it down in the middle of the room where I could keep an eye on everything and everyone. I found *The Adventures of Piglet and Rabbit* to

be quite enthralling, and as I turned handfuls of pages at a time I began to read aloud, pointing out Rabbit as he scurries about. "Nana yaa bunny" I say loudly. I quickly forgot about the rest of the room and became immersed in my story. I poke the animals on the pages as I see them, nodding my head from side to side. As I narrate my story I get into a bit of a rhythm, and soon my whole body is wiggling back and forth on my cushion.

SOURCE: Photos and text courtesy of Kimberly Hoesen

Tape Recordings

Tape recorders are used quite frequently in early childhood settings and have been part of the early childhood educator's repertoire of educational tools for at least three decades. Teachers know that sounds are extremely important to young children in sorting out what the world is all about. Children love to listen to themselves and others sing and talk. Do you remember the first time you heard yourself talk or sing on a tape recorder? Most people's reaction is one of stunned amazement, followed by "That's not me. That's not what I sound like!" We know the reasons why we sound different on tape, but children generally do not, and this is a great opportunity to teach them about how our ears function and what sound is, and to expand the subject to include animals' ears, animal sounds, and so on. Children also love to identify themselves and their friends on tape and take pride in participating in recorded group singsongs, whether just for fun or for a special musical event. What would you like to record on a tape recorder? Any ideas? Here are a few examples:

- Story-time expression of ideas during/after a story
- Role playing in the dramatic centre, i.e., a karaoke band
- Informal interviews between adult and child/ren
- An infant practising sounds while playing, or crib sounds
- A child talking to himself or herself

This text's definition of "observation" includes *watching and* **listening.** Sounds often tell us as much about what is going on as sight does. In familiar surroundings, the sounds you hear will be enough; you do not have to look around to confirm what you heard. Children who live in rural Saskatchewan or northern Manitoba will learn different auditory cues than those of children who live in downtown Vancouver or Halifax. Sounds are part of a specific environment. Think of the sounds in the playroom that are alarms for teachers: sudden crashing sounds, cries, and screams. Teachers can tell you quite easily, "The group is louder today than usual," or "They're very quiet; it must be Monday morning." Experienced teachers will observe with their ears as well as their eyes to gauge the mood or feeling of the group during the day. Observations also give the teacher opportunities to listen to what children are saying and how they use language, which are indicators of cognitive and social development. As a teaching tool, audio recordings can develop awareness and assist in the process of ordering and classifying sounds, associating sounds with objects, and using sounds to make beginning rhythms in music.

A tape recorder can be used effectively to capture samples of children's speech and language. Perhaps a parent, a speech pathologist, or an audiologist is interested in a profile of sounds that may further clarify the patterns of a child's speech and language development. In an ECE setting, the familiar environment helps professionals assess how the child is using language to imitate sounds, to repeat key words, or to name familiar objects and people.

PHOTO: Humber Institute of Technology & Advanced Learning

Tape recordings can serve as a substitute for writing. A teacher could conduct a one-on-one interview with a child for a variety of reasons. The tape recording Moyra used for the sociogram in Exhibit 6.6 is a good example of a way to use one medium to assist in collecting information for an alternative type of documentation. Tape-recording observations is also helpful when writing is not feasible at the time or is not fast enough to keep pace with what is occurring.

Once they finish recording, teachers should transcribe their findings in writing immediately. If you are wondering why, just listen to a spontaneous, five- or ten-minute tape-recorded session in a daycare. Recordings can be full of background noise, some voices being heard over others, and include a general cacophony of sounds that may not be easily understood, never mind interpreted! Even researchers who use tape recorders in a wide variety of ways in a team approach state that if they had the choice, they would just as soon skip the tape recorder and have a real live person write it down. Still, tape recordings can be an option for teachers. Tape recordings may record for the amusement or the education of the children, or they may record specific information on one or more children. The important point to remember is: the *purpose* of collecting information utilizes all means of communication. If a tape recorder works, use it.

Videotapes

Videotapes combine the visual aspects of photos with the audio aspects of tape recordings. In informal child-care settings, videotapes are used to record special events or brief clips of children at play to share with parents. During parent meetings or parent get-togethers, videos can provide an entertaining and educational means of sharing "A Day in the Life of Your Child." Parents appreciate being able to see their child playing spontaneously. By watching the video, they can become part of that day, which was invisible to them before. With parents working long hours and commuting between home and child care, they seldom have the time to stop and observe their child at play. Having video clips available for parents and teachers to view together encourages communication and can be an interesting starting point for dialogue. The immediacy of a videotape helps those watching to see firsthand and respond spontaneously. Parents who may not feel comfortable sitting with a teacher at a desk with written communication might find viewing a clip of their child at play with a teacher a more comfortable experience.

Videotaping with a Special Focus

The area of socioemotional development in young children has been highlighted in current literature, along with other topics such as redefining diversity, resiliency training, and brain research. This is not to say that socioemotional development is new but, rather, that it is new in light of the changes in families, the reordering of social structures, values, and socioeconomic factors. Whatever affects the family affects the child. Many of these effects require educators to challenge themselves to re-evaluate their perspectives, strategies, and curricula. For example, immediately after the terrorist attacks of 9/11 in New York City, student-teachers reported examples of the children's reactions to this event. One child repeatedly smashed toys into tall towers of blocks while engaged in **self-talk** about the event. Another child expressed fear that the tall buildings in his city too would be broken. As he saw the constant replays on television of the twin towers in New York City, he believed that each reply was a separate event. He thought that each replay of the same event was actually many, many new and separate attacks.

Kazim Alat wrote in the article entitled "Traumatic Events and Children: How Early Childhood Educators Can Help" that research of post-traumatic stress disorder (PTSD) reveals the impact of traumatic events on the social and emotional lives of children. The key to assisting children was first to clearly observe children for the symptoms of PTSD. Documentation of children from a variety of ages noted the differences in their responses to such events. With this evidence from a number of observers, intervention supports could be put into place, and follow-up was provided for individual children. The major intervention strategies to restore children's level of normal functioning were play-based physical activities, discussion groups, art activities, storytelling and writing activities, and **bibliotherapy.** Documenting specific behaviours was critical initially to determine which children had been adversely affected by traumatic events. Later, other types of documentation were used to monitor the children's daily functioning. Pictures, tape recordings, and videotaping of special projects or discussion groups were highly effective. They illustrated to the children's families that special activities are an effective way to monitor the social and emotional effects of tragedies like that of 9/11 on young children.

In their article "The Volcano at the Day-Care Centre," Barbara Kaiser and Judy Sklar Rasminsky discuss children who represent a special challenge with their extreme, violent behaviour: "Sometimes, it is hard to identify the high-needs child because he instigates so much tumult around him. Very anxious children are particularly vulnerable and may react to him with equally disruptive behaviour, creating a group of four or five difficult children" (1996, 12). Among other suggestions, they say that observation plays a key role in this challenge: "To assess what's happening, ask the educators to observe the child and the group, recording behaviours and situations in which they occur. As soon as the educators see any sign of a pattern—which may take days or weeks—they should let you know. They may want you to observe the child, as well" (1996, 12).

As researchers, psychologists, and educators discuss the socioemotional development of young children, it is no wonder that we have again looked to early childhood to learn more about the importance of social relationships and to understand the role of play in the child's social development. We can learn about the complexities of social learning by observing and recording. In studies done by Brown, Odom, and Holcombe, videotape technology was used to record highly complex social behaviours. Videotaping in a naturalistic setting allowed the researchers to monitor children "who are at-risk for social competence problems, particularly peer rejection, and to select children who need to participate in social competence intervention programs" (1996, 20).

Inclusion

Videotaping is often used to record the interactions of children with special needs in an integrated or inclusive setting. Teachers like to get a sense of how all new children are settling in, but for a child with special needs, this process is perhaps more critical. Videotaping may be vital in addressing the concerns of parents. Viewing a videotape of the child with the teachers and other supporting professionals is an excellent opportunity for discussion. With parental permission, these videotapes on integrating children can serve as educational as well as observational tools.

Videotaping a child with special needs in a social, informal environment often attempts to address fundamental questions, such as "To what extent is the child's learning influenced by peer models?" or "What is the function of imagination in a social play setting?" In their article "The Naturalistic Observation of Children with Autism: Evidence for Intersubjectivity," Toomey and Adams describe their interest in children with autism and their ability to demonstrate different forms of social experiences. In their videotaped sessions, the authors recorded language, gestures, use of pragmatics, and contexts of behaviour. They videotaped the children during the school day, including free play, lunch, and recreational activities. Studies like these attempt to gain an understanding of how children—in this case, children with autism—learn in social situations, what they learn, and the implications of their learning. Studies involving the social domain often investigate whether the social learning changes over time and is influenced by a social context.

Video modelling is a new method used with children with autism. Liana Malone and Pat Mirenda suggest that "video modeling procedures have been used successfully to teach children with autism a variety of adaptive behaviours including social play, requesting, self-care, purchasing, and academic skills. Although many advantages are cited for the use of video modeling, only a few studies have evaluated the outcomes to date and it remains a tool for further investigation" (2006, 2).

Is This an Effective Method?

When videotaping, there is a planning process: decisions have to be made in terms of time, resources, responsibility, and management. If applicable, an editing process may be necessary once the data have been recorded. The technical aspects of set-up, editing, maintenance, repair, and storage of any mechanical or electronic media can be an involved process. As with every method of observation, evaluating whether or not this method is the most effective for the purpose or event is a major consideration. The information from the media-assisted documentation must still be interpreted, organized, and compiled with other information. (Using media-assisted documentation does not mean the teacher escapes his or her responsibility for interpreting and communicating that information.) Partly due to the organization required and costs involved, videotaping is used far less than photographs in early childhood settings.

ADVANTAGES/DISADVANTAGES: MEDIA-ASSISTED OBSERVATION USING CAMERA, TAPE RECORDER, AND CAMCORDER

ADVANTAGES

- Visuals/audios of children are engaging and appeal to our senses; they capture the hear and now
- Does not require command of the written word to record behaviours
- Documentation with media gives a presentation effect

DISADVANTAGES

- People are often under the assumption that using media to assist in documenting children's activities means that it is easier or less work. Actually, the more tools you use, the more complex is the task. The more complex the task, the more planning is required. Using camcorders, cameras, or tape recorders means that equipment has to be available to you when you need it.
- The information you collect—photos, tapes, and videos—have to be labelled, catalogued, and stored in such a way that they can be easily retrieved. In tropical climates, the growth of mildew and mould on photos and tapes can be a challenge.
- Although digital photography is relatively efficient to use, the overall costs of maintaining, repairing, and storing this and other media methods must be considered.
- Children will often behave differently when they know they are being filmed or photographed. For example, children may hide behind peers or begin "hamming it up" for the camera, or just stand and stare. Alternatively, the stampede to be in the picture can also pose dilemmas for the photographer!

Observation Areas

A discussion of observation areas—areas that are designed specifically for observations—could appear in many sections in this text. The primary reason for including this topic here is to illustrate the unique function these areas provide.

An observation area can be a corridor or hall with a one-way mirror or an actual observation room that affords a view into one or more rooms. The one-way mirror allows adults to observe unobtrusively. The parents and/or teachers can see the children, but the children cannot see them. Either option allows parents, teachers, and others to observe children interacting without intruding on the children's activity. The observation area can also be a specialized place for staff and families to observe, discuss, and share their observations, feelings, and ideas.

Many lab schools connected to early childhood college/university programs have observation facilities. These rooms are specifically designed for observation. Headsets are connected to microphones in each room, allowing the observers to hear as well as see the activity of the children. In college/university environments, student-teachers and professors use the rooms for practice observation sessions, applying classroom theory to the actual process of observing the behaviour of active children and then discussing the findings.

Use of the observation room may be scheduled with the supervisor/director. Some centres may have log-in books that visitors, staff, and students sign, indicating name, organization, purpose, date, and times. Other centres take a less formal approach by posting a sign stating "Please use the observation room!"

The other option, which is more popular because it is less costly, is the one-way mirror along a common corridor. Along the one-way mirror may be a ledge with stools underneath so parents can put down their belongings and sit and watch their child at the beginning of the day ("Has she stopped crying?") or the end of the day ("Look at him put that puzzle together!"). Either way, the parent has the luxury of observing his or her child along with a few minutes of reflection during a busy day!

You may have a field placement in a centre with an observation room or a one-way mirror. New teachers or student-teachers state they feel a little nervous about that; not knowing who is observing or when is unsettling initially. However, as teachers gain confidence in their abilities and feel more comfortable with the idea, being "under the glass" is no longer a concern.

Teachers value the opportunity to take time out and observe the children without having to respond to them. The old saying of "Can't see the forest through the trees" applies here. They also value these times as they can focus more on just one child without being pulled in several directions at once. Teachers appreciate time to discuss a child's needs with parents, and other professionals, such as a speech pathologist or physiotherapist. A quiet observation area is ideal for just such conversations.

The observation room looks into the playroom. Children cannot see observers.

PHOTO: Humber Institute of Technology & Advanced Learning

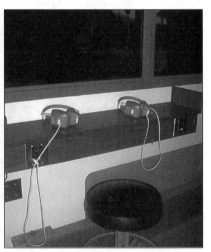

Inside: headsets, ledge, and a stool provide ease of observing.

PHOTO: Humber Institute of Technology & Advanced Learning

Benefits to Parents

Although supervisors and directors understand the value of observation areas for staff participation, they are generally more interested in their value to parents. One supervisor's face lit up when she talked about how important the observation area was for the parents of her centre. She recounted numerous examples of how parents would use the window to ease their anxieties about separating from their child and to relax for a few minutes after their workday, watching their child play.

Specialized programs for parents and children often have designated observation areas. Here, parents and teachers can discuss specific issues in concrete, interactive ways while observing the child. Seeing and hearing the child at play provides opportunities to link "before-your-eyes" examples of behaviour to the discussion topics between parents and professionals.

ADVANTAGES/DISADVANTAGES: OBSERVATION AREAS

ADVANTAGES

- Private area for observing unobtrusively
- Ideal for student-teacher training in observation skills
- Reserved area for other professionals to observe and consult with parents and teachers without interruptions
- Observing directly with teachers or other professionals can ease parents' anxieties; concerns or fears are addressed "there and then" and feedback given without waiting for written documentation or not being sure of what it means

DISADVANTAGES

- Installation and maintenance costs of the observation facilities and equipment
- Finding "equal time" so staff/parents/others can all access the areas

---

Observation and the Uses of Computer Technology

Get Interactive!

A few locations in Canada have Internet interactive access within the daycare; it is a concept that is emerging. If a daycare centre is wired with video cameras and has brokered a deal with an Internet provider, then parents can observe their children from work or home using Internet technology. With special access codes, parents can view their child during the day at any time. Some professionals in the child-care field feel that parents logging directly into their child's playroom is intrusive, while others herald this concept as a positive opportunity—a "window" for the parents into their child's day. It would be a good idea to discuss the benefits of this direct viewing by families into a child's day. What are the advantages or disadvantages for everyone concerned? How does this access affect the way families and teachers communicate? Observation takes on another dimension, doesn't it?

Recording Data and Visual Representations

Professionals in the field are applying the benefits of computers to record data and monitor children's progress. This recording can be done directly on a laptop computer in the playroom or by transcribing handwritten notes and saving them onto a memory stick or CD. Educators can use or modify forms readily available on the market through the Internet or they can design their own record-keeping methods.

EXHIBIT 6.12 ANECDOTAL OBSERVATION FORM		
Date: _____		
Child's Name: _____	Age: _____	DOB: _____
Recorder: _____	Time: _____	Activity: _____
Observations:	Interpretations:	

EXHIBIT 6.13 AT-A-GLANCE FORM	
Date: _____	Time Frame: _____
Age Group: _____	Recorder: _____

This form is left blank. The observer can choose to record any behaviour(s) that appear significant during that time frame on a particular day.
An At-A-Glance Form can be used for the entire group or one child.

Exhibits 6.12 and 6.13 are just two examples of the types of open-ended forms that can be easily formatted for general use by all teachers in a centre.

Forms or templates can be devised for any type of record, such as a checklist, and then be used generically for any child or age group in the centre. Participation charts could also be used to graphically present a child's curriculum interests over a period of time. Inputting basic information on a spreadsheet and then turning those data into a graph provides opportunities to look at the same information in different ways. In Exhibit 6.14, Karen's participation chart on Josie shows how Josie participated during indoor play for 35 minutes. Assuming Karen continued to document Josie's participation for several weeks, Josie's participation information could be converted into graph form.

With a graph, staff and Josie's parents could get a quick overview of Josie's activities over several weeks. Interestingly enough, Josie's graph could be used for other purposes as well. For example, in looking over which curriculum areas were most or least frequented by Josie, the teachers would quickly note her interests over that period of time. If they had other charts on other children in the same room, and their charts also noted the most/least, the graphs would quickly indicate patterns of the children's preferences. If the sensory sand was the area least frequented by all the children, then this is a signal for curriculum change.

EXHIBIT 6.14　CONVERTING DATA TO GRAPHICS WITH A COMPUTER

Participation Chart 1

Child's Name: Josie　　　　　　**DOB:** December 5　　　　　**Age:** 5

Group: Blue Jays (Seniors)　　　**Observer(s):** Karen　　　　**Date(s):** March 5

Activity: Free indoor play　　　　**Time:** 10:00–10:35

Item	Frequency	Comments
1. Dramatic centre (post office)	_	6 min. Plays independently. Talks to herself as she stamps envelopes. She licks each envelope and presses it down to seal. She did this with three envelopes. Smiles. Solitary
2. Block centre (Dinosaurs)	_	5 min. Sits nearby and watches three other children.

(continued)

Item	Frequency	Comments
3. Bucket toys		
4. Construction toys		
5. Stamp printing	–	8 min. Participates independently. Leans on table but does not sit on chair. Talks to herself. Makes sure she uses all colours. Puts materials away when done and asks for permission to put page in cubby.
6. Easel painting	–	6 min. Smock on. Uses pincer and with bingo dabbers palmar grasp. Uses all colours (4) on the full page. Makes careful marks in patterns. Calls to teacher, "Come and see!"
7. Sensory (goop)	–	Less than a minute. Sticks fingers in for a moment while walking by.
8. Puzzle area		
9. Apple matching game	–	5 min. Plays with two boys. She is quiet. Matches apples

CHART FOR JOSIE

Name: Josie   Age: 5   Date April 8

	Paint	Blocks	Outside	Water	Sand
Wk 1	2	1	3	5	3
Wk 2	3	3	5	4	1
Wk 3	5	3	4	4	1
Wk 4	4	4	2	1	1

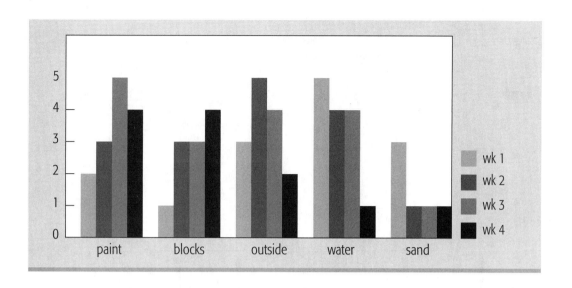

Weekly Curriculum Sheets

Teachers in licensed programs across Canada use weekly curriculum sheets (Exhibit 6.15). Using different colours, fonts, and graphics, weekly postings can be made attractive and eye-catching in appearance. Recording simple, brief statements on a weekly curriculum sheets helps parents know what experiences are planned and/or the opportunities their child was offered during the week. Planning sheets follow the philosophy of the centre and reflect planning with a top-down, detailed theme set by teachers or a loosely constructed play-to-learn, bottom-up, child-centred plan to be constructed as it happens during the week.

EXHIBIT 6.15	TODDLER WEEKLY CURRICULUM SHEETS			
Day	**Sleep**	**Snack/ Lunch**	**Washroom (time)**	**Activities/ Experiences**
Monday		S L S		Sensory Dramatic Circle Blocks Creative Cognitive *(continued)*

Day	Sleep	Snack/ Lunch	Washroom (time)	Activities/ Experiences
Tuesday		S L S		Sensory · Dramatic · Circle Blocks · Creative · Cognitive
Wednesday		S L S		Sensory · Dramatic · Circle Blocks · Creative · Cognitive
Thursday		S L S		Sensory · Dramatic · Circle Blocks · Creative · Cognitive
Friday		S L S		Sensory · Dramatic · Circle Blocks · Creative · Cognitive
Messages:				

SOURCE: Courtesy of Humber Child Development Centre

Record keeping, whether it is keeping track of weekly curriculum sheets or updating the children's portfolios, is a necessity. With computer memory not an issue, data can be stored and cross-referenced to maintain records for a variety of purposes. Computer use is seen as a time-saving and efficient means of logging, storing, and retrieving the large number of forms involved in child care, and the yearly curriculum events.

Teacher Computer Use

Teachers could daily, if computers are available,

- keep children's records up-to-date,
- enter new observations,
- track or monitor children's progress,
- manage reports on each child in the program, and
- adapt curriculum based on ongoing observations of the group.

Maintaining records electronically and finding more efficient ways to do so is a constant administrative function. Whether they are simple observations forms or essential documents utilized in child-care settings, appropriate staff need to peruse a variety of sources such as online websites, journals, magazines or organizations such as the National Association for the Education of Young Children (see Exhibit 6.16) for technology applications. Sources are constantly changing, so

---

EXHIBIT 6.16 NATIONAL ASSOCIATION FOR THE EDUCATION OF YOUNG CHILDREN—SOME RECOMMENDATIONS

Following are specific recommendations for early childhood professionals as they advocate for more appropriate technology applications for all children.

- Promote the development of software and technology applications that routinely incorporate features that cater to the needs of learners with different abilities.
- Advocate for software that promotes positive representation of gender, cultural, and linguistic diversities and abilities. Software publishers should create a balance of programs that appeal to both boys and girls.
- Encourage software publishers to create programs that support collaboration among learners, rather than competition. Fostering cooperative learning enhances the acceptance of the abilities of all learners.

SOURCE: National Association for the Education of Young Children. Young Children. NAEYC Position Paper. Washington, DC: NAEYC, April 1996

finding information on these topics requires a periodic Internet search! Bookmark and share a good website for future use.

Technology in Early Childhood

With Internet resources, websites, and databases, educators can now easily connect with one another, and investigate the latest research in early childhood. They can research for themselves the cultures and countries of our newcomer parents and children to Canada so that they may understand and respond intelligently and with sensitivity to the children and their families.

The reality of our profession is that knowledge of computer technology and electronic networking is now expected. College and university online services and courses over the Internet, CD-ROM instruction, and other technologies continue to enhance our education. How will the observation of young children continue to be changed by technology?

Summary

In this chapter, alternative, less print-reliant ways of observing children have been examined. Many reasons exist for choosing these types of documents of children's activity. One of these reasons could be that educators may not demonstrate strong written communication skills and for a time may be more comfortable with these less print-dependent methods. Some parents may also be more comfortable with information presented in a pictorial or graphic mode rather than a written report. Reviewing the advantages and disadvantages of each method gives the reader the information he or she needs to select the best method for the purpose. Pictorial or graphic representations add to the educator's ability to capture the necessary information using a variety of methods.

The types of media-assisted observations utilized in ECE settings have been discussed. Such media as the camera, tape recorder, and camcorder assist in documenting children's behaviour. When possible, special observation areas can also provide unique opportunities to unobtrusively observe children.

With families able to view their child through Internet connections, even when they are at work/school/home, new possibilities for dialogue are created. Technology changes the ways in which we communicate. Computer programs have also expanded the ways in which educators can develop and save data on children, as well as how they can use Internet resources to further understand and support children and their families.

In Singapore, early childhood education teachers have entered the phase of integrating computer technology–enriched learning in the classroom, as well as using computer technology in teaching strategies.

Students enrolled in a full-time early childhood education diploma course in Singapore undertake two modules in Information Technology and Applications, which are conducted in the first two years of their course. Apart from acquiring the basic computer skills, they learn to integrate computer technology in teaching, curriculum-specific learning, record keeping of progress reports, using charts and tables to analyze data, creating Web pages, and designing software for children's activities.

Knowledge and skills in computer technology support the use of graphs, sociograms, and mapping as they can be computer-generated, saved in the computer, and made easily accessible to teachers to compare present outcomes with previous data.

Media-assisted observation using digital and video cameras to complement or illustrate records of children's behaviour enhances the concept of total communication. This is true especially with the additional possibility of linking the camera to the computer to store pictures for reference and comparison and to share them with parents via e-mail.

Using alternative, less print-dependent observations certainly dispels the notion that not being able to write effectively means the individual is not a good observer. For teachers who are apprehensive about their writing ability, the use of less print-dependent observations can provide teachers with alternative, more achievable, means of observation. Less print-dependent observations certainly open new doors to teachers, encouraging them to embark on the important, yet achievable, journey of observation and documentation, so as to support children's holistic development.

—Theresa Lu,
The Regional Training and Resource Centre in Early Childhood Care and Education for Asia

KEY TERMS

bibliotherapy	palmar grasp	self-talk
interview	pincer grasp	total communication

DISCUSSION QUESTIONS

1. What are the alternatives to print-dependent methods used to document children's activities?

2. What are the types of media used to assist observation? What are some examples of their use?
3. What are some of the benefits to both parents and teachers when they utilize a specialized observation area?
4. How could you combine some of these methods to create observations that are interesting and relevant to parents?
5. How have computers and related technologies enhanced the role of the teacher–observer?

ADDITIONAL READINGS

Allen, Eileen K., and Lynn R. Marotz. *Developmental Profiles*. 5th ed. Clifton Park, NY: Delmar Learning, 2007.

The fourth edition displays a well-organized, easy-to-follow format complete with generous coloured pictures throughout the text. The main focus of this text is still to outline the major characteristics for each of the developmental areas from infancy through middle childhood. The text provides a comprehensive, yet non-technical, guide to child development, with photos and figures supporting the text with reader-friendly visuals.

Good, Linda. "Snap It Up: Using Digital Photography in Early Childhood Education." *Childhood Education: Infancy Through Early Adolescence* 82.2 (Winter 2005/06): 79–85.

This article reminds us of the many reasons why children are photographed in early childhood environments, such as promoting feelings of security and building self-esteem, rather than narcissism. Many ideas are presented supporting the use of digital photography to build a sense of community.

Gronlund, Gaye, and Bev Engle. *Focused Portfolios TM: A Complete Assessment for the Young Child*. St. Paul, MN: Redleaf Press, 2001.

This text demonstrates how to combine a variety of methods used in documenting children's activities using photographs with checklists, anecdotal notes, and parent collection forms. The information is used to plan individualized curriculum while reflecting on sharing that information with families.

Koster, Joan Bouza. *Growing Artists: Teaching Art to Young Children*. 3rd ed. Clifton Park, NY: Delmar Learning, 2005.

This text is a good antidote to the notion that one must only observe a child when there is a problem. When children create, educators learn. This text has many informal references to what can be learned from the creative process of a child. The author also devotes a chapter to assessing growth: how can artistic growth be assessed, how to share this information with families and how the observed process of the artistic product is used in a portfolio.

Part 3

USING OUR OBSERVATIONS

No matter how much you learn about children, there is always more to learn. That is the mantra of a good observer. Uncovering, discovering, and making the learning process visible to others is exciting not only for the observer to do, but to share! That is what Part Three of this text is all about.

Part Three is about uncovering what children are learning in order to share this with parents, and finding ways to communicate this information in meaningful ways. It is about making the learning process, which is invisible to parents during their workday, visible. When the teacher takes the time to photograph, map, chart, or write about a child and then shares this with the family, everyone is given an opportunity to pause, discuss, and reflect. Through documentation, teachers can develop their knowledge of each child and perhaps something about the cultural and familial influences in the child's life.

Part One started us on our journey with the basics of the observation process and provided the following definition: "Observation has been the means of discovering what we know about children today. Observing young children and recording their behaviour is considered essential practice in every quality child-care setting." From Chapters 1, 2, and 3, you learned "how to observe children and how to record that information."

Part Two introduced two major categories of records and three chapters full of different types of records used to document the activity of young children. Having explored all these methods, it is now time to make use of what has been learned.

At the beginning of the 21st century, early childhood in Canada is a kaleidoscope of programs, from small, rural, private home daycare, to large, urban daycare centres accommodating over a 100 children. Not only does the field range demographically, it also ranges in quality. All quality child-care programs should reflect practices demonstrating that educators

- document meaningful observations,
- plan reflectively, considering each child in the group,
- communicate responsively with children and families, and
- develop relationships with the children, families, and the community.

Opportunities for communicating with parents and families regarding the documented learning and activity of young children is integral to quality care. Questions to aid in reflecting on quality practices might be:

- What do parents *want* to know about their child?
- What are the ways teachers can communicate their interest in and knowledge of the children with families?
- With the diversity of families, how can you avoid a one-size-fits-all approach?
- How can the documentation of children's behaviour enhance the shared joys and responsibilities of socializing and educating young children?

Chapter 7 begins by exploring two current, differing philosophies in early childhood, and then illustrating how observation and documentation are used within these established philosophies. Each will be briefly discussed, followed by an explanation of how documentation is an integral part of each of their essential practices and principles.

As the focus of Chapter 7 is "making a child's world visible," two popular and well-used methods of using and sharing observations will be thoroughly investigated: (1) portfolios, and (2) report writing. Note that report writing could be part of assembling a portfolio, and collecting information in a portfolio may be the basis for a progress report. A parent–teacher interview can be a vehicle for sharing information and how this might be done is outlined at the end of the chapter.

"What do we do if there is not a strong philosophy like Reggio Emilia or a model such as High/Scope to guide us?" Many programs do not have or maintain an established philosophy or set of practices in regards to curriculum development, observation methods, or communicating with families. Chapter 8 will explore alternative methodologies that will support and guide educators in their investigations.

Chapter 8 is about expanding our ideas about observation. Two Canadian and one American assessment tool will be discussed, demonstrating how the assessment process complements observation and contributes to comprehensive documentation.

Throughout Canada, the field of child care is experiencing changes, such as unplanned for, but consistent, multiage groupings of children, children with challenging behaviours, and children whose families are experiencing difficulties navigating the sometimes turbulent waters of parenthood. How can we best use our skills of observation to assist children and their families? Lastly, but most importantly, how do our efforts to observe and document benefit children and families in our communities?

Chapter

(diamond with number 7)

MAKING A CHILD'S WORLD VISIBLE THROUGH DOCUMENTATION

PHOTOS: Humber Institute of Technology & Advanced Learning

Documenting and keeping records of children's growth and development is about making the child's day at a child-care setting visible to parents and families. A record-keeping system acts as a frame to begin to assemble and organize what is learned about children. Educators use that systematic process to communicate what they have learned with others—primarily parents/families.

Overview

Featured in this chapter are two philosophies in which observation is used in unique ways: (1) the philosophy of Reggio Emilia, and (2) the High/Scope curriculum model. We will examine how each model uses observation. Two methods of documentation and/or record keeping will also be examined, that of portfolios and report writing.

The two philosophies profiled in this chapter are child-centred philosophies based on the notion that children's interests are central in determining the curriculum and how it is constructed. Both philosophies consider the role of observation and documentation—the mirrors that reflect the activities of the children making the invisible visible. Both the philosophy of Reggio Emilia and the High/Scope curriculum model guide the educator to reflect, analyze, provoke, and evaluate, creating a co-construction of knowledge and a positive approach to learning for all concerned.

This discussion on documentation speaks to the role of the teacher as documentor, whether it be documenting children's progress in portfolios, record books, reports, or on document panels. This chapter focuses on the role of the teacher as observer. He or she helps children see connections, observes their responses and interests, and guides the work through collaboration with parents and children. It is a very reflective process demanding sensitivity to interactions of all children and adults; assisting everyone to express their knowledge through representational work. Such highly collaborative work requires not only the skill of an observer but the art of observation.

After reading this chapter, you should be able to:

- Identify the two philosophies that utilize observation in unique ways.
- Describe the process of developing a portfolio.
- Develop a report based on observations.
- Explain how families can be involved in the documentation process.
- Give details about the parent–teacher interview process.

The Reggio Approach

Over the past two decades, the Reggio Emilia approach to early childhood education has invigorated teachers in North America and inspired pilgrimages to the schools of Reggio Emilia in Italy. This city-run educational system for young children was started by educators and parents. At the end of World War II, as the legend goes, some parents built the first school with proceeds from the sale of a tank, a few horses, and some trucks. Over the last 30 years, many schools have been added to accommodate children aged from three to six years. During that time, the Reggio approach has been influenced by contemporary theorists, such as Lev Vygotsky, Erik Erikson, Howard Gardner, and Jerome Bruner.

The early childhood programs in this approach are unique in that they combine the concept of social services and education. The schools are based on a high degree of parental involvement. The man who founded and influenced the development of the ECE programs and guided the Reggio approach was Loris Malaguzzi (1920–1994).

The scope of this text is too limited to give an in-depth account of the philosophy, its successful experiences over the years, and the impact that the ideas from the book *The Hundred Languages of Children* have had on our image of the child and the role the community plays in connecting and activating members into a wider social environment. If you are interested, conduct an Internet search using the descriptors "Reggio Emilia Preschools" or "The Hundred Languages of Children." Bookmark these websites and others!

From the example in Exhibit 7.1, what is the role of the teacher? How is the curriculum (making an Inukshuk) developed? Did the adults believe that the toddlers

EXHIBIT 7.1   BODY AWARENESS PROJECT: BUILDING AN INUKSHUK

The children had been talking about body awareness, and Kathy (our artist) was driving by an art gallery and noticed an Inukshuk on the front lawn. This particular one looked like a person standing, with the arms out.

After discussing the idea of making a real-life Inukshuk in our program meeting, Kathy brought in some stones and a resource book about Inukshuk. Through the book, we learned that the plural for Inukshuk was Inuksuit and that each different Inukshuk had a different meaning to travellers passing by.

The toddlers made their first Inukshuk in November. After revisiting the documentation, books, and pictures, the stones were brought out again. . .

Leah examines her work so far. . .

Camron brings over stones to add to the top of the Inukshuk.

Can you stand like the Inukshuk? Laine puts her arms out to each side.

(continued)

SOURCE: Courtesy of McMaster Children's Centre.

were capable of this active construction? Does this activity reflect a particular culture? What do you think the families of the toddlers thought about this creation that these young children had made together?

The Inukshuk in this example evolved from a child-care centre whose teachers and families have embraced the philosophy of Reggio Emilia. Part of their philosophy is to create images of the projects the children work on—both during the process and in the final product. Photos, as we saw in Chapter 6, are an integral part of collecting information and documenting the learning process.

Reggio Emilia: Observation and Documentation

When teachers of Reggio Emilia schools talk about observation, they talk about documentation and communication, and relationships and inclusion. From the use of those words you cannot help getting a sense of community. Immediately, the power of intent in those words conveys a togetherness and openness, and a willingness to share. At this point, it should be quite clear that the teachers are not talking about a few isolated observations left in a folder in a drawer in the office. In the little text called *Spreading the News: Sharing the Stories of Early Childhood Education,* authors Carter and Curtis refer to "the Skill and Art of Observation" as "Making the News." The "news" they are referring to is making the lives of children visible— visible not only to others, such as parents and teachers, but also to the children themselves through their art, their accomplishments, and their projects. These authors write, in Exhibit 7.2, regarding observation and the role of the teacher.

Children and adults (parents and teachers) learning together form the basis for project documentation in the Reggio schools. The documentation can take many forms and include group murals, sculptures, and paintings. The documentations can be a series of photographs taken over time, visually documenting a construct of materials by a group of children. Photos can be mounted on boards and accompanied by written observations of teachers, or words written by the children themselves or transcribed by the teachers. As the teachers learn from the children, along with them,

We must shift our focus from paperwork and regulations to children's needs and interests. Primary roles for caregivers and teachers should be observing and detailing what children do and then broadcasting to others why these activities should be taken seriously. More than anything, children need us to become advocates for play and guardians of childhood.

As we focus more on children and their activities, we better know and plan for each individual. We learn more about child development theory because we see it in action.

SOURCE: Carter, Margie, and Deb Curtis. Spreading the News. St. Paul, MN: Red Leaf Press, 1996. 17.

Daniel revisits a technique learned earlier in his exploration of pipes. A teacher helps him to see a project he initiated and later added to with the help of Justin.

As a follow-up to this, straws were provided to begin to more fully realize the nature of pipes. They are also quite simply fun to join. Here, we see Daniel on tour with his newly created, very long pipe.

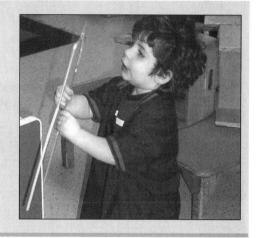

SOURCE: Photo and text courtesy of Jason Avery, Artists at the Centre.

they, in turn, show the children what is of interest to them, and the parents also contribute to this process. The flexibility and responsiveness to children's interests is documented by the staff in Exhibit 7.3.

Over months, the evolution of interest, skills, and concepts is documented, showing how the children support each other's learning and enlist the adults' participation during these discoveries.

Principles Supporting Documentation

Documenting brings alive the underlying ideas, skills, and interactions of children engaged in an activity. The behaviour of children does not have to be connected to a special event or contain a "WOW" factor to merit documentation. A daily event or a sudden interest in a common object is all that is necessary to begin the process of discovery. Teachers who are aware and responsive to the actions and ideas of children will recognize their importance. According to the Reggio Emilia approach, documentation is about being committed to openness and dialogue. Three of the Reggio principles are as follows:

1. *The image of the child,* with a belief that children have preparedness, potential, curiosity, interests in social interactions, construction of their learning, and ability to negotiate their environment. Teachers, therefore, work to be aware of the children's potentials and plan the work and environment with regard to children's experiences and responses.
2. *The three subjects of education include children, parents, and teachers,* and the well-being of children is connected with that of parents and teachers. By recognizing that children have a right to the best education that society can offer, parents are assured the right to be involved in the education of their children, and teachers' rights for professional development are guaranteed.
3. *The interdependence of cooperation and organization* is recognized through the minimum of six hours per week that are scheduled for meetings with colleagues and parents, preparation, and service training. Everything from teachers' schedules to the dietary needs of children is discussed and organized with great care. All are committed to this level of organization and cooperation because it is believed to be necessary in order to offer the best possible experiences for children. (Billman and Sherman, 2003, 260)

The philosophy that merges children, teachers, and parents together as "co-constructors of knowledge" displays their work as projects or as **document panels.** From the interests of the children and through the research and diligence of the teachers, simple stories may emerge about simple topics, such as hats or coloured glass. If interest in these topics is supported by the adults, then the stories become rich in examples about that topic. As the documentation is assembled, whether it be written or visual, a documentation panel can be organized. This panel would represent the process of investigating and researching this topic. The toddlers' Inukshuk in Exhibit 7.1 represents just a portion of the discovery process that lends itself to a document panel.

The High/Scope Model

The High/Scope model began in Ypsilanti, Michigan, to serve at-risk children from poor neighbourhoods. In the course of the past decades, this purpose has expanded to include children with special needs and children from diverse backgrounds and cultures from all socioeconomic levels. Over the years, this model has also changed its name from the Perry Preschool Project to The High/Scope Research Foundation. The major publications it produces are internationally acclaimed. David Weikart, the originator of the model, used Piaget's work on intelligence as the framework for the curriculum model he developed. The two main concepts that form the core of Weikart's High/Scope model are that children are active learners, and their learning can be reflected in a series of statements describing the social, cognitive, and physical development of children, called "key experiences." The four main components needed to support active learning are adult–child interaction, learning environment, daily routines, and assessment.

The High/Scope model where active learning is central has been represented as a wheel of learning (see Exhibit 7.4). From the Wheel of Learning, you will note that assessment has four components: teamwork, daily anecdotal notes, daily planning,

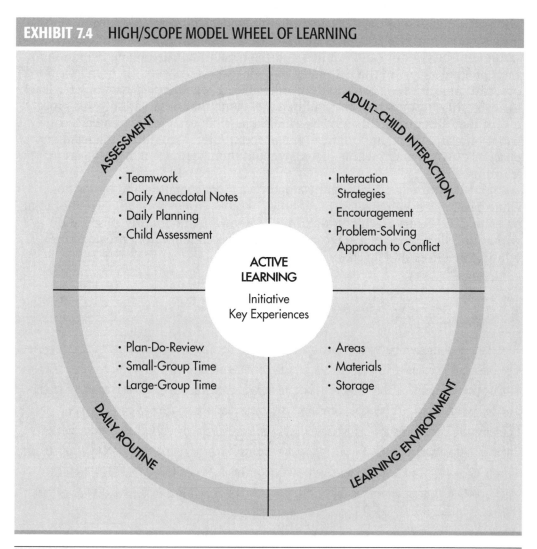

EXHIBIT 7.4   HIGH/SCOPE MODEL WHEEL OF LEARNING

ASSESSMENT
- Teamwork
- Daily Anecdotal Notes
- Daily Planning
- Child Assessment

ADULT–CHILD INTERACTION
- Interaction Strategies
- Encouragement
- Problem-Solving Approach to Conflict

ACTIVE LEARNING
Initiative
Key Experiences

DAILY ROUTINE
- Plan-Do-Review
- Small-Group Time
- Large-Group Time

LEARNING ENVIRONMENT
- Areas
- Materials
- Storage

SOURCE: M. Hohmann and D. Weikart. *Educating Young Children.* Ypsilanti, Michigan: High/Scope Press, 1995, p. 6. Copyright 1995 by High/Scope Press. Used with permission.

and child assessment. Assessment is based on the daily observations of each child in the group. How this model uses observation to learn about children, assess their development, plan curriculum, and involve parents is examined below.

In the scope of this text, it is impossible to do justice to the High/Scope model with only a brief introduction. The High/Scope model's history and use within the international community spans decades. The focus, therefore, will be on the Child Observation Record and the most recent revisions.

The High/Scope Child Observation Record (COR)

The original design of the COR assessment booklet supported the notion of long-term observation. High/Scope is well known for its documented longitudinal studies on the children and families and the benefits accrued by participation in their programs. One of the hallmarks of their success has been their approach to observation—observers participating and working together to pass along feedback to each other in support of the children. Believing that observation is reciprocal meant that differing points of view were exchanged; each team member's contribution was deemed important to the process. After discussions, the team of observers (which may include parents), could then begin to plan strategies for learning.

A main feature of COR is that it supports staff collaboration and interactions while developing their observations of the children. Problem solving, whether adult-based or child-centred, is highly valued in this model. Importantly, observation within the High/Scope model recognizes diversity—children from other cultures, ethnic differences, and diverse backgrounds.

EXHIBIT 7.5   HIGH/SCOPE RATIONALE FOR COR 1992

Assessment of children's progress in programs employing developmentally appropriate practices relies on careful observations of children by teachers and parents. Accordingly, the NAEYC and the National Association of Early Childhood Specialists in state departments of education (1991) regard the teacher or caregiver as the child's primary assessor and they expect assessment to depend primarily on their observations and anecdotal records of the child's performance and products. They criticize the use of artificial test situations for this age group, arguing that assessment instruments should focus on young children's strengths and achievements, rather than their undeveloped skills and abilities. The COR meets all these criteria; it relies on the teacher's or caregiver's careful observation of children as they engage in their daily program activities throughout the year.

SOURCE: High/Scope Research Foundation, *Child Observation Record Manual*. Ypsilanti, Michigan: High/Scope, 1992, p. 3. Used with permission.

The 1992 Child Observation Record (COR)

In the early 1990s, the High/Scope Educational Research Foundation introduced the 1992 version of the High/Scope Child Observation Record (COR) for children aged from two and one-half to six years. The rationale for developing the Child Observation Record resulted from the educational discussions during the 1980s, as increasingly, developmentally appropriate programs focused on young children learning by doing rather than testing their learning in an artificial testing situation. An excerpt from the High/Scope COR illustrates that focus in Exhibit 7.5.

Revisions to the Child Observation Record (COR)

Revisions to the original Child Observation Record have resulted in the Preschool COR, Second Edition, and The High/Scope Child Observation Record for Infants and Toddlers. These observational assessment tools focus on children aged from six weeks through three years (Infant and Toddler) and from two and one-half to six years (Preschool). The revisions seem to reflect the importance of relating the results from the COR items and levels to strategies and teaching plans for the individual child or group. Two other new additions, Child Information and Developmental Summary forms, and Family Report Forms, reflect the need for meaningful and useful ways of sharing observations with others. What is relevant to our discussion in this text is that the Family Report Forms have a blank section for a Developmental Summary, Supporting Anecdotals, and a Parent Observation. The importance of family participation will become more evident as we continue in this chapter and the next.

Changes and additions to the original COR are clearly outlined on the High/Scope website with assurances that even though there are changes, the transition to the revised Child Observation Record is relatively easy for those already versed in the COR process.

What has been expanded is the coverage of language and literacy and the change of one of the key six categories from *logic and mathematics* to *mathematics and science*. Instead of Observation Forms, a *Child Anecdotes* booklet is provided along with a user guide. These booklets are used to record the detailed development of each child, and are shared with parents. A Parent Guide in English/Spanish assists parents in understanding what the COR is and how they may be involved in the process. Additionally, High/Scope offers an online version of the COR assessment tool. The High/Scope website (http://www.highscope.org) offers valuable resources for teachers and child-care providers, administrators, and families.

In Part One of this text, we started out by defining the purpose of observation by saying that it was a process of discovery. What we have discovered in this chapter, after examining two major philosophies and beginning to examine the many ways to use observation, is that we are just beginning to uncover the world of children and be amazed at how much there is to learn!

Portfolios

Some Initial Questions and Answers

What Is a Portfolio?

Although the definition varies, there seems to be general agreement that the portfolio is a purposeful collection of work that conveys relevant ideas of a child's growth and development. A portfolio is a chronological collection that shows how a child changes over time; early works can be compared to current information.

What Is the Purpose of Developing a Portfolio?

A portfolio should be a work in progress; a dynamic process that reflects the individuality of child. The purpose is the heart of any portfolio and should reveal what is important to the children, teachers, and families. However begun, a portfolio offers opportunities for interpreting growth and development, revisiting ideas, and reflecting. There doesn't seem to be a right way to assemble a portfolio, and therefore some confusion exists about how to go about developing one.

A portfolio could

- reflect how curriculum was used,
- be open-ended so the collection process represented a child's interests, skills, participation and areas to improve,
- if relevant, compare a child's current level of learning and functioning with previous material, and
- reflect the child's current development and indicate appropriate developmental levels of functioning.

What Is in a Portfolio?

- Artwork samples (paintings, colouring, masks, rain sticks)
- Photographs (individual children, a group, or the process of a project)
- Observations: examples from open methods, such as anecdotal records, as well as records that target specific behaviours, such as checklists and rating scales
- Combination methods such as ecomaps and anecdotal comments, or sociograms with accompanying audio recordings

What Else Could Be Included in a Child's Portfolio?

- References to the environment (space, lighting, materials, equipment)
- Past discussions/goals for the future, reflecting input from family
- Plans of the centre/room staff, e.g., transitions from one room to another
- Resources: community events and trips, professionals involved

Who Collects This Information?

Teachers, children, parents, volunteers, student-teachers.

How Would Parents/Families and Teachers Be Involved?

Documenting children's work and experiences in a portfolio provides opportunities for reflection and discussion. Imagine what a rich experience it would be to share a portfolio with parents. What possibilities could that engender? What might the parents want to share with you? As you share this information with families, more information could be added to the portfolio! But, of course, that would be your ultimate goal in creating the portfolios, as it offers an open-ended opportunity for dialogue and participation. It is an ideal way to integrate the family's experiences into a culturally appropriate curriculum for young children (see Exhibit 7.7). Then, as the children collectively explore the curriculum, more opportunities for documentation are created, and the cycle continues. This process helps ensure a playroom is rich in ideas from various perspectives, similar to the **anti-bias curriculum** of developmentally appropriate practice (see Exhibit 7.6), and invites reflection and discussion.

A Holistic Image of a Child

Making the child's day visible through anecdotal records, charts of their participation during the week, and notes about their social development reveals a **holistic** image of the child. Photographs of children interacting during the normal events of the day—outside chasing snowflakes, building, or painting at the easel—are the kinds of documentation found in portfolios and appreciated by families. A variety of documentation over time contributes to the understanding of the total child, which is more than a focus on cognitive skills, social interactions, or gross motor abilities. Having a portfolio that represents a child's activity recorded at different

---

EXHIBIT 7.6   IMPLEMENTING A MULTICULTURAL CURRICULUM

The ideal way to implement a multiethnic, multicultural, or anti-bias curriculum is to integrate it into the everyday curriculum of the classroom, rather than teach specific units or add-ons to units that relate to diversity. "Looking at curriculum through an anti-bias lens affects everything a teacher does" (Derman-Sparks 1989, p.8). According to Derman-Sparks, an anti-bias curriculum incorporates the strong aspects of multicultural curriculum but tries to avoid a "suitcase" or tourist approach, in which children "visit" a country or culture, its foods, holidays, and customs before packing the "suitcase" of materials away for the year. In addition, care must be taken so that the multicultural activities do not misrepresent, trivialize or stereotype the cultures…

SOURCE: Billman, Jean, and Janice A. Sherman. *Observation and Participation in Early Childhood Settings: A Practicum Guide*. 2nd ed. Boston, MA: Allyn & Bacon, 2003. 256.

EXHIBIT 7.7   WALKING THE TALK OF COLLABORATION

True collaboration requires a set of dispositions, beliefs, commitments, and skills. Even then, it isn't easy to collaborate, especially across significant differences in cultural perspectives, experiences, personal, or organizational histories. Above all, collaboration takes time, something rather scarce in most of our child care programs. . . .

To acquire a desire for and the ability to collaborate, most of us need some serious retraining of our minds and mouths. There isn't much in our overall culture that develops us into collaborators. To the contrary, so many things conspire to pull us in the opposite direction toward competition, complacency, defensiveness, or disregard for the collective body. It takes a concerted effort to discover the deeper benefits of collaboration and unlearn the attitudes and behaviors that undermine it.

Consider the organizational culture of your program. Do your policies and standard practices reflect and reinforce the value of collaboration? What things need revamping to be consistent with notions of collaboration? When families first visit your program or potential staff members arrive for an interview, how will they get a sense of the value you place on collaboration?

SOURCE: Carter, Margie. "Walking the Talk of Collaboration" *Child Care Information Exchange* 3 (2003): 72.

times of the day, during different events, and focusing on all developmental areas provides opportunities for the parent to appreciate their child in new ways. With documentation carefully organized in a portfolio, parents can then not only see what the child did—the products—but also gain insights into how and why—the process.

When Would We Begin?

Right away! Logistically, beginning an endeavour, such as developing portfolios for a centre with an infant/toddler preschool/kindergarten room, would take a lot of planning! The entire staff of the centre must be engaged in the process. Timelines or schedules would need to be created. The staff at the daycare would need to determine approximately how much time it would take to complete. Many other decisions would also have to be made so that everyone involved would have a role to play and an understanding of what to do and when.

A Collection Plan

In simplistic terms, portfolios represent a systematic process of compiling information with a specific purpose in mind. Just simply collecting information is not good enough; there needs to be an organized plan around a goal or outcome. Strategies should be in place to ensure that all children will be included in the process. How can teachers keep track? See some possible ideas for collecting information in Exhibit 7.8.

EXHIBIT 7.8   HOW TO COLLECT INFORMATION

How to collect information for a child's portfolio? Some ways could be

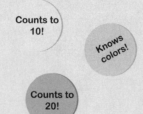

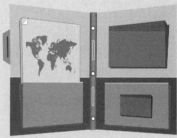

Label dots

using stick-on notes or colour-coded pages

Folio with pockets

keeping a notepad in your pocket

Pens, pencils, highlighters, and clipboard

using a clipboard and keeping it close by

File folders

having an "at-a-glance" folder in the room

Small tape recorder (for interviews)

keeping a camera or tape recorder nearby

Laptop computer

using laptop computers

Specially designed evaluation sheets

using key experience forms

Where Is It Stored?

The information collected could be stored

- in a file folder,
- in a pizza box,
- in a plastic container,
- saved electronically, or
- using a combination of these storage methods.

Portfolios: Different Types

The portfolio can be associated with a variety of curriculum approaches or philosophies, such as the Project Approach (covered in Chapter 8) and Reggio Emilia. The portfolio is similar to observation in that it, too, is setting-independent and can be used in programs with a broad-based or eclectic philosophy.

Danielson and Arbrutyn (1997) identified three types of portfolios:

1. display portfolios—scrapbooks with collected items without teacher comments
2. showcase portfolios—best pieces of a child's work
3. working portfolios—include selections of typical work along with teacher documentation to show the child's progress (Gordon and Browne, 2007, 242).

Portfolios became particularly popular in the United States in the 1990s, where their use was seen as an alternative to the standardized assessment and testing of young children. Portfolios were referred to as a type of **authentic assessment.** This term originated in the United States and it meant that the observation or assessment of children should be conducted in a familiar environment rather than a testing environment. It referred to the ongoing assessment of a child's learning and development as a means of evaluating progress, rather than a one-time standardized test.

Much information regarding portfolios that appears on the Internet refers to early childhood in the United States. Early childhood in the United States includes kindergarten *and* the primary grades. The field of early childhood education in Canada is different; it does not typically include the primary grades. Therefore, performance criteria and assessment indicators that are often topics included in portfolios from Internet sources do not reflect the reality of the portfolios typically used in early childhood settings in Canada.

Although the field of early childhood in Canada has not been part of the battle over authentic assessment versus standardized testing, we have benefited immeasurably from the dialogue, new ideas, and useful methods that have resulted from it. From decades of research into authentic assessment, we have uncovered or rediscovered truths about how children learn and ways to document that process. We've learned that portfolios can serve an assessment function or an instructional function, or act as a reflective activity for parents and teachers. At the end of the chapter are several additional readings dealing with the diverse ways in which portfolios are used.

Stages of Collection

Before beginning the actual collection, educational and managerial decisions are made in terms of the purpose of the observations, timelines, implementation strategies, participation of others, and portfolio organization. A systematic collection process could resemble the example shown in Exhibit 7.9.

In Exhibit 7.9, the timelines were defined by the purpose. The selected dates were grouped into two-week intervals to allow educators and parents time to observe while also serving as guidelines for the systematic process. Getting that initial portfolio started at the beginning of enrollment reflected the decision of the educators to establish a baseline of information on each child and to have opportunities to confer with families.

EXHIBIT 7.9   TIMELINES FOR OBSERVATION

September 1–14	-	Anecdotal observations/running records Meet with parents to explain portfolio process Collection samples of creative work
September 15–30	-	Continuation of anecdotal observations/running records, and collection of creative work samples plus photographs
October 1–15	-	Checklists (areas targeted for observation, depending on an age group and focus)
October 15–30	-	Team/parent discussions regarding each child in group
November 1–15	-	Based on six-week observation timeline and discussions, further observations: ABC analysis/event sampling, mapping, sociograms, participation charts, profiles, tape recordings and/or rating scales
November 15–30	-	Continuation of further observations using a variety of documentation.
December 1–20	-	Team/parent discussions regarding each child in group

How would the process and content change for an early childhood education setting? Not all the information has to be collected at the same time. There could be stages of collection within each of the rooms in the centre. Those initial stages could vary, depending on the purpose of the collection at the time. They may be categorized or organized according to projects, themes, or key experiences. All records of observations could be organized chronologically. Photographs could be mounted on coloured paper with anecdotal records attached to explain a particular feature of the photograph. Obviously, the portfolios would contain some things that would be the same for all children. But there would also be a variation between individual children and certainly between the infant room and kindergarten room.

What would be the purpose of developing a portfolio in an infant room? With many developmental milestones occurring during infancy, the portfolio would be filled with examples. The same could be said about the toddler age group as well, with examples of language development, **autonomy,** and self-help skills such as dressing, eating, and toileting. What would be the main purpose of a portfolio in a kindergarten class? How would the construction of a portfolio in this age group vary from that of a portfolio for an infant?

Standardization and Individuality

All portfolios for each child in the group will contain items that will be generic: a class picture or documentation of the trip to the apple orchard. Each portfolio will be standardized to the extent that everyone will have that photo or record of that trip.

As seen in Exhibit 7.10, children will have some of the same kinds of documentation in their portfolio. That standardization forms the foundation for all the portfolios. However, as noted in Exhibit 7.10, portfolio content should then begin to diverge and reflect individual differences.

EXHIBIT 7.10	JULIANNA AND REBECCA	
Dates	**Julianna**	**Rebecca**
Sept.–Oct.	4 anecdotal records	3 anecdotal records
Sept.–Nov.	2 work samples	8 work samples
Nov.	1 class picture	1 class picture
Oct.	1 language checklist	1 language checklist
Nov. 10	1 ABC analysis/event sampling	
Nov. 24	1 ABC analysis/event sampling	

Becoming an Editor: A New Role

Some children are very prolific, with multiple pieces of artwork and project work participation. Over time much can be compiled, and at some point, a judgment may need to be made as to whether only some types of information should be kept that clearly represent the child's growth or all the work should be considered. This process invokes a new role: that of an editor. Questions should be asked such as: Should teachers edit out a child's work? What is the role of the teacher-editor? How comfortable is a teacher in making those decisions? What are the teacher's biases? These questions are posed to encourage reflection and discussion of this unique role prior to the second stage of analysis, reflection, or evaluation of the collected materials.

PHOTO: GOH SIOK HIAN/Shutterstock

The onus of responsibility lies with the teacher to construct and organize the information within the portfolio to reflect the whole child. It does not mean that the teacher dictates the content, but rather develops the content. The teacher ultimately collects, organizes, and presents the material in a parent-friendly manner. Even though ideally the parents have collaborated informally with the teacher throughout the collection process, at some point they will want to discuss the contents of the portfolio in a formal way. Methods of informal and formal parent–teacher communication are discussed near the end of this chapter and in Chapter 8.

Commitment to the Process

Ideally, everyone collectively needs to take part in developing a portfolio or it will fall short of its potential. Those in a supervisory capacity can support this process of collecting and compiling information by assisting with

- schedules for data collection,
- negotiating timelines with families for parent interviews,
- editing reports and making recommendations for improvements, and
- organization of portfolios and reports.

These efforts should support teachers in their commitment to the portfolio collection and parent interviews. Commitment to the process of portfolio development will help inspire collaboration as teachers investigate methods of documentation to guide their progress. If there isn't administrative or peer support, and only one brave soul wishes to develop a portfolio collection, what then? As colleague of mine once said, "One staff member can begin and lead by example." Maybe the journey will begin with the step of asking "What happened today that is important to share with parents?" Discovering what is meaningful is crucial to the communication process.

Some teachers will choose to focus on such information as "He knows his primary colours, can count by rote to 20, and is beginning to differentiate between squares and rectangles." Perhaps parents would prefer to learn about their children's creativity, industry, and play. Some teachers will focus on the social interactions of the children in their groups and observe helping and **prosocial behaviours.** What will you believe to be important?

Benefits to Students

Students of early childhood benefit from completing a portfolio at least once prior to graduation and employment. Assembling a portfolio helps to develop a student's sense of organization, critical thinking, reflection, knowledge, use of different types of records, and writing skills. As with any multistage project, instruction is helpful to guide and assess how the information is collected, organized, and presented. Students have indicated that, even though assembling a portfolio is a lot of work, they are glad of the opportunity. Completing a portfolio gives students a sense of the organization required for such a multi-phase project. Students have to consider such components as the types of documentation to use, the strategies needed to collect information, and the time frame allotted to each phase. It also gives them a sense of accomplishment and pride at having completed a complex process involving many people over time; it represents a sustained effort.

Documentation in a portfolio can stand alone, or the information found in running records, participation charts, and profiles can be organized and summarized into a report for parents. Writing a report from the information gleaned from the portfolio process represents yet another stage. Information collected over time will need to be compiled and analyzed before beginning to write a report.

Report Writing

The key to writing a good report is to identify the target audience: whoever will read the report. For whom is the report intended? From that beginning, the rest follows. Basically, a report, like a good conversation, considers the purpose (the focus of the conversation), the content, and the tone. It has been said that in conversation, the tone of voice and body language of the sender is considered more by the receiver than the actual words spoken. What about in written communication? What else is important in a written message other than the actual words? It could be said that the wording or tone of a message is important as well as the style and mechanics (spelling, grammar, punctuation, sentence structure). The **affective** aspect of report writing is very important to consider when the reader of the report is the parent/family of the child in your care.

The Affective Aspect of Report Writing

When writing a report for parents, colleagues, or other professionals, ask yourself the following questions:

- What do the readers want to know?
- What do the readers need to know?
- How can they use the information you are giving them?
- Who will benefit from this report?
- In what context will the information be conveyed to the readers? At a conference or parent meeting? Formally? Informally?

Considering these and other questions before you begin will help ensure that you develop an "others" perspective. In other words, you are considering the affective *response* of the reader before you begin the written communication. This consideration is a reflective approach to writing. It includes people's possible responses to the information instead of being solely fixated on presenting the information.

After reading over the report, ask yourself these questions one last time:

- Do my comments describe the uniqueness of the child?
- Is the tone positive and encouraging?
- Is the information accurate?

Reports should be clear, concise, and detailed without being overly wordy and contain objective observations with professional interpretations. Such reports are usually about two pages in length. Exceptions may occur if many other professionals are involved with the child/family. Written reports of this depth are typically compiled no more than twice a year. Educators may provide other kinds of mini-reports or weekly updates between any major written reports. What kinds of reports are there, and how are they organized?

Types of Reports

- Entry/intake
- Conference
- Assessment

- Progress/portfolio
- End of year/discharge
- Telephone/e-mail update/home visit

Each of these reports differs in its purpose. The entry/intake and end of year/discharge reports are self-explanatory. A brief report is written on a child enrolling in a program and the other report when the child is leaving the program. The conference report may support the parent–teacher conference. Short reports or updates with a particular focus are written for contacts with family via phone or e-mail, or home visits. The assessment, progress, or portfolio report are the type of reports that are written from two to four times a year, and represent one of the most common types of reports found in early childhood settings.

How Are Reports Organized?

The format or organization of any report can be customized to suit a specific purpose. Large organizations use letterhead and a specific, standardized format that is followed by all programs in the organization. Although a wide variety of templates exist for reports, for our purposes we will examine a common, generic format used within the early childhood community. This format can be divided into the following sections:

- Section A: Essential Information
- Section B: Background Information
- Section C: Physical Description
- Section D: Summary
- Section E: Recommendations

The format of the first page of a report should be consistent for each child.

Section A: Essential Information

Child's Name (first and last): _____

Child's Date of Birth (D.O.B.): _____

Age of Child (years, months & days): _____

Date of Enrollment: _____

Date of Report: _____

These five pieces of information should be presented in the essential information section.

Having an accurate date of birth is absolutely critical. Depending on centre practices, other information may be included in this section, such as date of referral or dates of assessment. Listing essential information at the beginning of the report provides vital information at a glance. Readers do not want to have to look through pages of a report to find it. You may also include (optional) a sentence or two that indicates the dates you began your observations on this child and all subsequent dates (taken from the actual records), the settings in which the observations took place (rooms, outdoors, trips), and lastly, a list of the types of records and work samples that were used to collect the information about this child.

Section B: Background Information (optional)

If the child has attended the centre for a substantial period of time, a brief paragraph here may be included, detailing in which age group the child began and where the child is now (e.g., school-age room). If the child is attending kindergarten for half-days or is working with a resource teacher, this section could include information that refers to the dual programming and professional(s) involved.

This section also includes any information that would further clarify the findings in the report to others, such as medical history, special adaptations, previous referrals or assessments, or significant family history.

Section C: Physical Description (optional)

A brief paragraph describing the child could be included. This gives readers, usually other professionals, an image or holistic view of the child so he or she is perceived as a child first. The reader will then move on to the discussion of developmental areas in the summary.

Section D: Summary

This section is the summary of collected information in the child's portfolio. The summary should be written in the narrative (see Exhibit 7.11). The purpose of the summary is to present an overview of the child in a way that is clear, organized, and parent-friendly. The summary is based on the accumulated documentation you have collected, including the various methods we discussed in Chapters 4, 5, and 6.

There are many ways to organize this information. A generally accepted practice is to organize the report using the areas of child development as this gives structure to the content. Using these domains as a guide presents an overall perspective of the child. This balanced perspective cannot be emphasized enough. The educator's professional responsibility to the child, the parents, and the field is to present any information on a child as objectively, ethically, and sensitively as possible. Frame the information in terms of child development and report the conclusions in behavioural and developmental terms. Examples of development to support the summary

EXHIBIT 7.11   EXAMPLES OF SUMMARY STATEMENTS

Maliha's fine motor skills are apparent during activities involving activity boards, stringing beads, and playing board games with small pieces. She is able to complete intricate lacing cards with ease. We are introducing her to prewriting skills, and she is just beginning to trace along vertical and horizontal lines.

Maliha's self-help skills are age-appropriate; she is able to dress, undress, and attend to her toileting needs independently. She is working on fastening and unfastening zippers, snaps, and ties.

Maliha's speech and language skills are improving and she is beginning to initiate conversations with peers with confidence. She is able to ask for food at the table, deliver simple messages, and respond appropriately to questions involving choices.

statements can be drawn from the anecdotal observations, profiles, checklists, rating scales, sociograms, or a combination of methods.

The summary should indicate the strengths and interests of the child, with the areas to improve stated in a positive manner. Include what skills the child may be just beginning to develop or has begun to master, as well as variables that may influence behaviour.

STRENGTHS AND NEEDS FORMAT

Particularly, although not exclusively, when writing a report on a child with special needs, a strengths and needs format is used. This format can be used as part of any report such as a portfolio or progress report. The strengths and needs section can be expressed in point form or narrative as part of a report, or it can be used as a rough draft to aid in constructing a formal report. A **strengths and needs list** might look like the one in Exhibit 7.12. Basically it is organized by listing the child's

Strengths	Needs
What the child can do	Areas to improve/areas to monitor
What the child likes to do	
The people who are willing to help	
The resources available	

EXHIBIT 7.12 STRENGTHS AND NEEDS UNDER DEVELOPMENTAL AREAS

GROSS MOTOR

Strengths	Needs
• pulls on handle to open door	• to begin to pedal tricycle forwards
• pedals tricycle backwards	• to mount stairs using railing or adult hand
• climbs up stairs on hands and knees	

FINE MOTOR

Strengths	Needs
• uses Lego to build two- to three-piece structure	• to demonstrate threading skills
• uses pointer finger to push buttons	
• nests three to four cups in gradation	

WRITE IT POSITIVELY

When stating a child's area of need, write it positively. For example, instead of saying "Marc has trouble holding onto a crayon or marker," say:

- "Marc has yet to grasp a crayon or marker with ease."
- "The focus of learning for Marc will be grasping and writing with crayons or markers."
- "Our program emphasis for Marc will be drawing with various crayons and markers until he is able to hold them and draw with ease."
- "Marc's skill to acquire is the comfortable handling of utensils, such as markers and crayons."

Instead of using the word "cannot" to describe an area of need, remember the more positive ways of phrasing. Student-teachers wonder if that is not just "dressing it up." Actually, what lies between "cannot" and "has yet to" is *potential*. It is not that the child *cannot;* he just has yet to accomplish that skill. It could speak to lack of experience or practice or familiarity. Positive phrasing is respectful language. Parents of children with special needs, in particular, may need to feel encouraged and hopeful about their child's progress, however small. Reading information about their child that is phrased in a positive manner conveys caring and respect not only for the child, but for themselves as well.

OUTLINE OF STEPS IN WRITING A REPORT

To organize and develop a report, there are several basic steps to follow. An outline of steps in writing a report in the early childhood field is as follows:

1. Collect all the records you have documented including photographs, artwork, observations, and any other materials that will be part of the child's portfolio.
2. Assemble the information to begin your first draft. Your first draft represents the first attempt to organize your information; it is only the beginning. Following an outline gives the information structure. For example, if you are writing about a developmental area such as *social interactions,* you might begin by listing key words or phrases from your anecdotal records, charts, and ecomaps, such as: understands games with rules, follows directions, explains things to her peers, plays Snakes and Ladders, Monopoly Jr., Clue, and checkers, and plays catch outside with friends.
3. Some of the behaviours recorded in anecdotal records, participation charts, or sociograms may fit into more than one area. For example, "yelling" could be recorded under language but could also fit under the social–emotional domain. You have to decide how to organize the behaviours from your observations. How would you group the following behaviours?

   - Names family members
   - Sits in circle and listens to a story for 10 minutes
   - Uses "no" in speech
   - Usually uses two- to three-word sentences

4. For each paragraph or topic, support your opening sentence with examples from your observations. Be descriptive in your examples so the reader will clearly understand how the examples illustrate your main points. Remember this is your rough draft, so don't fret over every word. Do not try to make it perfect the first time around.
5. Read through your rough draft. Ensure that all the essential information is complete and accurate. Read it again. This time consider the audience, for example, the parents. Have you stated things positively? Read it aloud. Does it make sense to you when you hear it? Remember to use words to express, not impress!
6. Ask a colleague or team member to read over your draft. Listen to their feedback, including criticisms. In his *Guide to Report Writing,* Lawrence Gulston provides an interesting section on "Writing in Teams." In this section are helpful ideas to building a writing team and approaches to team writing. When compiling reports within an organization, teachers utilize the many advantages to a team approach to writing. Doing so assists them with the writing process as well as ensuring consistent agency standards in their reports.
7. Edit and rewrite. Again, read over the essential information for accuracy. Check to ensure that you have used all the relevant information from your portfolio. Read over the content again so that content is coherent and follows a sequence;

in short, it is easy to read. There is an old saying that the more the writer works, the less a reader must. Here's when you check again for errors in spelling, grammar, and punctuation.

8. Read it again. Check it again. Your professional credibility and the reputation of your agency or organization depends on the quality of your reports.

HOW DO I SAY THIS?

If a report contains a topic that teachers know parents may not wish to hear, it is even harder to write it in a report. "How do I say this?" is a common teacher lament. No matter how long you've been writing reports, finding the right way to convey an idea can be a real challenge. Juggling words around to see how they sound is a good practice. Even if you *feel* that "Joel can't get along with anyone in the room," you will have to find another way to say that. How about writing "We are currently working on Joel's interactions and communication with his peers"? Follow through with examples that support that statement. Write about what strategies have been effective. Stating things positively does not mean that inappropriate behaviours are conveniently ignored and only the positive things are said. Nor does it suggest that we write that things are fine when they are not. We all have to hear things we do not like sometimes, but most people feel less threatened if the message is phrased in a positive way. Think, reflect, and write positively and with sensitivity.

Section E: Recommendations

The recommendations should be positive, realistic, and appropriate. One to three main recommendations might be a better idea than trying to write about every possible area. Stick to only a few, as it will be less daunting and perhaps less intimidating to parents. Write each recommendation clearly in paragraph form. When moving on to the next recommendation, ensure the reader understands that by perhaps beginning each topic with "I recommend that . . ."

Indicate how these recommendations could be put into action. If you and the family have agreed that Tim should be enrolled in a community program, indicate why you are making this recommendation. Relate the recommendation to areas covered in the report. "Tim is beginning to understand that games have rules, and he appears to enjoy telling the younger children how to play! Perhaps team games with children of his age group that involve the 'way to play the game' would be gratifying to him, such as soccer, hockey, T-ball, or lacrosse." In making these recommendations with input from the family, you need to be aware of what is available in the community! Check your community information bureaus. Ask around. You will want to find out if the family is able to afford such sports, considering the cost of equipment or resources that can be accessed to defray the costs. Talk with the family about their readiness to support Tim in this sport. Observations have taken us a long way!

Parent–Teacher Interviews

The parent–teacher interview or parent conference involves the early childhood educator and the parent/family. This interview provides a focused opportunity to share mutually inclusive time.

Preparing for Parent Interviews

The formality of scheduling and conducting a parent interview gives weight to its importance; an endorsement that an unscheduled discussion may not otherwise have. Parent interviews are scheduled not only for teachers to convey information they wish to share with families, but also for parents to share their perspectives of the child or any other pertinent information. Parent interviews are really an extension of the work that has already been accomplished—the child's portfolio. The interview is a highlight; an event anticipated by staff and families; an opportunity to celebrate the lives of the children.

The number of children in a child-care setting may vary from five to ninety-five. The larger the number of children involved, the more planning is required to prepare for parent interviews. Details of the parent interviews are planned during staff meetings, as the cooperation of all concerned is essential. The following topics are considered:

- The dates and times of the interviews
- Any special arrangements that have to be made, for example, a translator for some families
- The location(s) of the interviews: playrooms, staff room, or office
- How to notify parents of the interviews
- How to confirm actual dates and times

These topics should be addressed at least three weeks before the actual interviews. This gives parents three weeks to schedule their appointment, arrange for a baby-sitter, if necessary, and check work schedules. Contacting parents for the meeting often involves more than one strategy. Here are some examples:

- Telephone, e-mail, fax, BlackBerry
- Letter to go home with the child that includes a tear-off portion to be returned
- Sign-up poster on the front door or bulletin board
- Notice in centre newsletter with a clip-out portion to be returned
- Person-to-person communication followed by a written reminder

Whichever method(s) is chosen, it is important to remember that parents are busy people with full calendars. Sometimes it almost takes the talents of an air traffic controller to keep track of all the communications with the families in one centre.

The Parent Interview: What to Consider

Staff should be clear about how the parent interviews will be conducted and their role in the interview. In some organizations, the administration clearly gives directives about how long the interviews will be, the format, the location—even the content of the children's reports. In other centres, interviews are less structured. Here are some factors to consider when conducting parent interviews:

- *Interview length.* Most experienced teachers say that 20 minutes is satisfactory for a parent interview. If further discussion is needed, find another time to meet so you will not feel rushed and the parents will not feel that you are putting them off.
- *Discussing the child.* Over the years, teachers have used what is commonly called the "sandwich approach," which means alternating between discussing the child's positive areas and the areas that need improvement. To begin or end with a topic that is stressful for the parents ensures that they will mainly remember only that part of the meeting, so try to begin and end on a positive note.
- *A systematic, professional approach.* Being organized and having the child's portfolio, artwork, or even favourite toys at hand gives the parents and teacher a good place to start the interview. Using the progress/portfolio report, the teacher and parents will be able to discuss and reflect upon the collection of information. The report shows how it is based on representative samples of the child's work over a period of time. The teacher's collection of photographs, running records, and profiles will support any statements made about the child and clarify what the teacher is talking about. Following a systematic model ensures a more professional approach and also provides the parents with a more balanced overview of their child's interests and skills.
- *Perceptions.* Do not expect that parents will talk about their child the same way you do: their child is family, and their perceptions may be very different from yours. Parents are often reassured by the calm yet caring perspective an early childhood educator demonstrates when discussing the child's problems or difficulties. Parents take heart from the fact that teachers can give examples of certain behaviours and talk about how they handled these and how they felt. Parents are doubly delighted when the teacher asks for their opinions and ideas.
- *Discussing other areas.* Part of the interview should be set aside to share information about any changes or decisions coming up in the near future. For example, if the parents and teacher feel that the child should be moving from the toddler room to the preschool room, discussing an appropriate time for this transition to occur is important. If the parents agree with the move, then they will be able to support the teachers and the child in the transition from one group to another. The hardest transition for the parents is moving their child from the infant room to the toddler room because it means their baby is growing up. Moving on from child care to school is also a huge change for children and parents alike!
- *Listening and observing.* Parents do not attend a meeting about their child with nothing to say. Extend the courtesy of listening. This practice extends to all parents, but especially to parents who are shy, who have difficulty with English, or who have recently immigrated to Canada. Parents may have rehearsed what they want to say and may have waited for this time to speak. Depending on

their culture, the mother may defer to the father, or both parents may quietly sit and nod to whatever you say. Parents may come into the conference with their own ideas for discussion: special things the teacher may need to know about the child or family matters, questions about how the child gets along with others, or how the teacher feels about such issues as discipline or language development.

Use your observation skills during your discussions with parents. Do they appear comfortable? Do they seem interested in what you are saying, or do you feel that they are just waiting to talk? Some family members will want to take the initiative in the meeting, while others will choose to follow your lead. Diversity in families ensures that you will be a lifelong learner.

Summary

This chapter has examined the unique perspectives of two different philosophies/approaches and how their principles and practices are reflected in their documentation. The documentation gives families and educators opportunities to see in concrete ways what interests the children on a daily basis and how they problem-solve and use their imagination. Portfolios are developed by educators to organize the accumulated documents in a systematic way that records the learning process. Part of a portfolio may be a professional report that thoroughly summarizes the importance of the documentation for the reader. What is important to remember from this chapter is the reciprocal nature of communication and documentation. When families and educators perceive themselves as partners in the lives of children, there will be genuine cooperation and respect. Documentation is better seen as a process rather than as a product; a process that involves everyone concerned from the beginning.

PROFESSIONAL REFLECTIONS

Early childhood educators in Hamilton who have been exploring the Reggio Emilia approach have come to recognize the richness that documentation has brought to their work. Perhaps even more than an "observe-to-plan" approach, this is an "observe-to-learn" approach. As with all complex ideas, this, too, has many layers.

It was important for our community of learners to recognize why we document. It follows from a fundamental view of the child as having ideas and interests that are worth pursuing, as having the ability to reflect on his or her own thinking and to maintain interest in a topic for a prolonged period of time. It also follows from the view of the teacher as a researcher and co-learner. It soon became apparent to us that documentation is far more than a record of what happened. At first, though, until these educators gained experience, they were trying to do just that—record everything. New skills were needed—stenographer, photographer, videographer, editor, graphic display artist. It seemed overwhelming. But this may be a necessary stage; the pendulum may have to swing too far before it finds what is just right.

We have discovered that documentation allows educators to see and reflect on their own teaching. They are recognizing missed "teachable moments" and have responded by slowing down the pace and allowing themselves to be more present with the children. These are reflective educators who are excited about their work.

The benefits for the children and parents are obvious. Children feel validated when someone takes the time to listen and record their activity. Parents become eager participants in the curriculum when their children's thinking and learning is made visible to them on an ongoing basis.

Another layer of benefit involves the broader community. Documentation panels allow others to see and celebrate children's thinking and ability to represent it. Our experience has shown us that the response is often, "What can I do to help this to continue?"

—Karyn Callaghan,
Mohawk College

KEY TERMS

affective

anti-bias curriculum

authentic assessment

autonomy

document panels

holistic

prosocial behaviour

strengths and needs list

DISCUSSION QUESTIONS

1. How are observations used in the Reggio Emilia approach and High/Scope model? Provide concrete examples in your answer.
2. What is involved in the process of developing a portfolio?
3. In what ways does report writing depend upon documentation found in projects and portfolios?
4. How can families be involved in all of the approaches, documentation, and record-keeping systems?

ADDITIONAL READINGS

Bullock, Ann Adams, and Parmalee P. Hawk. *Developing a Teaching Portfolio: A Guide for Preservice and Practicing Teachers*. New Jersey, NJ: Prentice-Hall, Inc, 2001.

Chapter One begins, "It is an exciting time to be an educator." This text is interested in presenting information to busy people as it is easy to read, organized, and relevant to the topic of developing portfolios—both process and product portfolios.

Fraser, Susan. *Authentic Childhood: Experiencing Reggio Emilia*. 2nd Can. ed. Toronto: Thomson Nelson, 2005.

This text would be an excellent start for those just investigating the approach educators take when building on the curiosity and intelligence of young children that is Reggio Emilia. The author has not sought to transplant Reggio Emilia in Canada, but rather deconstruct her own practices and be inspired by the words and actions of Malaguzzi. A new section in this edition speaks to students, relating the principles of Reggio to their learning.

High/Scope ReSource: A Magazine for Educators 20.3 (Fall/Winter 2001).

This magazine is one of the many publications of the High/Scope Educational Research Foundation. *ReSource* is published by the High/Scope Press, a division of the Foundation. This particular issue introduced *The High/Scope Child Observation Record for Infants and Toddlers: A Tool for Meaningful Assessment*. The articles in the issue discuss how to accurately track and document the development of children in this age group, enabling parents to further understand their infants or toddlers.

Gulston, Lawrence. *Nelson Guide to Report Writing*. 2nd Can. ed. Toronto: Thomson Nelson, 2008.

This guide includes the issues central to writing a report, such as how to organize information and write in a clear, readable style. Chapter 1 begins with the topic of audience and purpose. This chapter is extremely relevant when writing a report for parents and professionals. "Writing in Teams" is another chapter that should be read by all educators as it stresses the collaborative approach to writing and the value of reviewing each other's work.

Chapter

WHAT OBSERVERS DISCOVER

PHOTO: Courtesy of George Brown College

At the end of one of our classes, Tara, a third-semester early childhood education student, showed me a portfolio. It was a huge scrapbook bulging with papers. The cover was decorated in bright colours with her daughter's name on it. Tara explained that her daughter's teachers had assembled the scrapbook and had presented it to her the previous week. "How wonderful!" She was overjoyed at this! As a mother and future early childhood educator, she understood its value from both perspectives. It certainly was an inclusive portfolio, representing months of work. She then told me that some of the parents did not bother to take their child's portfolio home. "Why not?" I asked. "I don't know," Tara said, "but maybe it was because the parents didn't know anything about it. It was a surprise. They didn't know what to make of them." I asked, "Didn't the teachers tell the parents about what they were going to do? Didn't they get the parents involved?" "No, I don't think so," Tara replied, "I didn't know about it until they came up and gave it to me. I was very impressed, but they were disappointed because I was one of the few who gave them any good feedback." Is this true story about documentation, or communication and relationships? What could have been done differently to ensure a more positive outcome for everyone?

Chapter 7 summarized the philosophy of Reggio Emilia and the High/Scope model to illustrate two differing ways of documenting children's behaviour. Each was intentionally selected for discussion to show how two quite distinct philosophies both excel in that process. By exploring each, you were able to gain an awareness of how observations were developed, a brief glimpse of the teacher's role, and how communication and relationships with families are central to the educational and social values of both models.

Educators using the Reggio Emilia approach or the High/Scope model would have a clear, yet differing, idea of how observation is used. They would know how to record the activity of young children from their professional preparation within the philosophy's practices.

But not every program has such a strong philosophy and set of practices as those of Reggio Emilia or High/Scope. Many programs do not have a "plan to observe," "observe to learn," or "observe to plan" methodology as part of their defining philosophy and practices. Even if some programs *do* follow a philosophy or have a set of practices, they may not be articulated or clearly understood within the organization. In either case, where do the educators begin, and how do they proceed?

PHOTO: Sonya Etchison/Shutterstock

Overview

Chapter 8 explores the question of how educators develop an observation process, and answers those questions raised in the opening scenario. Finding a systematic process or a framework with which to begin observing and recording the activity of young children can be challenging. In this chapter, three different models, those of webbing, the project approach, and traditional planning, illustrate the possibilities that exist to document the activity of young children and to use those observations in meaningful ways. Observations and curriculum should reflect the diversity of each child and his or her culture. Formulating an observation/curriculum cycle connects the child-care setting with the influences of the child's family, home life, culture, and general community. In the opening scenario, the educators who compiled portfolios for all the children should be commended. But would not their efforts have been better received and appreciated had they considered including the families at the beginning of the process?

In a society that is ever changing, and with research that constantly evolves and reframes our thinking, we need to utilize our observation skills and explore alternative methodologies that assist us in creating the most useful, meaningful ways of uncovering and sharing the incredible development of a child.

After reading this chapter, you should be able to:

- Explain how educators plan to observe, observe to plan, and observe to learn.
- Examine how curriculum is developed through webbing, project approach, and traditional planning.
- Identify how societal changes influence practices in the field of early childhood.
- Examine the role of parents/families in the documentation process.
- Describe informal opportunities to share information with families.
- Consider the influences of the environment when observing.
- Explore how observation plays a vital role in early intervention.
- Look at the role of two forms of evaluation in this process.

Change in the Field of Early Childhood

During the past few years, we have witnessed changes in the field of child care in Canada. Some of the changes identified by workshop participants at the 2001 Kitchener-Waterloo AECEO (Association for Early Childhood Educators—Ontario) annual meeting were as follows:

- Cultural, linguistic diversity in children and their families
- Mobility of families
- Turnover of staff in centres
- Attitudes in society
- Financial cutbacks/downsizing, restructuring, and administrative reorganization
- New directives from provincial/territorial or municipal governments
- Increasing popularity of the Reggio Emilia approach and High/Scope curriculum model in communities
- Shift from theme-based curriculum to emergent curriculum
  (Axford, Muriel, and Sally Wylie. From the workshop "Planning for Multi-age Groupings: Are you Crazy?")

These identified changes indicate that there has been a shift in our experiences in early childhood settings. Change is also noted in the United States by Jennifer Bradley and Peris Kibera, who state: "Three trends are of critical importance in preparing early childhood professionals to meet the needs of children and families. These trends are demographic changes in the U.S. population resulting in the increased diversity of families' cultural backgrounds (Brewer & Suchan 2001); the movement toward inclusion and recognition of the rights of all children to be cared for in natural environments (Odon, Teferra, & Kaul 2004); and the increased prevalence of emotional and behavioral problems among preschool children (Koppelman 34)."

Why is it important to note change in the field? Early childhood professionals must recognize and identify the changes in order to respond appropriately and act conscionably. As indicated, one of the key changes for the field of early childhood is the increase in the number of newcomer families, who bring with them new ideas and values from different cultures. If families and early childhood educators are indeed the child's first teachers, then we have an amazing opportunity *and* responsibility at hand!

In Canada, for the most part, we are familiar with the obvious ways teachers demonstrate their acknowledgement of new cultures in the playroom. Examples include culturally inclusive books, music, food, games, artifacts, examples of festive dress, posters, and words of greeting and comfort in many languages. Acceptance is a value that is part of Canada's multilingual, multicultural society. Yet, in the field of child care, we must constantly ask ourselves if, through our attitudes and practices, we are creating an appropriate atmosphere to meet the needs of our diverse communities.

In the article entitled "Respecting Culture in our Schools and Classrooms," Robin Pearson uses the image of an iceberg to reflect the idea that some cultural indicators are visible at the tip, while a vast number are hidden below the surface (see Exhibit 8.1).

How often have we noted and looked for examples of "the hidden iceberg"—the part under the surface? Do we acknowledge others' concepts of tempo of work, notions of leadership, concepts of beauty, approaches to problem solving, incentives to work? If we do acknowledge different perspectives, such as those noted under the iceberg's surface, how is that demonstrated in early childhood settings? How are the differences and similarities acknowledged in a quality ECE program?

One of the main reasons to investigate change is to gain new insights. From new insights, we can begin to appreciate anew the influences upon children and their families and understand their perspectives. In the article "Meeting the Needs of Refugee Families," Dr. Marlinda Freire says, "The immigrant child when he leaves his country has been part of a plan. . . . [T]he youngster has had the possibility to dispose of his/her belongings, to say goodbye, to think of what type of precious things that he may want to bring . . . like his toys for example or books" (*SWIS News & Notes*). Understanding the reality of just one child should give us pause for reflection. From the knowledge of this child's experiences, we may be better able to provide a program more responsive to the interests, strengths, and needs of the child and his

EXHIBIT 8.1 THE CULTURAL ICEBERG

What do we think of when we hear the term, culture? Common responses are food, dress, music and dance. If we ask a group of students what they understand by the term, they may also include language, manners, relationships and religion. When a newcomer arrives in another country, s/he brings a rich cultural background from his/her country of origin. Much of this is unspoken, much of it is subconscious, and the most important aspects are generally not visible. Culture is effectively compared to an iceberg: there are some indicators above the surface, but much more is hidden below the surface.

SOURCE: Pearson, Robin. "Respecting Culture in our Schools and Classrooms." Child & Family 9.2 (Summer/Fall 2006): 37.

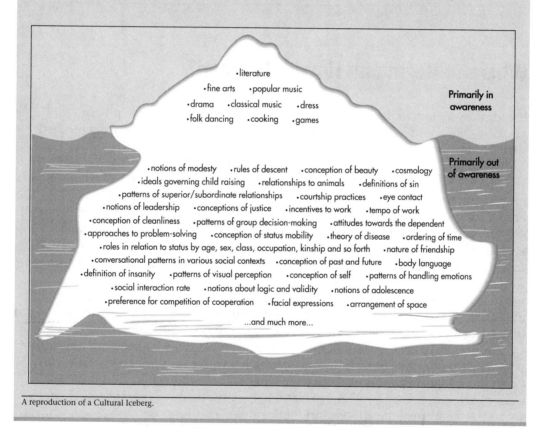

A reproduction of a Cultural Iceberg.

or her family. Based on our observations and an appreciation of their experiences, we could network in the community and **advocate** for needed family resources or services. When the care and education of young children is viewed as a collective of relationships, then we can all become collaborators in creating a better world. As shown in Exhibit 8.2, observation is the foundation upon which opportunities can be built with windows for new perspectives.

Where to Begin and How to Proceed?

If educators in a program, for whatever reason, don't have a philosophy or set of practices, the question is: where do the educators begin and how do they proceed with documenting the activity of young children?

Remember the definition of observation in Chapter 2? "Observation is a systematic process of watching and listening to children and recording their behaviour in a meaningful way for future use." Teachers using the High/Scope model or the Reggio Emilia approach have developed meaningful ways. What are some other meaningful ways of using observation? Documentation could reflect an "observe-to-plan" approach, such as an emergent curriculum model, or a "plan-to-observe" approach, such as a theme-based curriculum. Another way to use observation could be solely as a means to learn or an "observe-to-learn" approach.

In Chapter 4 the anecdotal record exhibits showed the form or format currently used to record observations in early childhood settings. Two other formats or graphic organizers, the T-Chart and the KWL chart, are illustrated in Exhibit 8.3.

The anecdotal record form or T-Chart organizes what we know about a child and separates our objective observations from our subjective interpretations. The KWL Chart provides three columns to record what we know about the child, what we want to know, followed by what we learned. L = how further observations changed, shaped, or confirmed our perceptions of the child. This form encourages educators to continually examine the growth and development of each child.

Observations can be used in conjunction with the inferences of the teacher's role and that of the environment as a way to start looking at the behaviour of children *in context,* such as those in Exhibit 8.4.

Karyn Callaghan of Mohawk College comments on the use of this form:

> The form was intended very specifically to encourage reflection on the impact of the environment and on the role of the educator on children's

EXHIBIT 8.3   TWO DIFFERENT FORMATS

The T-Chart

Observation
for Karen: _____

Observation	Interpretation

The KWL Chart

K	W	L

K = What I/We Know
W = What I/We Want to Find Out
L = What I/We Learned

EXHIBIT 8.4   OBSERVATION–INFERENCES FORM

Child's Name: _____   Date: _____   Time: _____

DOB: _____   Setting: _____   Teacher's Name: _____

Observer's Name: _____   Centre Name: _____

Time	Observations	Inferences (Child's Development)	Inferences (Teacher's Role)	Inferences (Environment)

SOURCE: Courtesy of Mohawk College

behaviour. By its design, it conveys that each individual child's development and behaviour occur in a context. The intention is not just to provide a rationale for planned activities, but rather to reveal the complex interplay among and between children, environment and educators.

If what is revealed is a lack of thoughtful interactions with adults, or environments that are not engaging or challenging, the onus is on the educator to make changes. These changes will have impact on children's behaviour and on how they feel about being in the community of the playroom. It is much easier to change what we are doing, and to experiment with elements in the environment and schedule than it is to try to change children's behaviour directly without addressing those other aspects. Our form is designed to encourage reflection as a starting point to help us to think about the meaning of teaching and learning.

The observations and inferences concerning child development, the role of the teacher, and the environment become the basis for reflection. Further observation can provide teachers with

- an awareness of the individual children within the group;
- an understanding of the group dynamics;
- an evaluation of how the materials and space are used; and
- a basis for child-centred curriculum reflecting daily events and activities.

The observation-based curriculum represents each child's interests and emerging skills and group interactions as illustrated by the example in Exhibit 8.5.

What role did the teacher play in the activity of Neena and Sabrina in Exhibit 8.5? How did the environment (materials) support their ideas?

EXHIBIT 8.5   WHAT DAY SHOULD WE HAVE?

During setting up of a wake room program, I was observing Neena and Sabrina at the creative table. The girls were drawing lines up and down and across their papers. Next, they began to print numbers starting with the number one in each of the boxes they had created. Neena then posed the question to Sabrina, "What day should we have on number one?" The girls used their cognitive skills 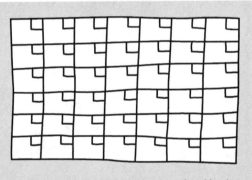 and their imagination to think of creative and fun days to add to their calendar. Neena thought of having a magic wand day. This led the girls to creating their own magic wands using glitter, tissue paper, and left-over cardboard tubes. Sabrina thought it would be a good idea to have an "H" day when all the children could bring in something that started with the letter "H." The girls continued to fill up all their spaces with a small picture representing what each day meant. This type of activity promoted the girls' concept of time and awareness of the difference in each day. Their cognitive skills played a great role in promoting their organizational skills. The girls used the teachers as their role models as they had previously seen the teachers put together the monthly calendar.

SOURCE: Documentation by Josephine Lopez, Vincent Custodio, and Essen Chavez, 2002.

Exhibit 8.5 is a good example of the observation/curriculum cycle. Materials are provided and activities developed that will be interesting, appropriate, and relevant to the children. Creating a curriculum based on observations offers teachers opportunities to

- keep the idea of what constitutes a curriculum flexible and responsive,
- develop their observation skills,
- interpret/analyze information on an ongoing basis,
- build upon new information, and
- revisit the curriculum reflecting on what is meaningful to all concerned.

A curriculum based on the spontaneous interests of children must be flexible and responsive. As the children play and learn, the teacher will look for new ideas in their play.

Planning Curriculum Based on Observations

"Does conducting observations mean that I have to observe all the children all the time on top of everything else I do in my already busy day? Does it mean I have to plan my curriculum *and* compile observations?" If teachers respond in this way, then they have not understood how observation and curriculum are really part of the same cycle. Observation and curriculum need not be seen in isolation! On the contrary, observation and child-centred programming could be visualized as the two wheels on a bicycle. The teacher's role then becomes that of the cyclist: getting those two wheels (observation and curriculum) working together and going in the same direction (Exhibit 8.6).

As the wheels of observation and curriculum are engaged, the teacher moves the curriculum forward, followed by further observation, and then revised curriculum, together in tandem. Documenting children's activities ensures a dynamic curriculum that is meaningful to children based on their everyday interests—from the inquiring ("Why is nighttime dark?") to the inspiring ("Why can't we build a spaceship in the playground?"). The documentation as shown in Exhibit 8.7 clearly demonstrates how the teachers' observations captured the children's interest in building.

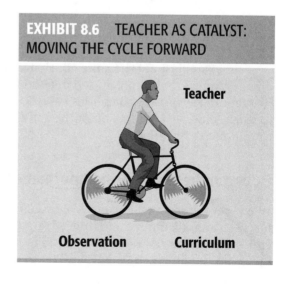

EXHIBIT 8.6 TEACHER AS CATALYST: MOVING THE CYCLE FORWARD

Teacher

Observation   **Curriculum**

EXHIBIT 8.7   BUILDING A HARDWARE STORE

One morning, Gabriel came into the classroom with a sample piece of wallpaper of his favourite Marvel Comic heroes. "Cool! Where did you get that?" asked Lionel. "The lady at the hardware store, when my mom and dad were buying stuff, me and Josh were looking at the wallpaper and the lady gave us a piece," responded Gabriel.

Ryan was listening to their conversation, and he said, "Hey! I know, we can build a hardware store in the dramatic area so people could buy wallpaper and stuff." "Okay," agreed Gabriel. The boys proceeded to the dramatic area to begin the set-up of their hardware store.

Ryan began by placing two large wooden blocks at the entrance of the dramatic area. "This can be the door to come into the store," Ryan proclaimed. "Wait! We need a 'Closed' sign 'cause we're not ready yet," said Gabriel, who then went to the creative area to print out a "Closed" sign and then taped it to the "door" of the store. Lionel came back from the block area with his arms filled with blue and yellow waffle squares saying, "They sell carpet at the hardware store." "Yeah, let's set it up so people can see what it looks like," answered Ryan. The two boys began to interlock the waffle squares to create the "carpet." From across the room, Gabriel was gathering some books to bring back and said, "These are the building books, so you can learn to build stuff," as he placed them on the shelf next to the tools he had neatly organized.

Soon, Adam joined the boys in their "hardware store," carrying cardboard boxes and a small measuring tape. "You could pretend that this is wood, and I will measure it," he suggested as he held up the boxes. The boys continued to set up their store until lunchtime, when Gabriel pronounced, "We have to close the store down because nobody came to buy things. Let's tidy up."

SOURCE: Documentation by Josephine Lopez and Vince Custodio, June 24, 2002.

This example and others previously featured reveal the personalities of the children, as well as their problem solving and ideas, and how, through creative documentation, the individual child is valued. The teachers in Exhibit 8.7 took the time to listen, observe, and document the activity, which illustrates and clearly validates the children's learning.

Opportunities for Sharing Information

When developing a child-centred curriculum, everyone could be involved: parents, teachers, administrators, and, indeed, anyone significantly connected with the child-care setting. Take a look at Exhibit 8.8 for examples of the many informal opportunities in which parents and teachers can share information.

EXHIBIT 8.8 SHARING INFORMATION INFORMALLY

DAILY INFORMATION–INFORMAL CHATS

When someone once said, "It's the little things that count," he or she must have been referring to the day-to-day brief conversations between teachers and parents. Research shows that the more the parents are involved, the better is the quality of care in early childhood education settings. *These informal opportunities are ideal times to share a sample of a child's learning.*

INFANT/TODDLER DAILY CHARTS

Infants and toddlers need adult assistance communicating their wants and needs. The daily chart is shared by parents and teachers and is available for parents in the morning and evening. In the charts is relevant information about the child, written so that everyone can access it. These pages are used primarily for reference regarding physical maintenance of the child's daily needs, such as sleeping, eating, or toileting information. *Couldn't daily charts also include a space to log examples of "Look what I did today!"?*

PARENT INFORMATION BULLETIN BOARD

Licensed centres often have two bulletin boards: one for the information that must be posted (e.g., menus), and the other for topical issues, relevant information for parents, information on community events, or an open-ended section for informal messages.

That open-ended section is perfect for some daily observations!

PARENTS' CORNER

This is a resource area for parents, containing books, pamphlets, and comfortable chairs so that parents can sit and read or chat with other parents/teachers. *Include books or panels created by the children for all to view!*

TWO-WAY COMMUNICATION BOOKS

These are for parents whose children are dropped off and picked up by bus or by someone other than the parents. Communication books could also used for parents of children who do not have time to share daily occurrences before or after work. The two-way book accompanies the child to and from the centre so that there is a constant flow of communication between the centre and the family. These feedback books can often contain wonderful exchanges of information because both parties take the time—when they are able—to write in them. These books with their quick messages and anecdotes from home/school could be considered a form of running records.

(continued)

TELEPHONE, TEXT-MESSAGING, E-MAIL, FAX, BLACKBERRY

In an increasingly busy world, more than one means of ensuring communication is necessary. Early childhood educators and families need to be able to access each other through a variety of technological means.

NOTES AND LETTERS

Notes and letters can be left in cubbies and sent home with the children. These methods tend to focus on news items relating to special events or specific messages. *Older children could create their own newsletter with special messages, a description of their projects, and their perspective on special events.*

PARENT INTERVIEWS AND MEETINGS

Interviews and meetings between parents and teachers are discussed in Chapter 7. These interviews and meetings can be informal or formal, held at various times of the year, and have an interactive social and educational focus.

A Good Partnership

A good partnership between teachers and parents will generate a varied menu of opportunities for participation, geared to the diverse needs of the families and their children and to the particular focus of each centre/program. Respecting the wishes of families both in principle and practice is the key to a healthy partnership. To determine how to accommodate the communication preferences of the parents, questions could be posed for a good discussion, such as the following:

- What kinds of information do families want/need from the teachers?
- How do they wish to have that information conveyed?
- What kinds of information do teachers want from parents/families?
- What are some of the ways parents *and* teachers can share information?
- What kinds of work can be dedicated to this process by both parents and staff?
- What resources are available to make this happen?
- What feedback mechanisms are in place to determine if parents are content with the level and kinds of opportunities to dialogue and participate?

Doing and Reflecting

The teachers' observations will focus not only on the children but also on their activities and how they use materials and express ideas. Capitalizing on the

EXHIBIT 8.9 WORLD CUP FEVER

WORLD CUP FEVER!

Week of June 3–7, 2000

On Monday morning, Gabriel, Kaitlyn, and Adam were talking about the World Cup Tournament, which is currently being held in South Korea. Victoria and Ayla were talking about the many different flags that they had seen hanging out of car windows and apartment windows, and others were simply talking about their own soccer games.

That morning Josephine and I sat down with the children to talk more about this wonderful sport. We talked about the many different countries that were involved in this year's tournament and even made a class list of which countries we thought might win the World Cup.

We then decided together that this week would be Soccer Week here in the kindergarten room. "Soccer Week" was an opportunity for all of the children to bring in any soccer-related items from home to share with the class. Shannon, Ayla, Keara, and Ryan helped make our interest table into our "soccer table" by cutting out World Cup pictures from newspapers and sticking them up on the wall, while Josephine and a small group made soccer balls at the creative table for the class door.

The following day Kaitlyn and Gabriel brought in their soccer jerseys to hang by our soccer table while Adam wore his.

That morning I took a small group of children who were interested in playing a friendly game of soccer out on the field. Here, we learned the importance of passing and sharing the ball with our teammates, and even good sportsmanship, as all the players shook hands and congratulated each other on a good game. Lionel even suggested switching shirts with each other like some soccer players do, but later on decided it wasn't such a good idea.

SOURCE: Documentation by YMCA teacher.

children's interests means flexibility, not only in how teachers document the children's behaviour, but also in how they expand upon their interests with further ideas and materials. This point is well documented in Exhibit 8.9 where the teachers and children decided to name that week, starting on Monday, "Soccer Week."

Building on the children's interests, teachers, parents, and children were encouraged to bring in newspaper clippings, soccer jerseys, trophies, and any other soccer-related materials. Parents, especially dads, were keenly interested. Both home and school were involved during World Cup Fever!

The better the documentation, the more visible the whole process becomes. With solid documentation, we can see how children learn about the topic, how they share ideas, and collaborate. What becomes evident through documentation is how children listen, negotiate, and express their thoughts. Children learn best by doing. Be ever aware of what excites their interests and share that knowledge with family members. This information gives parents a concrete feel for what their child contributed and his or her interests. It gets parents involved!

Observe to Learn

Not all observing in the playroom is purposely related to the development of curriculum. Observation can be used for many other reasons, as outlined in Chapter 2. Asking the questions of why, how, who, when, where and what motivates us to learn about the children in our care. In Exhibit 8.10, the purpose for observation is clearly identified: "How Beth observes and records David's progress." The focus of Beth's observations is three-year-old David's progress in using words and sentences. Beth is interested in discovering David's use of language in a variety of contexts. Note the section entitled "How Beth uses her records." This section illustrates the ways in which Beth relayed her findings to parents and indicates how her records influenced curriculum and how she will follow up with further observation to learn more about David's progress.

EXHIBIT 8.10 LANGUAGE AND LITERACY

CHILD CARE KNOWLEDGE AT WORK: HOW BETH OBSERVES AND RECORDS DAVID'S PROGRESS

Beth regularly observes all the children in her care, both to be able to report to their parents on what and how they are doing and to pinpoint any problems that may require a formal assessment by a professional, such as a speech language pathologist.

With three-year-old David, for example, Beth uses a range of observation strategies to develop a complete picture of his progress—over one month—in using words and sentences and in other skills important for reading and writing.

STRATEGY 1: STORY-TIME CHECKLIST

Beth has created an easy-to-use checklist that focuses on language skills. She uses it at least once a week while watching David during story-time. She also asks her colleague Jennifer to use the same checklist occasionally, so she can compare their observations. When Beth reviews her checklists at the end of the month (she completed five; Jennifer completed two), she sees that, while David sometimes looks like he's not listening, he can retell the story in his own words later. He also seems to talk more when the story really interests him. If it's a story about dinosaurs, especially, he has no problem asking and answering more than five questions.

STRATEGY 2: ACTIVITY RECORD

Beth supplements her story-time checklist by keeping a record of David's behaviour during individual and group play. She quietly watches (he does not even notice) to see what he does and how he interacts with the other children, then writes up her notes later, including all the details she can remember. She tries to keep an accurate and objective record by writing down his specific behaviours and actions one part of the page, and her feelings, comments and conclusions on another.

STRATEGY 3: FOLDER

Beth works with David to put together a folder of items—such as scribbles and pictures, stories, lists of books he has "read," excerpts from Beth's observations or a couple of her checklists—for his parents. David understands the concept of the folder, and is very interested in showing his parents what he has been doing over the past months. He is also able to tell Beth exactly which pieces of his work he thinks are best, but understands why she wants to include some of the others as well.

HOW BETH USES HER RECORDS

Beth uses her records when talking to David's parents, to help her recall important or interesting events. She also uses them to help her make informed decisions about her programming—for example, she plans to add more non-fiction stories to her reading list, because David really responds to them. Next month, she will compare these records to her new observations to track David's progress and help identify any problems (so far, she thinks he is doing very well).

SOURCE: Adapted from: Canadian Child Care Federation and the Canadian Language & Literacy Network. "Resource Sheet #3". *Language and Literacy, From Birth . . . For Life*, Ottawa: Canadian Child Care Federation, 2007.

Developmentally Appropriate Practice and Webbing

In Chapter 1, the concept of developmentally appropriate practice (DAP) was introduced.

Webbing is integral to developmentally appropriate practice. Webbing is a visual way of representing a key concept, idea, or event, and a process whereby children and teachers brainstorm a curriculum topic from that interest. Webbing is considered to be developmentally appropriate practice as it builds on the ideas of the children, as illustrated in Exhibit 8.11. Webbing gives flexibility to planning yet provides a construct from which to work. Once a topic has been decided upon, one of the most exciting parts of the process is brainstorming strategies to create the actual web. During this initial phase of the project approach, the teacher and children

EXHIBIT 8.11 **STARTING WITH A WEB**

"The function of the web is not to create an elaborate set of teacher-planned activities—the 'curriculum plan for the month'; rather, it serves as a starting place for teachers to focus their thinking. As one teacher said, 'I see this initial web more as a guidebook for travelling, with reminders to 'be read for . . .,' 'Be sure to spend some time at . . .,' and 'Bring along. . . .' This web would not be a map marked in red to be followed unwaveringly. Webbing allows teachers to be creative and playful in their planning, rather than just logical and linear" (Gestwicki 57). Starting a web with sand could resemble the following:

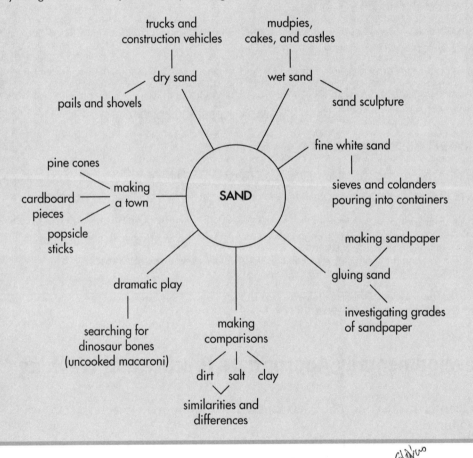

consider sub-topics based on discussion or answers to questions. The teacher will assist the children in this process to guide and support their interests. The documentation or evaluation of the process of developing a web is both formative and summative. The forms of evaluation will be detailed near the end of this chapter.

Developing a web means creating a tentative plan that is woven with the threads of the children's interest. For example, one of the mothers in the program brings the new baby to the centre. Imagine the interest of the children! How can teachers capture that interest, expand on their questions, and introduce new ways to learn about what it means to have a new baby in the family? Observing and documenting this process can begin with the teacher writing down what the children said or taking pictures of the baby with the children. On the basis of their responses, what are some of the ideas that support further discussion and learning? How could the mother assist in this process? Could other family members contribute their ideas to this learning? What materials could families bring in for the children to see?

Could these materials be used to bathe a doll? Teachers could generate ideas and concepts and activities *with* the children. Out of this enthusiasm for the subject of "a new baby" comes a tentative plan that could look something like the one in Exhibit 8.12.

EXHIBIT 8.12   TENTATIVE PLAN FOR NEW BABY

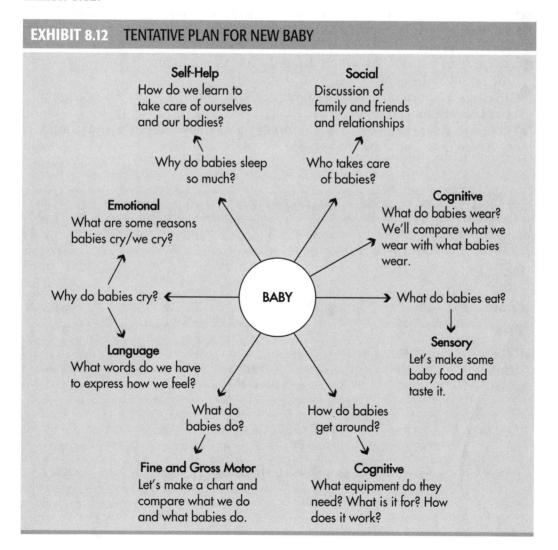

One of the myths surrounding the notion of a child-centred curriculum is that the children do whatever they want and the teachers follow along, providing no structure or direction. Actually, the teacher's role in co-creating a curriculum with the children (and hopefully their families) is to use their observations in ways in which the *children's* learning will be represented. A Board of Education curriculum addresses the learning that *should* take place at a particular grade level and the evaluation is geared to demonstrate if the educational objectives of that curriculum have been met. A curriculum based on the spontaneous interests of children must be flexible and responsive, one that can only be achieved with ongoing observations and documentation.

What Is the Purpose of Webbing?

1. To create a curriculum that is based on the daily observations of the children
2. To create a curriculum that reflects the three guiding principles of developmentally appropriate practice
3. To create a curriculum based on the individual strengths, needs, and interests of each child in the group
4. To create a curriculum based on appropriate guidelines and solid knowledge of child development
5. To create a curriculum based on the family's background, lifestyle, and culture (Adapted from Gestwicki, 1999, 8–11)

EXHIBIT 8.13   SHOES: A DEVELOPMENTAL APPROACH TO PLANNING

Curriculum: <u>Shoes</u>

Date: <u>Monday, October 9</u>

Gross Motor	Fine Motor	Cognitive	Self-Help	Socio-emotional	Speech and Language
Hide and seek for lost shoe	Lacing boards	Matching the same shoe pairs	Finding own shoes after nap or outdoors	Dramatic play: shoe store	Listening to stories about shoes
Trying on various kinds of shoes	Painting shoes with "shoe polish"	Ordering and classifying shoes by function	Taking off and putting on shoes by self	Showing and telling about our favourite shoes	Naming different kinds of shoes

Webs with a Developmental Approach

Constructing a web around a concept or even around skills in a developmental area gives flexibility to planning yet provides a construct from which to work. The curriculum model represented by the use of webbing can use concepts or topics to generate activities that will enhance and develop skills in all areas of development. Webs can be created with such topics as dinosaurs, space, islands, or sea creatures. These topics can then be the focal points to brainstorm activities for children covering all the developmental areas. Exhibit 8.13 demonstrates this concept using the curriculum topic of *shoes*.

The Project Approach

What is the project approach? The project approach is an in-depth investigation of a topic focusing on a unifying topic around which activities are planned. The project can be undertaken by a small or large group of children. The project approach affirms the child as an active learner and incorporates opportunities for parental involvement. The teacher facilitates the progress of the project, but the children's interest is the driving force. The project approach has been around for decades in the United Kingdom and North America enjoyed a revival with the popularity of the Reggio Emilia approach. The project approach to learning has been part of many different models of curriculum. In the school system, the project approach is used to complement the curriculum, especially in the elementary grades. In Exhibit 8.14 Katz & Chard, Helm and Katz offer more insight into this approach.

In the project approach, the child is seen as the protagonist, the initiator, and the constructor. The assumption behind this approach is that children will become more

---

EXHIBIT 8.14   THE "YOUNG INVESTIGATORS"

"A project is an extensive study undertaken by an individual child or a group of children that incorporates writing, measurement, drawing, painting, model making, reading, creating stories, dramatic and fine arts," (Katz & Chard, 1993, p. 209) according to the abilities of the participating children. The project typically involves the following activities: collecting information through observation, interviewing experts about the topic being studied, performing experiments, collecting artifacts, and preparing oral and written reports and displays. Because of their engagement in these types of activities, Helm and Katz (2000) refer to children involved in a project as "Young Investigators."

SOURCE: Billman, Jean, and Janice A. Sherman. Observation and Participation in Early Childhood Settings: A Practicum Guide. 2nd ed. Boston: Allyn & Bacon, 2003. 256.

engaged in learning if they are intrinsically motivated to learn. In the beginning of the project, the topic is initiated and reviewed with the children's knowledge and interest as the base, and the teacher observes and assists them in their exploration. The key is that learning is concrete-based, and often, but not always, projects may begin with field trips or people coming into the classroom. Inferred is the notion that this information may be new and, therefore, may trigger a great deal of interest and a quest for new experiences.

The documentation of the project is carefully supported by the teacher in various ways that encourage experimentation while following the child's lead. The role of the teacher is more of a facilitator–observer who watches, listens, and offers suggestions and support, rather than one who provides facts or asks convergent questions.

Observations are central to the role of the teacher but may take the form of transcriptions of children's discussions or comments of the parents. These documentations could include the child's written reflections on their work and certainly photographs, pictorial representations, and tape recordings. All this work of the teachers, children, and others becomes part of the project. In the end, this process of documentation can be displayed. For examples of children's projects, you may want to visit any website using the descriptors "Project Approach" or "Project Examples."

Traditional Planning

If This Is October, We Must Be Doing Apples!

The traditional, theme-based approach is patterned after an elementary school–style curriculum. Within the school system, the teacher bases her plans upon the curriculum set by the Ministry of Education. Early childhood educators have patterned themselves after this model for many reasons. One of the reasons is that this approach offers predictability for teachers. "If this is October, we must be doing apples" is a typical example. The preordained themes are complemented by bins of appropriate resources and plastic tubs of related materials, all of which have been accumulated over the years with great dedication and much cost. Within the theme parameters, teachers organize not only their resources and materials, but time, efforts, and planning such as special projects or trips. What can be planned using apples as a theme? We may all remember bits of that curriculum from childhood memories in Canada: matching pictures of the different types of apples, talking about seeds, or going to the apple farm. These memories not only give a sense of predictability and comfort, but they also gives a sense of continuity and a sense of time that is inherent in the cycle of seasons in Canada.

Another reason that early childhood educators have patterned themselves after the schoolteacher role model is that it represents what we imagine a teacher should be! The role of the teacher in our minds has been partly shaped by all the years we have spent in school and all the teachers we have encountered. Therefore, even though the academic and field placement experiences in early childhood education at the college level promote many different perspectives of what it means to be a teacher of young children, student-teachers still cling to that ideal/idea of "the teacher." Those personal beliefs or values fashioned over the years by school experiences do influence how student-teachers approach the concept of developing curricula and teaching young children. Where does your image of a teacher originate?

Traditional Curriculum Planning

Some educators confess that is it easier to follow a traditional, theme-based approach that is teacher-focused than a child-centred approach. Many programs still organize their curriculum in a way similar to the following September–December model:

Month	Week	Theme
September	1 & 2	All about Me
	3 & 4	All about Family
October	1 & 2	Apples/Harvest/Thanksgiving
	3 & 4	Halloween
November	1 & 2	Farm Animals
	3 & 4	Zoo Animals
December	1 & 2	Winter
	3 & 4	Christmas Holiday

Perhaps each week a new theme is introduced, rather than using a two-week time frame for each topic. The point is that the curriculum is already set before the children arrive and is rarely changed.

Traditional method supporters believe that implementing a child-centred curriculum is more demanding than a teacher-driven curriculum where the teacher establishes the topics or themes and sets out preselected activities "for the toddler group." In the article "Making Lemonade from Lemons," Sue Grossman recounts her difficult experiences as a student teacher, as well as sharing her learning:

> Teachers sometimes have difficulty asking reflective questions rather than dispensing advice. It is something I work on all the time. The centuries-old traditional role of a teacher was to tell the truth—to give information, advice, answers. We were to be the font from which all knowledge flowed. Children were to sit quietly and listen and absorb our words. . . . Now we know not only is this not possible—witness the explosion of information due to modern technology—we also know that merely *telling* is perhaps the least effective way of teaching anyone anything—even adults. (Grossman, 2004, 252)

Documentation Reflects Traditional Curriculum

In the traditional curriculum approach and teacher role, the form of communication between parents and families also took traditional forms: report cards, formal parent meetings, worksheets, and workbooks. Parents expected this kind of communication from the teacher. The teacher did not expect the parents would need further communication (see Exhibit 8.15).

Observing the Physical Environment

Observing the environment is an important part of the entire approach to systematic observation in the playroom. Children are highly influenced by their environment. Some reasons to observe the environment could be

- to maintain a safe and healthy environment;
- to offer a balanced curriculum according to the interests, needs, and strengths of the children;
- to maximize the influence of families and community;
- to increase awareness of special needs and adaptations; and
- to evaluate the effectiveness of program goals, the curriculum, and sufficient play space.

The next time you are in a playroom, take a look around. Is the lighting adequate? Is there natural light, and are there windows at a child's level? Would you want to spend the day in this room? A playroom should be more than just a physical space. It needs

PHOTO: Paul Till

to reflect the values of those in it. Service industries, such as hotels or restaurants, spend thousands, if not millions, of dollars on just the right design, colours, and textures to create a special atmosphere. How well do we attempt a special atmosphere that caters to the well-being of the children in our care? Creating an atmosphere involves defining what is important to the children, teachers, and parents, organizing resources, and communicating daily our thoughts and expectations. What kind of quality child-care setting do you envision?

Materials and the Environment

Materials refer to many things in the environment, but can best be seen as those items that can easily be added to or deleted from the setting. They are of a temporary nature: puzzles, toys, games, constructs, and investigative lures, for example. Materials can be permanent items, yet may be stored and retrieved as required. Materials also include such things as beautiful junk (scraps of paper, boxes, bows), creative supplies (paint, paper, glue), sensory bin selections (rice, macaroni, sand, beans), or

EXHIBIT 8.16   DISCUSSION OF THE ENVIRONMENT

Years ago, I was involved in the design of a new centre, and the architect had a colour chart that ascribed emotional value to certain colours. Choosing colours for a playroom may not need to be that programmed; however, colours *are* important in making a room attractive. Certain colours are more visually comforting than others, and some colour combinations work well. Colour coordinating is an important aspect of a workplace being an attractive place for both children and adults. An appealing environment is important if teachers and children will be spending most of their day in one or two rooms. Montessori and Reggio Emilia philosophies place importance on the design and attractiveness of the environment. Perhaps I am showing my Montessori training, but I believe that if the room is attractive, children learn to respect the environment, to be careful, to put things back, and to take responsibility for their space.

SOURCE: Courtesy of Linda Chud, Sheridan College, Oakville.

specialty items, such as dramatic play accessories or block play additions. Materials can be adapted quite easily, whereas equipment tends to be rather stable items in the playroom along with furniture. Furniture and equipment may be rearranged, of course. However, they are less likely to be replaced frequently and actually represent a sense of permanence in the room.

Many centres use artwork to create colour and texture in their rooms from these materials. Children enjoy the sensory stimulation of textures, colours, and design. Wrapping themselves, dolls, or teddy bears in soft, cuddly blankets soothes and comforts. Carpeted areas are more likely to be resting places or building places than are tiled floors. Tiled or linoleum floors tend to be high traffic areas and areas for painting, messy creatives, and sensory items. Colours and textures throughout the room are important, if not vital, to some schools/philosophies as described in Exhibit 8.16.

Informal Evaluation of the Environment

Chapters 4, 5, and 6 outlined several types of records such as the participation chart, event sampling, mapping, and sociograms. These types of records not only provide information about the child, but also contextual information about the environment. These types of records are used to evaluate the role of the environment in relation to children's behaviour. For example, the participation chart records the participation of a child or group of children as they participate in the daily activities. From these observations, teachers can not only determine which areas are the most popular or least popular, but also how the children use the materials. Sociograms and ecomaps tell us how children play among themselves, and also how they interact with the environment.

Centres may devise their own environmental evaluation method in the form of a checklist or report. Organizations or municipalities may compile a manual of operating criteria that relate to the environment: indoor or outdoor. Many options exist for appropriately evaluating child-centred environments. These types of evaluations are typically informal, depending on the practices of a particular child-care setting.

Formal Evaluation of the Environment

Formal evaluations refer to the standardized, commercial types available to child-care operators. Informal types are setting-specific, whereas formal or standardized evaluations tend to be used in more than one location and across provinces/territories.

Among the formal types of evaluation in the early childhood education field, none is more renowned than the Harms, Clifford, and Cryer Environmental Rating Scale (Table 8.1).

This scale has been devised for rating environments for infants, toddlers, preschoolers, and the family. It can be easily administered after a brief training period. The scale is **standardized** and has proven **reliability** and **validity.** This rating scale

- includes a section for comments,
- helps identify strengths and needs of a particular environment,
- provides identified criteria for highlighting,
- assesses particular aspects of the environment, and
- allows for graphing the results for easy interpretation.

Whether observing the environment or how an individual child or a group of children utilize aspects of the environment, these observations should engender awareness and dialogue. Observations provide feedback for developing appropriate environments that reflect genuine consideration for all children.

The Affective Environment: Daily Interaction with Parents

Parents working or going to school sometimes feel guilty or anxious about leaving their children in group care. They may feel particularly vulnerable and sensitive to any concerns or worries about their child. Knowing the concerns of the families gives

TABLE 8.1　HARMS, CLIFFORD, AND CRYER RATING SCALE

Item	Inadequate		Minimal		Good		Excellent
Space and Furnishings	1	2	3	4	5	6	7
1. Indoor space		1.1 Insufficient space for children,[1] adults, and furnishings. 1.2 Space lacks adequate lighting, ventilation, temperature control, or sound-absorbing materials. 1.3 Space in poor repair (e.g., peeling paint on walls and ceiling; rough, damaged floors).		3.1 Sufficient indoor space for children, adults, and furnishings. 3.2 Adequate lighting, ventilation, temperature control, and sound-absorbing materials.		5.1 Ample indoor space that allows children and adults to move around freely (e.g., furnishings do not limit children's movement; sufficient space for equipment needed by children with disabilities).	7.1 Natural light can be controlled (e.g., adjustable blinds or curtains). 7.2 Ventilation can be controlled[2] (e.g., windows can open; ventilating fan used by staff).
2. Furniture for routine care, play, and learning[3]		1.1 Insufficient basic furniture for routine care, play, and learning (e.g., not enough chairs for all children to use at the same time; very few open shelves for toys).		3.1 Sufficient furniture for routine care, play, and learning.		5.1 Most furniture is child sized.[4]	7.1 Routine care furniture is convenient to use (e.g., cots/mats stored for easy access).

3. Room arrangement for play	1	2	3	4	5	6	7
		1.1 No interest centres defined.[5]		3.1 At least two interest centres defined.		5.1 At least three interest centres defined and conveniently equipped (e.g., water provided near art area; shelving adequate for blocks and manipulatives).		7.1 At least five different interest centres provide a variety of learning experiences.
		1.2 Visual supervision of play area is difficult.		3.2 Visual supervision of play area is not difficult.		5.2 Quiet and active centres placed to not interfere with one another (e.g., reading or listening area separated from blocks or house-keeping).		7.2 Centres are organized for independent use by children (e.g., labelled open shelves; labelled containers for toys; open shelves are not overcrowded; play space near toy storage).
				3.3 Sufficient space for several activities to go on at once (e.g., floor space for manipulatives, easel for art).		5.3 Space is arranged so most activities are not interrupted (e.g., shelves placed so children walk around, not through, activities; placement of furniture discourages rough play or running).		7.3 Additional materials available to add to or change centres.
				3.4 Most spaces for play are accessible to children with disabilities enrolled in the group.				

Notes:

[1] Base space needs on largest number of children attending at one time.

[2] Doors to outside count as ventilation control only if they can be left open without posing a safety threat (for example, if they have a locking screen door or safety gate to keep children from leaving the room unattended).

[3] Basic furniture: tables and chairs used for meals/snacks and activities; mats or cots for rest or nap; cubbies or other storage for children's things; low open shelves for play/learning materials. To be given credit for low open shelves, they must be used for toys and materials that children can reach by themselves.

[4] Since children are of different sizes at different ages, the intent here is that furniture should be the right size for the children in care. For chairs to be considered child-sized, the children's feet must rest on the floor when seated. Table height should allow children's knees to fit under the table and elbows to be above the table.

[5] An interest centre is an area where materials, organized by type, are stored so that they are accessible to children, and appropriately furnished play space is provided for children to participate in a particular kind of play. Examples of interest centres are art activities, blocks, dramatic play, reading, nature/science, and manipulatives/fine motor.

SOURCE: Harms T., R.M. Clifford, and D. Cryer. Early Childhood Environment Rating Scale. New York, Teachers College Press, 1998, 9–12.

you key areas in which you can provide meaningful information about the children. First-time parents tend to need the most reassurance, the most detailed observations on a daily basis, the most feedback in terms of their parenting skills, and the most information on community resources, books, and appropriate toys and activities for their children. Their concerns are not just about how the child will manage or cope in a group setting but also about how the teacher will care for the child and involve the family. Daily sharing of information with parents creates not only a positive affective environment, but also strengthens the bonds of trust so necessary to the well-being of parents as well as children.

Educators need to be active observers and be ready to act on their observations. For example, observations relating to a child's health (ear infection, contagious disease) and welfare (bumps, bruises, changes in behaviour) need to be communicated. Early childhood educators need to be attuned to each child's growth and development and share those observations. Development of trust between parent and teacher sets the cornerstone for a professional yet personal relationship. Creating an openness to share information encourages many parents to become involved in meaningful communication. If time allows, parents enjoy engaging in an activity with their child (see Exhibit 8.17). These times also offer opportunities to talk informally with the teachers. Documenting the parent–child mutual experience also creates ties with the teacher who took the time to photograph and write about the process of making the doll.

If you intend to observe a child for a particular reason, talk to the parents— preferably face-to-face. Indicate your intention—why you want to observe and record their child's activities. Also let them know that you will be sharing your observations with them. Talking with the parents beforehand provides an opportunity to explore *their* feelings about their child's behaviour. Their responses during the conversation will give you a sense of their interest.

Early childhood educators, like many other related professionals, must maintain a sensitive balance between being a qualified service provider and responding in that role with an emotional and personal relationship.

Observation: A Vital Role in Early Identification

Responsible educators reflect carefully on what is seen and heard in the playroom and develop a keen awareness of what is age-appropriate behaviour. With experience, educators become sensitized to what is appropriate behaviour for children and are able to identify patterns that alert them to possible emerging concerns. Their child development expertise and knowledge of individual differences of each child in the group make them quite able to "flag" behaviours. Early identification of a child's lack of age-appropriate behaviours must be taken very seriously. Once there is suspicion that a child may be demonstrating a possible delay in any area of

EXHIBIT 8.17   MAGGIE AND HER MOTHER

Maggie, aged four years, and her mother look at the possibilities of making a doll using an existing figure as a model. Attempts to model using a very soft Play-Doh result in repeated failure, and they are offered Plasticene. When shown how to use a drinking straw for a central support, Maggie is free to concentrate on the details that catch her interest.

Although it is difficult to see in the photograph, these include a beautifully draped shawl.

Mom cuts hand shapes out of construction paper, but when it comes to feet, Maggie decides that the number of toes make them too difficult to render. They are left out.

SOURCE: Photos and text courtesy of Jason Avery, Artists at the Centre

growth and development, the teacher must clearly communicate these concerns to the supervisor, and the family. The importance of educators as the frontline in the identification of possible developmental problems cannot be stressed enough. Educators play a key role in the early identification process.

Observations and Assessments

All assessment tools used in ECE settings are based on observation. There is simply no other unobtrusive way to assess children other than through observation.

What is assessment? In this context, assessment refers to the process used to identify those children whose development may deviate from the **norms** of that age group. There are three stages to the assessment process.

Three Stages of Assessment

There are three stages of assessment: screening, functional, and diagnostic. Depending on the screening tool, some **paraprofessionals** or parents may conduct the assessment. However, the functional assessment tool is usually administered by a professional such as a resource teacher/consultant/early interventionist. A diagnostic assessment can only be conducted by a highly trained, specialized professional, such as an audiologist, doctor, or speech pathologist. The functional and diagnostic assessment tools are beyond the scope of this text; however, it is instructive to briefly investigate the screening tool and its function. What are some of the terms or jargon associated with the topic of assessment tools? First, the kinds of assessments conducted in early childhood settings tend to be those which are criterion-referenced. What does that mean? **Criterion-referenced assessment tools** are those assessment tools that measure a child's progress against a **fixed standard,** rather than comparing them with the skills/knowledge of others. What is a fixed standard? It is an item or competency that is typical for children of that age group to perform, such as tying shoelaces, completing a single insert puzzle, running without falling, or following a two-step, related direction. If a child can accomplish these skills independently, that competency or fixed standard is checked off as being achieved. If the child is unable to achieve that task, then a different kind of scoring is noted to indicate that the child has yet to accomplish that competency. The teacher/resource teacher/consultant records the observations in the assessment tool: "Yes, the child has achieved that skill," or "No, the child has yet to achieve that skill." If the person using the screening tool (Exhibit 8.18) records many "no" responses in an area where most children of this age can accomplish these skills, then it may indicate a possible delay.

The Nipissing District Development Screen (see Exhibit 8.18) is a good example of a criterion-referenced assessment tool where groupings of age-related behaviours can be checked off as a "yes" or "no." The Nipissing District Screen could be described as a form of a checklist.

EXHIBIT 8.18   DEVELOPMENTAL SCREEN "30 MONTHS"

Child's Name _____   Birth Date _____   Today's Date _____

The Nipissing District Developmental Screen is a checklist designed to help monitor your child's development.

✓   ✓

By 30 Months of Age, does your child . . .

Yes   No

Yes	No	#	Question
☐	☐	1.	Usually have healthy ears and seem to hear well?
☐	☐	2.	Put a toy in and put a toy under when asked?
☐	☐	3.	Join three words together, like "Me want ball"?
☐	☐	4.	Recognize the names and pictures of most common items (i.e., "Show me the ball")?
☐	☐	5.	Use pronouns I, you, me, and mine?
☐	☐	6.	Lift and drink from a cup and replace it on the table?*
☐	☐	7.	Imitate drawing vertical and horizontal lines? (Picture A)
☐	☐	8.	Remove clothing already unzipped or unbuttoned?
☐	☐	9.	Run without falling most of the time?
☐	☐	10.	Kick a ball forward?
☐	☐	11.	Jump off the floor with both feet? (Picture B)
☐	☐	12.	Try to join in songs and rhymes with you?
☐	☐	13.	Listen to simple stories?
☐	☐	14.	Act out daily routines with toys (e.g., feed doll, sweep floor)?
☐	☐	15.	Wait briefly for needs to be met (e.g., when placed in highchair at meal time)?
☐	☐	16.	Recognize self in mirror or picture?

*Item may not be common to all cultures.

A   B

Always talk to your health care or child care professional if you have questions about your child's development or well being.

(continued)

ACTIVITIES FOR YOUR CHILD

♡ Emotional   ❦ Fine Muscle   🏃 Large Muscle

🔤 Learning/Thinking   ❀ Social   ☺ Speech/Language

> *Nipissing District*
> ## *Development Screen*™

The following activities will help you play your part in your child's development.

- I want to help you shop for groceries. Keep me interested by talking about the things we are buying. Ask me questions and wait for me to respond.

- When we go for a walk collect rocks, seeds, leaves, twigs, and flowers, and so on. Feel the objects while we look at them and talk about the different weights, colours, shapes and sizes.

- Let me help sort the clean laundry. Make a pile for each family member. Pull out an item and ask, "Whose shirt is this? Yes, this is Mom's shirt. Put it on Mom's pile." This will help me learn to observe and compare.

- Play my favourite music and encourage me to move in and out, over and under furniture, roll on the carpet, run, bend, lie, stretch, jump, march, and walk. As the music changes, my movements can be fast, slow, or graceful.

- I like a challenge. Play movement games with me where I change my speed and direction. Give me easy directions, such as: stop and go, run to the door, walk backwards, sway side to side, clap fast, crawl slow, and so on. I will learn to follow directions.

- I like to knock things down. Set up large plastic bottles, empty cans or milk cartons. Let me have a ball to roll and knock them over. Give me the words for what happens. Let me set them up again.

- I like to explore play dough by poking, cutting, rolling or pressing it. I can use a Popsicle stick, safety scissors, and cookie cutters to cut the play dough.

- Let's do puzzles of different sizes, textures, number of pieces, and colours. We can take turns adding one or two pieces at a time and continue this way until I can do the whole puzzle on my own. Give me a hint when I need help.

- It's fun to use markers, crayons, paint, or chalk to make a picture. Ask me to tell you about my picture when I am finished. Make a book of all my pictures and we can look at it together.

- Dressing up is fun. I like hats, old clothing, jewellery, household objects, dolls, or anything I can use to make believe. I will act out things that are familiar, and this will help me learn about relationships.

- My actions will tell you how I feel. Celebrate with me when I am happy, and be patient with me when I am sad or angry.

I need a chance to play with other children my age. Let's go to a play group often.

A screening tool does *not* diagnose, nor does it indicate a clear, thorough summary of all the necessary skills in all developmental areas. Results from screening tools should *not* be used for planning a program for a child with special needs. So, what is the purpose of a screening tool?

Purpose of a Screening Tool

The *primary purpose* of a screening tool is to assist in identifying problem areas in a child's development and indicate if that child *may* need a **referral** for a further assessment. The purpose of a screening tool may be also to target services that may be required or determine program eligibility. There are many screening tools on the market, but only a handful are commonly used.

Two of the most commonly used Canadian screening tools are the DISC Developmental Preschool Screen (DPS; Exhibit 8.19) originating in Kitchener-Waterloo, Ontario, and used extensively across Canada, and the Nipissing District Developmental Screen, which was compiled in North Bay, Ontario.

If you are interested, conduct an Internet search using the names of the assessment tools. Bookmark this website and others!

Documentation for Each Child: Individual Program Plan

Most early childhood settings include children from diverse backgrounds and cultures and children with special needs. If a child has been diagnosed as having special needs, then that child is entitled to a special program designed to meet his or her unique needs. An Individual Program Plan (IPP), is a long-term written plan of action that is designed by all concerned to maximize the child's optimal growth and development. The IPP is also used to coordinate personnel and resources. The IPP is based on the observations from family, playroom teachers, resource teachers/early interventionists, and other professionals. These observations can be informal and *nonstandardized*, such as those you discovered in Chapters 4, 5, and 6. Further assessments may be completed on the child on the basis of more formal observations. When all the information about the child is compiled, goals for the child can be determined. From the process of reviewing and discussing the information (parents and professionals), ideas and strategies to achieve the goals will be made and implemented at home/school/centre. Ideally, the child with special needs should be included in the activities of the playroom along with the rest of the children. In a child-centred, play-based curriculum, the children's initiative may take that curriculum in a number of different directions and vary from day to day. If a child with special needs has daily programming expectations that require consistency, repetition, and individualized instruction, how do educators plan and observe for the individual child and the group? Adapting the child's individual program plan to complement the activities planned with the other children offers a balanced curriculum for all children. By welcoming diversity, we expand the learning of all children as in the example shown in Exhibit 8.20 and Table 8.2.

EXHIBIT 8.19 THE DISC DEVELOPMENTAL PRESCHOOL SCREEN

Materials	Starting Point by Month	Does the Child . . . ?			
Crayon, paper	36 & 37 months	Imitate both vertical and horizontal lines. Demonstrate 1/3 trials	YES	NO	REFUSE
	38 months	Repeat phrases. "little boy" _____ "big red truck" _____ "nice warm coat" _____ 2/3 phrases	YES	NO	REFUSE
6 cubes	39 months	Match colours. "Find another one like this one—the same colour." blue _____ red _____ green _____ 2/3 matches	YES	NO	REFUSE
Picture book p.1	40 & 41 months	Answer questions using related words. "What is the boy/girl doing?" girl crying _____ boy swinging _____ girl sleeping _____ girl skipping _____ boy sitting _____ boy reading _____ 3/6 answers	YES	NO	REFUSE
	42 months	Stand on one foot for at least three seconds. Demonstrate. 1/3 trials	YES	NO	REFUSE
Picture book pp. 2–3	43 months	Discriminate pictures Apple _____ cup _____ doll _____ baby _____ 3/4 pictures	YES	NO	REFUSE
Crayon, paper	44 months	Imitate a cross (+). Demonstrate. 1/3 trials	YES	NO	REFUSE

SOURCE: For further information regarding the DPS: www.discmainland.ca or contact DISC Research Coordinatior, Marian Mainland: mmainland@rogers.com.

EXHIBIT 8.20   COMMUNICATION CHECKLIST

Child's Name: Joshua   **DOB:** October 5, 2001   **Age:** 4

Observer(s): Frank   **Date(s):** September 15–19, 2005

Behaviour	Comments
Visual tracking	Follows objects within sight. Looks at people move around the room.
Auditory tracking	Consistently turns to sounds in the environment. Turns head to sudden sounds.
Selective attention	Focuses when interested. Will attend 5–10 minutes at one activity.
Pointing	Can point to objects upon request. Points to familiar people in the room.
Reaching	Shows initiative at reaching for and taking toys he wants. Holds arms out to adults.
Body language	Shakes head for "No." Nods for "Yes." Shakes and flaps arms when excited. Slaps own body when frustrated. Turns head away to indicate refusal.
Gestures	Waves "bye-bye." Puts hands and arms out in front of his body when he wants you to go away.
Speech sounds	Seldom emits intelligible sounds. Makes loud sounds when vocalizations excited. Cries. Coos and gurgles. Squeals. Imitates motions.
Imitates motions	Will imitate most gestures and motions. Especially likes to imitate active circle songs, e.g., "Wheels on the Bus" (round and round).
Initiates sounds	Makes sounds during circle time, but has yet to imitate specific sounds.
Other	Often uses his body to sway back and forth or rock back and forth; we are not sure why he does this.

Adapting the Observation/Curriculum Cycle for Inclusion

Using Exhibit 8.20 (Examples of Joshua's Communication) and Table 8.2 (Topic: Under the Sea) you can see how Joshua's areas of communication programming are integrated into the theme "Under the Sea" for the group. Let's take a look at this process.

One day the speech pathologist asked the teacher to keep track of the kinds of communication Joshua used from Monday to Friday. (Joshua is four years old. Read through the examples of what he was observed doing/saying. Are Joshua's skills in

TABLE 8.2   TOPIC: UNDER THE SEA

Gross Motor	Fine Motor	Cognitive	Self-Help	Socioemotional	Speech and Language
• Play the octopus game.	• Make an under-the-sea collage using beautiful junk.	• Play a matching game, (e.g., match dolphin to dolphin, shellfish to shellfish).	• Care for and feed fish in aquarium.	• Work together and share materials and activities.	• Label the new names of sea creatures.
• Imagine and imitate sea creatures (e.g., crabs, whales).	• Weave a fish net using chicken wire and a variety of interesting materials.	• Compare homes of sea creatures to homes of people.	• Make decisions about taking turns in games and activities.	• Interact and share ideas, listening to others' ideas.	• Joshua will imitate some sounds in songs.
• Make and play the fishing game.		• Explore ways in which sea creatures get around and compare with people.	• Try for independence in activities.	• Complete games and toys and return materials.	• Sing along to "sea creature songs" and others during circle time.
				• Cooperate with teacher and peer requests.	• Joshua will repeat sounds and gestures with teachers and peers.
					• Discuss the various features of sea creatures: fins, legs, tails, gills, and shells and compare with human body parts.
					• Express feelings and ideas during games and activities.

this area age-appropriate, or would he need to receive extra assistance in this area?) Joshua's mother, the teachers, and the speech pathologist met to discuss what he can do and ways they could encourage further vocalizations and sounds. They talked with the teacher to find out how they could incorporate what Joshua needed to learn with what the other children were learning and doing. As it turns out, one of the children had been to Florida on holiday and had brought back seashells, beaded necklaces, and other souvenirs to the playroom. The children had become intensely interested in the subject of the ocean. That interest encouraged another child to bring in a video, "The Littlest Mermaid." They began singing songs, such as "Under the Sea." Another child brought in a snorkel and goggles. The teachers began to plan around the topic "Under the Sea." See Table 8.2 for their creative programming focusing on the areas of child development. Note especially how the teachers integrated the daily programming for Joshua, for example, "Joshua will imitate some of the sounds in the songs."

How did the teachers incorporate Joshua's individual program plan of increased vocalizations and sounds into this topic? Did you find all the opportunities for Joshua to be involved with his peers and have lots of chances to vocalize?

By adapting the specialized focus for Joshua into the topic "Under the Sea," the true spirit of inclusion was achieved along with the specialized objectives for his development in the communication area.

Evaluation: Summative and Formative

The intent of observation is to uncover the realms of a child's everyday learning and development. That process asks the questions: "What will be discovered?" "What will it mean?" Evaluation asks the questions: "What happened?" and "Was it meaningful?"

In the article "Reflection—The Key to Evaluation, Elaine Ferguson states:

> Evaluation begins, proceeds, concludes and starts over again with reflection. We begin by reflecting upon why we are evaluating and what we will evaluate. We use reflection to collect information on what is being accomplished. We reflect upon the information collected, share our reflections with others and distinguish what we have learned about what we did. These new learnings and affirmations of previous learnings are used to develop new insights that will help us identify how we are going to use what we've learned. (Ferguson, 2004, 17–18)

All too often the notion of evaluation is perceived as a threatening experience; however, if it is seen to bring meaning to the experience, then it can be a supportive activity. In that context, "What happened?" is a question of interest. Whether evaluating the curriculum or a child's progress, those involved from the beginning should be involved at this stage. Why? We need to review the purpose and then determine where we are now. Have we arrived? Evaluation is when questions are answered and decisions are made. Is it necessary to wait till the end of an observation/curriculum cycle before an evaluation takes place? Ideally, there should be two types of evaluation with any process: formative and summative.

Formative evaluation refers to an evaluation that is ongoing. This type of evaluation is informal and is used to make changes as the process evolves. During this time **monitoring** occurs; a brief, up-to-date check of progress. Using the observation/curriculum cycle itself as an example, let us consider where some key junctures would be to monitor the progress of this cycle.

- Decision points—what are the decisions to be made?
- Actual observations—are the types of records appropriate for the kinds of information that is being sought?
- Compiling information—how long would observations continue or stop being collected? Who would compile the information?
- Planning—how will the observations be used in planning the curriculum? Who will guide the planning?
- Organization of resources—what kinds of materials/space/equipment will be needed?
- Implementation—where, when, and how will the curriculum be introduced, expanded upon, and concluded? Who will be responsible?
- Evaluation—when will the summative evaluation be concluded?

Summative evaluation is usually perceived as being a more formal type of evaluation. A summative evaluation takes place at the end of a timeline, such as an observation/curriculum cycle, when the process has come full circle. The summative evaluation will summarize the process.

This type of evaluation

- involves all the people in the process;
- takes place at an appointed interval;
- is done at the end or at key junctures: semiannually, yearly; and
- provides accountability for the process.

This process of evaluation does measure more than is at first apparent. What else does evaluation measure? It could measure

- the impact of the affective and physical environment;
- practices that represent centre philosophy;
- skills and knowledge of teachers/caregivers;
- involvement of all concerned—team functioning; and
- quality programs in the community.

Elaine Ferguson states that "reflection allows us to review what we've done, know why we did it and incorporate new ideas into our practice. We can do something with what we've learned and enhance what we already know. The quality of our practice is affected and we become active agents in our growth and development" (Ferguson 18).

A child-care setting with a good reputation in the community has educators who believe in and work toward a consistent quality program for children. A quality program is recognized as such by the commitment, caring, and dedication of educators and families working together. It starts with the mutually agreed-upon decisions of parents and teachers. It continues in the daily efforts of early childhood educators and families who believe in children and document their collective learning for all to see. Through the observation and documentation of a child's growth and learning, communication and relationships thrive benefiting all concerned.

Summary

What do observers discover in observing and recording children's behaviour? What may be concluded from the material in this chapter is that observation is a highly complex activity. The discovery of the complexities began with looking at the changes in the field of early childhood and raising awareness of ways to consider culture. Fundamental to this chapter has been the notion that formulating an observation/curriculum cycle connects observation with curriculum; it does not separate observation from curriculum. Observing to plan, planning to observe, or observing to learn are choices that reflect our philosophy about how children learn, and our image of what an educator could be or do. Three examples, webbing, the project approach, and traditional planning, have illustrated this process. When developing a curriculum with young children, the influences of the child's family, home life, culture, and the general community must be considered. From this chapter we have learned ways information can be shared with the parents about what the child learns and how he or she develops. The sharing of information with families is a work in progress. The examination of the influences of the environment and the role of early identification at the end of this chapter have contributed to the understanding of the complex world of observation.

 PROFESSIONAL REFLECTIONS

There are many sources of information that can assist early childhood educators in understanding a child's developmental progress: documentation collected while the child attends a child care program, the use of parent questionnaires, and standardized developmental screening tests. While the use of any *one* of these sources will provide useful information, the *combination of all three* provides the most comprehensive, valid, and reliable record of a child's developmental progress.

The value of parental input is well documented. In most cases, parents are the "experts" when it comes to their child. They can sense that something is not quite right with their child, but they lack the specific skills necessary to identify the area in which their child is struggling. The early childhood educator has the unique advantage of being in a position to *observe* the skills and activities of the child, to acknowledge the parent's concern, and assist the parent in whatever way possible.

(continued)

Before setting up a program for a child, we must document information on the child's strengths *and* the challenges. To focus only on the areas of need provides us with only half of the information, creating a "deficit-driven" approach to devising programs. Acknowledging the child's areas of strength provides us with ideas about "how" we can use the child's strengths to work on the area(s) of challenge while involving the child in activities in which he/she can be successful.

The early childhood teachers should never underestimate the value of their work in early identification and intervention. Their experience with large numbers of children over time gives them a better sense of what is *"normal development."* Knowing what normal development looks like assists the early childhood educator in identifying the children who may be struggling. The role of the early childhood educator is critical in the process of ensuring that young children get the support they need, at the time they need it.

—Marion Mainland,
College of Psychology of Ontario

KEY TERMS

advocate	monitoring	reliability
criterion-referenced assessment tools	norms	standardize
	paraprofessional	validity
fixed standard	referral	webbing

DISCUSSION QUESTIONS

1. How could the plan-to-observe and observe-to-plan approaches be debated using the project approach and traditional planning?
2. Is the developmentally appropriate practice of webbing a plan-to-observe, an observe-to-plan, or observe-to-learn approach to observation/curriculum? Explain why or why not.
3. Why is it necessary to consider the environment as an influence on young children's behaviour?
4. Why is it important to note societal changes that impact on the field of early childhood?
5. What is the role of observation in the early identification of children with special needs?
6. How could families be involved in the children's observation/curriculum development process?

ADDITIONAL READINGS

Allen, Eileen K., Carole L. Paasche, Rachel Langford, and Karen Nolan. *Inclusion in Early Childhood Programs: Children with Exceptionalities.* 4th Can. ed. Toronto: Thomson Nelson, 2006.

This Canadian edition provides an introduction to the education and care of children with special needs from birth through age six years. This edition continues to focus on supporting and responding to the developmental needs of all children in an inclusive early childhood education setting, including a chapter on second-language development.

Bradley, Jennifer, and Peris Kibera. "Culture and the Promotion of Inclusion in Child Care." *Young Children* 61.1 (January 2006): 34–38.

This article discusses cultural awareness and cultural sensitivity. It provides recommendations to support educators in their practice with families from diverse cultures who have children with special needs or challenging behaviours.

Crowther, Ingrid. *Creating Effective Learning Environments.* 2nd ed. Toronto: Thomson Nelson, 2007.

This text complements Chapter 8, as it illustrates the importance of the learning environment and how it influences young children. Chapters refer to observation and documentation techniques and areas that may be particularly useful to observe such as quiet areas, dramatic play areas, or sensory areas. It suggests, for example, that photographs and descriptions might best document water play or a portfolio be compiled to demonstrate the learning activity.

Lewin-Benham, Ann. "One Teacher, 20 Preschoolers, and a Goldfish: Environmental Awareness, Emergent Curriculum, and Documentation." *Young Children* 61.2 (March 2006): 28–34.

This insightful article demonstrates how commitment to learning can begin with just one goldfish. The four-year-olds and Mrs. Putnam first created a documentation panel, then revisited it, sparking further discussion. From observations to tape recordings, this article demonstrates how documentation can be used along with the children's interest to facilitate learning.

Logue, Mary Ellin. "Teachers Observe to Learn: Differences in Social Behavior of Toddlers and Preschoolers in Same-Age and Multiage Groupings." *Young Children* 61.3 (May 2006): 70–76.

This article will assist students in understanding the importance of behavioural observation in research and the importance of cross-cultural studies. These studies raise questions concerning the hypothesis that age-segregated groups may be contributing to social issues.

Shipley, Dale. *Empowering Children: Play-based Curriculum for Lifelong Learning.* 4th ed. Toronto: Thomson Nelson, 2008.

Section 3, "Planning the Curriculum," is an excellent resource to complement this chapter as it focuses on developing curriculum and planning appropriate activities that are either teacher-led or child-initiated. This edition provides more information on the project approach, emergent curriculum within a developmental framework, cultural aspects of play, and brain research. This text uses play-based methods as the medium for learning.

Glossary

abscissas
The horizontal axis of a graph.

accommodate
To bring into agreement, for example, adapt new information to previous knowledge.

advocate
Someone who amplifies a client's voice, gives support, and pursues objectives according to instruction while empowering the client to self-advocacy.

affective
Refers to the expression of feelings or emotions.

ambiguous word
A word that can express more than one meaning; indefinite, ambivalent.

analogue
Something similar in function or comparable with another; a model.

antecedent
Occurring before; prior; preceding.

anti-bias curriculum
A curriculum that embraces an educational philosophy and set of practices based on the notion that differences are good and that the "practice of freedom" enables children to build a healthy positive self-identity while respecting others.

at-a-glance records
Point form notes typically recorded by teachers; intended to be read quickly.

atypical
Different from the norm.

authentic assessment
An assessment which is connected to practical, pragmatic real world skills to demonstrate performance and understanding.

autonomy
The ability to care for oneself; to be independent; self-determination.

baseline of information
Information that profiles a child's current level of functioning in all developmental areas.

behaviour
Anything that can be seen, measured, or counted.

behaviour tallying
Counting a specific behaviour or monitoring the frequency of a behaviour and adding it up.

biases
Preconceived ideas or attitudes (personal or philosophical) that affect objectivity; prejudice.

bibliotherapy
The use of books that deal with emotionally sensitive topics in a developmentally appropriate way to help children understand and respond with positive coping strategies.

central tendency error
A judgment error that evaluates all children the same way, regardless of their individual characteristics.

checklist
A type of record providing a list of items that, if present, are marked or checked off.

child-sensitive
Attitudes, awareness, and practices that demonstrate care and sensitivity to the uniqueness of each child, his or her family, and culture in a group setting.

closed methods
Records or methods used for targeted behaviours.

Code of Ethics
Guidelines for responsible behaviour; principles and practices that guide the moral and ethical conduct of professionals in a field/discipline.

coding scheme
A design or diagram using a specific symbol to represent an idea, for example, colour coding to chart various activities.

cognition
The process of knowing; thinking; reasoning.

consequence
Relation of an effect to its cause; a natural or necessary result.

contextual information
Relevant information from the environment that directly or indirectly influences the behaviour of a child; information that helps to explain or give meaning to a child's behaviour.

continuum
A continuous line of reference.

contrived observation
Observation that is prearranged for a specific purpose in a formal or informal setting.

correlate
Two or more things that are so closely connected or associated with each other that one directly implies the other.

criterion-referenced assessment tools
Fixed standards used to evaluate an individual's performance; points of reference used when an individual is assessed against himself or herself, rather than compared with the performance of others.

current level of functioning
Up-to-date information in all developmental areas compiled about a child's skills/interests and areas to work on.

descriptor
A word/phrase that characterizes an idea or item; the adjectives used to rate the items of a rating scale continuum.

diversity
A reference to a range of categories, such as those of culture, religion, ethnicity, abilities, or beliefs.

documentation panels
A display panel illustrating artwork or photographs of any documentation about the activity of a group of children.

domain
A sphere of activity or function; psychology; area (of development), for example, cognitive, gross motor.

duration
The time frame within which an action occurs; how long something lasts.

eclectic approach
A method of selecting what seem to be the best practices from various philosophies or programs.

ecological approach
An approach for understanding a child's development in terms of the environment, which includes family, neighbourhood, or community.

evaluation
To examine and judge carefully; appraise.

event sampling/ABC analysis
A type of documentation that records a sequence of related events over time.

expectancy or logical error
An assumption made about two seemingly related behaviours, without a base from direct observation.

fixed standard
A rule, principle, or measure established by an authority that is accepted without deviation.

formal settings
Settings for observation that are structured in purpose, such as testing or research.

frequency
The number of times a specific incident occurs.

generic
Relating to or descriptive of an entire group or class; universal.

guide
To direct the way with the implication being that those following will benefit.

holistic (wholistic)
Information gathered and integrated from as many sources as possible; encompassing every aspect of a belief or approach.

indirect influences
Influences that have a subtle effect on behaviour, yet are not immediately observed or obviously connected to the behaviour.

inference
An opinion based on given data or assumptions; judgment.

informal settings
Settings for observation that are familiar and known to a child, such as private home daycare or a group daycare setting.

interpretations
Subjective responses to what is observed; personal or professional judgments or beliefs.

inter-rater reliability
The degree to which persons who are evaluating a particular behaviour or competency agree that the results are reliable; a method of controlling bias.

interview
A face-to-face meeting, usually within a formal context for a specific purpose.

intrinsic
Belonging to the nature of a thing; inherent; from within.

introspection
To look into or within at one's thoughts/feelings.

key experiences approach
A curriculum planning approach focusing on child development that utilizes the daily experiences and learning of the children.

labelling
To attach a term or phrase to a person or thing that classifies or characterizes him, her, or it.

leniency error
A common judgmental bias that occurs when the observer is overly generous when rating children.

longitudinal study
A study of an individual conducted over an extended period of time, usually months or years.

microcosm
A small representational system having characteristics of a larger system; a little world.

monitor
To check or test a process in a systematic fashion.

narrative/running record
The describing or telling of an event involving characters and setting; a story.

natural observation
Observation that is recorded as it happens within a familiar environment.

norms
A set of scores that represent the distribution of test performance in the norm group; standard against which others are measured.

observational drift
A common error made by teachers when observing a targeted behaviour whose definition is ambiguous in nature, for example, sharing.

open methods
Records or methods used for unanticipated behaviours.

ordinates
The vertical axis of a graph.

orientation
A process developed for creating awareness of and insight into existing procedures, policies, and expectations of a particular environment or field of study.

palmar grasp
A grasp whereby the tool or utensil lies across the palm of the hand with fingers curled around it, and the arm, rather than the wrist, moves the tool.

paraphrasing
To say the same thing, but in other words; a restatement; to give meaning in another form.

paraprofessional
A trained person who works under the guidance of a more qualified professional in that field.

pedagogy
The art, practice of a profession of teaching or instruction.

perception
An intuitive judgment often implying subtle personal bias; insight.

pincer grasp
A grasp whereby small objects are picked up using the thumb and forefinger.

play therapist
A therapist or consultant who specializes in working with children in a play-based environment to assist with their social, emotional, or communicative development.

pluralistic
The idea that there is more than one method, philosophy, or pedagogy.

portfolio
Information systematically collected about a child, which may include documentation, work samples, or photos, used for curriculum planning and sharing with families.

pragmatics
Dealing with events in a way that shows their interconnection; practical consequences.

prosocial behaviour
Positive, commonly valued social behaviours, such as sharing.

rapport
Relationship of harmony; affinity.

rating scales
A method of documentation that records behaviours targeted in advance and provides a continuum against which to judge the behaviour by degree or frequency.

reciprocal
Mutual; corresponding to each other as being equivalent or complementary.

referral
To send or direct someone to a treatment/program or service.

reinforcement
Consequences that increase the likelihood that a certain behaviour will occur again; in behavioural theory, any response that follows a behaviour that encourages repetition of that behaviour.

reliability
The extent to which a test is consistent in measuring over time what it is designed to measure.

segregate
Set apart; separate; to isolate, seclude, or set off from others.

self-talk
Thinking aloud; saying what is thought; private speech; using words to control attention, coordinate attention and thought.

semantics
The study of the meaning of language; the relationship between words (symbols) and what they refer to, and how these meanings influence behaviour and attitudes.

severity bias
The strict or severe treatment of a child by a teacher who is predisposed by a sometimes inexplicable dislike for that child.

specimen record
Detailed observations taken over a period of time and used for research purposes.

standardize
To apply a rule, principle, or measure established by an authority.

stimuli
Agents or environmental elements that are capable of influencing an activity; incentives.

strengths and needs list
A method that allows the observer to organize collected information on a child in a format divided into strengths and needs.

targeted behaviours
Behaviours that are preselected by the observer.

tenet
A principle, belief, or doctrine held as true.

total communication
An approach using as many kinds of communication as necessary for a child to understand an idea/concept, for example, sign language, hearing aids, pictures.

unobtrusive
Blending with the environment so as not to stand out; inconspicuous.

validity
Capable of being justified or supported; the degree to which something measures what it claims to measure.

webbing
A creative process of developing curriculum using ideas and/or developmental areas that reflect the integration of the subject matter.

References

Alat, Kazim. "Traumatic Events and Children: How Early Childhood Educators Can Help." *Childhood Education* 10.1 (Fall 2002): 2–7.

Allen, E., and L. Marotz. *Developmental Profiles: Pre-birth Through Twelve.* 4th ed. Clifton Park, NY: Delmar Learning, 2003.

Allen, Eileen K., Carole L. Paasche, Rachel Langford, and Karen Nolan. *Inclusion in Early Childhood Programs: Children with Exceptionalities.* 4th Can. ed. Toronto: Thomson Nelson, 2006.

Amdur, Jeanette, Marian Mainland and Kevin Parker, "The Disc Developmental Preschool Screen", Diagnostic Inventory for Screening Children, Kitchener-Waterloo, Ontario, 1984**.

Beaty, Janice, J. *Observing Development of the Young Child.* 6th ed. Toronto: Pearson, 2006.

Bentzen, Warren R., and Martha B. Frost. *Seeing Child Care: A Guide for Assessing the Effectiveness of Child Care Programs.* Clifton Park, NY: Delmar Learning, 2003.

Biggar, Heather. "NAEYC Recommendations on Screening and Assessment of Young English-language Learners." *Young Children* 60.6 (November 2005): 44–46.

Billman, Jean, and Janice Sherman. *Observation and Participation in Early Childhood Setting: A Practicum Guide.* 2nd ed. Boston, MA: Allyn & Bacon, 2003.

Bradley, Jennifer, and Peris Kibera. "Culture and the Promotion of Inclusion in Child Care." *Young Children* 61.1 (January 2006): 34–38.

Bullock, Ann Adams, and Parmalee P. Hawk. *Developing a Teaching Portfolio: A Guide for Preservice and Practicing Teachers.* New Jersey: Prentice-Hall, Inc., 2001.

Canadian Child Care Federation and the Canadian Language & Literacy Network. "Resource Sheet #3", *Language and Literacy, (From Birth . . . For Life).* Ottawa: Canadian Child Care Federation, 2007.

Capone, Angela, Tom Oren, and John T. Neisworth. *Childmate: A Guide to Appraising Quality in Child Care.* Clifton Park, NY: Delmar Learning, 2004.

Carter, Margie. "Walking the Talk of Collaboration." *Child Care Information Exchange* (03) (March 2003): 72–74.

Carter, Margie, and Deb Curtis. *Spreading the News.* St. Paul, MN: Red Leaf Press, 1996.

Cartwright, Carol A., and Phillip G. Cartwright. *Developing Observation Skills.* New York: McGraw-Hill, 1984.

Cohen, Dorothy, and Virginia Stern. *Observing and Recording the Behaviour of Young Children.* New York: Teachers College Press, 1978.

"Checklist Items from HELP", HELP for Preschoolers. VORT Corporation, 1995.

Crowther, Ingrid. *Creating Effective Learning Environments.* Toronto: Thomson Nelson, 2003.

Dichetelmiller, Margo, and Laura Ensler. "Experiences from the Field: New Insights into Infant/Toddler Assessment." *Young Children* 59.1 (January 2004): 30–33.

Doherty, Gillian. *Occupational Standards for the Child Care Practitioners.* Ottawa: Canadian Child Care Federation, 2003.

DPS: www.discmainland.ca or contact DISC Research Coordination, Marian Mainland: mmainland@rogers.com.

Early Childhood Education Department, "Observation and Inferences Form" Policy Manual & Field Placement Handbook—Year 1 & Year 2, Mohawk College of Applied Arts & Technology, (61).

Elliot, Barbara. *Measuring Performance: The Early Childhood Educator in Practice.* Albany, NY: Delmar Learning, 2002.

Ferguson, Elaine. "Reflection—The Key to Evaluation." *CCCF Interaction* 17.4 (Winter 2004): 17–18.

Feurer, I.D., A. Dimitropoulos, W.L. Stone, E. Roof, M.G. Butler, T. Thompson. John F. Kennedy Centre for Research on Human Development, Department of Psychiatry, School of Medicine, Vanderbilt University, TN. 13 March 2007 <http://www.ncbi.nlm.nih.gov/entrez/query.fcgi?Retrieve&db=PubMed&list_uids=10>.

Fraser, Susan. *Authentic Childhood: Experiencing Reggio Emilia.* 2nd Can. ed. Toronto: Thomson Nelson, 2005.

Freire, Dr. Marlinda. "Meeting the Needs of Refugee Families (2)." *SWIS News and Notes Newsletter.* 15 March 2007 <http://www.settlement.org/sys/atwork_library_detail.asp?doc_id=1003378>.

Gestwicki, Carol. *Developmentally Appropriate Practice: Curriculum and Development in Early Education.* 2nd ed. Albany, NY: Delmar Learning, 1999.

Gestwicki, Carol, and Jane Bertrand. *The Essentials of Early Education.* 3rd Can. ed. Toronto: Thomson Nelson, 2008.

Goleman, Daniel. *The Nature of Emotional Intelligence.* New York: Bantam Books, 1995.

Good, Linda. "Snap It Up: Using Digital Photography in Early Childhood Education." *Childhood Education—Infancy through Early Adolescence* 82.2 (Winter 2005/06): 79–85.

Gordon, Ann Miles, and Kathryn Williams Browne. *Beginning Essentials in Early Childhood Education.* Clifton Park, NY: Delmar Learning, 2007.

Gronlund, Gaye, and Bev Engle. *Focused Portfolios TM: A Complete Assessment for the Young Child.* St. Paul, MN: Red Leaf Press, 2001.

Grossman, Sue. "Making Lemonade from Lemons: Reflecting on Difficult Experiences." Annual Theme edition. *Childhood Education* (2004): 251–253.

Gulston, Lawrence. *Thomson Nelson Guide to Report Writing.* 2nd Can. ed. Toronto: Thomson Nelson, 2008.

Hanline, Mary Frances, Sande Milton, and Pamela Phelps. "Young Children's Block Construction Activities: Findings from 3 Years of Observation," Journal of Early Intervention, 2001, Vol. 24, No. 3, pp. 224–237.

Harms, T., R.M. Clifford, and Debby Cryer. *Early Childhood Environment Rating Scale (ECERS).* New York: Teachers College Press, 1998.

Hendrick, Joanne, and Patricia Weissman. *The Whole Child.* 8th ed. Upper Saddle River, NJ: Pearson Education, 2006.

Hohmann, M., and D. Weikart. Educating Young Children. Ypsilanti, Michigan: High/Scope Press, 1995, p. 6.

Kagan, Jerome. "The Power and Limitation of Being a Parent," Lecture given at the Centre for Studies of Children at Risk, Hamilton, ON: McMaster University, November, 1996.

Kaiser, Barbara, and Judy Sklar Rasminsky. "The Volcano at the Day Care Centre." *CCCF Interaction* (Winter 1996): 12–15.

Katz, Lilian G. "The Project Approach." *ERIC/EECE Publications-Digests* April 1994. 17 November 2002 <http://ericeece.org/pubs/digests/1994/lk-pro94.html>.

Katz, Lilian G., and Sylvia C. Chard. "The Contribution of Documentation to the Quality of Early Childhood Education." *Eric Digest* ED393608. Urbana, IL: Eric Clearinghouse on Elementary and Early Childhood Education, 1996-04-00.

Katz, Lilian G., "Trends and Issues in the Dissemination of Child Development and Early Education Knowledge." Perspectives from ERIC/EECE. Urbana, Il: ERIC Clearinghouse on Elementary Early Childhood Education, 1993.

Keyes, Carol R. "A Way of Thinking about Parent/Teacher Partnerships for Teachers/ Le partenariat parent/ensignant: un autre point de vue." *International Journal of Early Years Education* 10.3 (2002): 177–191.

Klein, Diane M., and Deborah Chen. *Working with Children from Culturally Diverse Backgrounds*. Albany, NY: Delmar Learning, 2001.

Koster, Joan Bouza. *Growing Artists: Teaching Art to Young Children*. 3rd ed. Clifton Park, NY: Delmar Learning, 2005.

Lee, Soyoung. "Using Children's Texts to Communicate with Parents of English-Language Learners." *Young Children* 61.5 (September 2006).

Lewin-Benham, Ann. "One Teacher, 20 Preschoolers, and a Goldfish: Environmental Awareness, Emergent Curriculum, and Documentation." *Young Children* 61.2 (March 2006): 28–34.

Lockwood, David, Instructional Materials, Humber College, 1997–1998.

Logue, Mary Ellin. "Teachers Observe to Learn: Differences in Social Behavior of Toddlers and Preschoolers in Same-Age and Multiage Groupings." *Young Children* 61.3 (May 2006): 70–76.

Malaguzzi, Loris, et. al. *The Hundred Languages of Children: The Reggio Emilia Approach to Early Childhood Education*. Norwood, NJ: Albex, 1993.

Malone, Liana, and Pat Mirenda. "Effects of Video Modeling and Video Feedback on Peer-Directed Social Language Skills of a Child with Autism." *Journal of Positive Behavior Interventions* 22 March 2006. 22 March 2007 <http://www.accessmylibrary.com/coms2/summary_0286-14794618_ITM>.

Marion, Marian. *Using Observation in Early Childhood Education*. Upper Saddle River, NJ: Pearson Education, 2004.

McClellan, Diane E., and Lilian G. Katz. "Assessing Young Children's Social Competence." *ERIC Digest* March 2001. 29 October 2002 <www.ericdigests.org>.

Ministry of Education. "Many Roots/Many Voices: Supporting English language learners in every classroom." Queen's Printer for Ontario 2005. 18 January 2007 <www.edu.gov.on.ca>.

Mooney, Carol Garhart. *Theories of Childhood: An Introduction to Dewey, Montessori, Erikson, Piaget & Vygotsky*. St. Paul, MN: Red Leaf Press, 2000.

NAEYC (National Association for the Education of Young Children). *Young Children*, NAEYC Position Paper. Washington, DC: NAEYC, April 1996.

Nilsen, Barbara Ann. *Week by Week: Documenting the Development of Young Children.* 3rd ed. Clifton Park, NY: Delmar Learning, 2004.

Nipissing District Developmental Screen, Inc., "The Nipissing District Developmental Screen", Compiled in North Bay, Ontario, 2002.

Pearson, Robin, "Respecting Culture in our Schools and Classrooms." *Child & Family* 9.2 (Summer/Fall 2006).

Pence, A., S. Griffins, and L. McDonnell, H. Goelman, D. Lero, and L. Brockman, Shared Diversity: An Interprovincial Report on Child Care in Canada. Canadian National Child Care Study. Ottawa. ON: Statistics Canada and Human Resources Development Canada, 1997.

Pence, Alan. "Seeking the Other 99 Languages of ECE: A Keynote Address by Alan Pence." *Interaction* 20.3 (Fall 2006).

Peterson, Evelyn A. *Early Childhood Planning, Methods, and Materials: The How, Why, and What of Lesson Plans.* Scarborough, ON: Allyn & Bacon, 1996.

Piaget, J. The Origins of Intelligence in Children, New York: International Universities Press, 1952.

Pimento, Barbara, and Deborah Kernested. *Healthy Foundations in Early Childhood Settings.* 3rd ed. Toronto: Thomson Nelson, 2004.

Portage Project, "Child Development Tool for Observation and Planning (TOP)", *The New Portage Project,* Portage, Wisconsin, 2003.

Quesenberry, Amanda, and Sharon Doubet. "A Framework for Professional Development Focused on Social and Emotional Competencies." *Young Children* 61.6 (November 2006): 30–43.

Read, Katherine, Pat Gardner, and Barbara Mahler. *Early Childhood Programs.* 9th ed. Orlando, FL: Harcourt Brace, 1993.

Rhomberg, Valerie. "Nurturing Young Minds: Linking Brain Research to Anti-Bias/Diversity Concepts." *CCCF Interaction* 20.4 (Winter 2007).

Shipley, Dale. *Empowering Children: Play-based Curriculum for Lifelong Learning.* 4th ed. Toronto: Thomson Nelson, 2008.

Tanner, Karen and Danielle Turney, "The Role of Observation in the Assessment of Child Neglect," Child Abuse Review, 2000, Vol 9, (337–348).

Tommey, Janice, and Lawrence A. Adams. "The Naturalistic Observation of Children with Autism: Evidence for Intersubjectivity." *New Directions for Child Development* Fall 1995: 75–89. <http://www.eric.ed.gov/ERICPortal/recorddetail?accno=EJ12438>

Valentino, Lucy. *Handle With Care.* 3rd ed. Toronto: Thomson Nelson, 2004.

(Videotape) The Unbiased Mind. Lake Zurich, IL: The Learning Seed, 1995.

Weiss, Amy L. *Preschool Language Disorders: Resource Guide.* San Diego, CA: Singular, 2001.

Wellhousen, Karen, and Rebecca M. Giles. "Building Literacy Opportunities Into Children's Block Play: What Every Teacher Should Know." *Childhood Education* 82.2 (Winter 2005/06): 75.

Willis, Scott. "Teaching Young Children." *Annual Editions.* Dushkin McGraw-Hill.

Wilson, Kim. "To Speak, Participate and Decide: The Child's Right to be Heard." *CCCF Interaction* 20.3 (Fall 2006).

Wilson, Lynn. *Partnerships: Families and Communities in Early Childhood Development.* 3rd ed. Toronto: Thomson Nelson, 2005.

Winzer, M.A. *Children with Exceptionalities: A Canadian Perspective.* 3rd ed. Scarborough, ON: Prentice-Hall Canada, 1993.

Wortham, Sue C. *Tests and Measurement in Early Childhood Education.* Columbus, OH: Merrill, 1990.

Wortham, Sue C. *Assessment in Early Childhood Education,* 3rd ed. Columbus, OH: Merrill, 2001.

Wylie, Sally, and Muriel Axford. "If Children Are So Different, Why Is Programming the Same?" *CCCF Interaction* 14.2 (Summer 2000): 11–12.

Index

High/Scope Model Wheel of Learning, 219

High/Scope Research Foundation, The, 218

Holcombe, 203

Holistic, 223

Holistic image/portfolios, 223–24

The Hundred Languages of Children (book), 215

I

Iceberg analogy, 246–47

Identification process, age-appropriate, 270–81

Individual Program Plan (IPP), 275

Inference(s), 43, 44

Informal settings, 30

Information, re children
    baseline of, 99–100
    consent and authorization forms, 65–66
    parent information bulletin board, 253
    parent interviews and meetings, 254
    sharing, examples re informal, 253–54
    telephone, text-messaging, email, 254
    two-way communication books, 253

Internal conditions, 42–43
    and ambiguous words, 44
    vs. behaviour, 42–43

Internet, 207–208, 214

Interpretation(s), 110, 118–22
    brief observations and, 119–20
    of charts and graphs, 169–70
    collection of observations, 120, 122
    expanded observation and, 120
    summary statement and, 120, 122
    terminology and levels of, 118–22

Inter-rater reliability, 96

Interview, 190

Intrinsic process, and children's play, 15–18

Introspection, 26

Inukshuk, and body awareness, 215, 216

Ireton, Harold, "Professional Reflections," 33

Itard, Jean-Marc-Gaspard, 24, 25

J

Judgmental error, *see* Bias(es)

K

Kagan, Jerome, 28, 29, 101

Kaiser, Barbara, 203

Katz, L.G., 30, 261

Kaul, 246

Kitchener-Waterloo Association for Early Childhood Educators–Ontario (AECEO), 245

Koppelman, 246

KWL chart, 248

L

Label(s), 45–46

Labelling, 45

Language
    clear image conveyance and, 77
    descriptive, 76–77
    development, in children 1– 5 years, 21T, 22T
    and key words, 75
    meaningful recording of observations, 73–74
    and observations, 73–74
    parts of speech, 76
    in playroom setting, 75
    semantics and, 78
    speech and tape recorder use, 200
    writing physical descriptions, 91–93

listening and tape recording, 200
location of, 59
meaningful recording of, 47–48
as means to learning, 256–57
media-assisted, *see* Media-assisted
   observation
methods of, 51–52, 55–58
and objectivity, 92–96
observational drift and recording,
   95–96
opportunity for, 85
overcoming obstacles to, 62–63
and parents' involvement, 11–12, 52
participatory mode of, 57–58
and perception, 117
permission to conduct, 10–11
and playroom environment, 53–54
and portfolios, 222
rapport with parents/families, 10, 12
recording, 77
and Reggio Emilia approach, 214–18
rough notes about, 81
and selection of ECE approach, 248–51
spectator mode of, 55, 57
strategies, 62–63, 100–101
as systematic process, 37, 38, 39
tape recording method of,
   200–201
and T-chart, 248
time periods for, 100–101
timing of, 58, 60–61
types of reports re, 93
understanding/interpreting, 111–13
unobtrusiveness of, 59
utility of, and discovery, 248
writing, 80–86
writing physical descriptions, 91–93
Observation areas, 199–201
   advantages/disadvantages, 201
   benefits to parents, 201
Observation guidelines, 86–90
   and accurate records, 87–88
   child selection and, 87

recording dialogue, 88
rewriting observations, 88
and staff, 86–87
spectator vs. participant mode, 83
Observation process, 244–45
   and family/societal issues, 245
Observation tools, *see also* Anecdotal
      records; Running records
   behaviour tallying, 165
   checklists, 142–47
   event sampling, 126–27
   High/Scope Child Observation Record
      (COR), 220–21
   and profiles, 158–65
   rating scales, 148–51
Observational drift, 95–96
Observations
   interpretation vs., 86
   interpreting, 111–13
   and interpreting behaviour, 118–22
"Observing Young Children"
      (video), 85
Occupational standards, 54, 55
Odom, 203
Odon, 246
Open methods, 139–40
Operant conditioning, 129
Ordinates, and graphs, 168
Orientation, 8
*The Origins of Intelligence in
      Children* (Piaget), 25

P

Paasche, Carole, "Professional
      Reflections," 102–103
Painter, Claude, "Professional
      Reflections," 68
Palmar grasp, 184
Paraphrasing, 88

standardization and individuality
of, 228
types of, 226–27
as work in progress, 222

Pragmatics, 78

Privacy, *see* Confidentiality; File(s)

Professional research, 28–32

Profile(s), 158–65
adaptation of, 160–65
advantages/disadvantages, 160
contextual/ecological approach, 158
and differing environments/settings,
160, 161, 162
format of, 159–60
and hospital setting, 162
"key experience" approach, ECE
centre, 160
purpose, 158
reasons/uses for, 159

Project Approach, the, 245, 261–62

Prosocial behaviours, 230

R

Rapport, 10
establishing with parents/families,
10–12

Rasminsky, Judy Sklar, 203

Rating scales, 148–51
adaptation for special populations,
150
advantages/disadvantages, 149–50
Childhood Autism Rating Scale
(CARS), 150
Children's Depression Rating
Scale, 150
and continuum, 148
format of, 148–49
judgment factor and, 149
purposes of, 148

Read, K., 23

Reciprocal learning process, 11

Record(s)
anecdotal, *see* Anecdotal records
at-a-glance, 123
behaviour and event sampling,
126–27
CD, etc., re playroom, 208–209
data, and computer use, 208–209
electronic, 213–14
files, 66–68
forms/templates, and
computerized, 209
mapping, 193–96
and playroom environment
evaluation, 266–67
pictorial representation, 184–87
recording data and visual
representation, 208–10
running *see* Running record(s)
specimen, 123
tape recording, 200–201
re targeted behaviours, 139
videotapes, 202–205
and unanticipated behaviours, 107

Recording(s)
closed method, 139
and computer technology, 207–11
congruence re observations, 73
dialogue, guidelines, 88
graphic, 248
observations of early childhood,
24–28
open method, 139–40
rewriting, and reflecting, 88
tape recording vs. paraphrasing, 88

Referral, 275

Reflection(s), 88

Reggio Emilia (preschool) approach,
245, 248, 261
children-parent-teacher interaction,
216–17
and co-constructors of knowledge
notion, 218
documentation principles, 217–18

Reggio Emilia (preschool) approach
(*continued*)
to early childhood education, 218–21
Inukshuk construction, 218
objectives, 216
observation/documentation, 216–18
as social services/education
combination, 214

Reinforcement, 129

Report(s)
background information
section, 23
child development structure for
summary, 233–34
essential information section, 232–33
format/organization of, 232–37
physical description of child in, 233
progress/portfolio, and parent-teacher
interview, 239
recommendation section, 237
special needs child and, 234–35
strengths and needs list in, 234–35
summary and child's strengths/
interests, 234
summary of portfolio information,
233–34
types of, 231–32

Report writing, 230–41
affective aspect, 231
and purpose/content tone, 230–31
of sensitive issues, 237
steps in writing, 236–37
types of reports, 231–32
writing with positive phrasing, 235

Reward system, 26, 27

Running record(s) (narrative
records), 122–25
advantages/disadvantages, 125
chronological feature, 122–23
format of, 123
longitudinal studies and, 125
and parents, sharing- with, 134

purpose of, 122–23
and special needs child, 133–34

S

Screening tool(s), 272, 275
Nipissing District Developmental
Screen, 275
purpose of, 275
referral, 275

Segregate, 25

Seguin, Edouard, 25

Self-help, 19
development, children 1–5 years,
21T, 22T
rate, 21T, 22T
skills, 97, 98

Self-talk, 202

Self-evaluation, writing/recording-,
89–90

Semantics, 78

Severity bias, 95

Sharing process, 90

Sherman, J.A., 59, 126, 223, 261

Skinner, B.F., 26, 27, 128, 129

Social development, children one to
5 years, 21T, 22T

Social emotional development, 19

Sociogram(s), 182–86, 266, 267
defined, 188
and family tree, 188
interview and, 190
variation/ecomaps, 189–90

Special needs child(ren)
frequency of observation, 100
Individual Program Plan (IPP), 275
mapping, 196
report summary and special needs
list, 234
videotaping, 203–204

Specimen records, 123

Spectator mode, 87

Stimuli, 37–38

Strengths and needs list, 234

Student-teacher-observer
  Code of Ethics, 8–9
  and confidentiality, 9
  and differing ECE philosophies, 9–10
  parent/family rapport and, 10–11

Student-teacher-observer role,
  development of, 7–10

Summary statements (interpretation),
  120, 122

Summative evaluation, 280

Systematic process, 37, 38, 39
  as cycle of observation, 40–41

T

Tape recordings, 200–201
  uses, 200

Targeted behaviour(s), 139
  behaviour-selection criteria, 143
  and behaviour tallying charting,
    165–72
  checklists and, 142–47
  frequency vs. duration, 141–42
  interpreting participation chart
    information, 153–55
  participation charts and, 151–58
  profiles and, 158–65
  rating scales and, 148–51
  recording, preparation for, 140–42
  types of records re, 139

T-chart, 248

Teacher(s), *see* Early childhood
  educator(s)

Teacher-observer(s), professional skills, 6

Tefenna, 246

Terman, Lewis, 27

Time, as behaviour variable, 47

Toomey, J., 204

Total communication, 198

Traditional curriculum
  its documentation, teacher's
    role in, 264

Traditional curriculum planning, 262,
    263–64, 265
  child-centred vs. teacher driven
    curriculum, 263–64
  pre-ordained themes and, 262

Traditional planning, 245

U

Unanticipated behaviour, 107
  anecdotal observation and, 110
  and anecdotal records, 108, 110
  contextual information and, 110
  critique of observation/interpretation,
    111–13
  and diaries, 122
  event sampling, 126–33
  interpretations and recording, 118–22
  observing process re, 111–13
  running(narrative) records and, 122–25

Unbalanced perception, and subjective
  inference, 117

Unobtrusive, 59

V

Verbs, 76

Video modelling, and videotaping, 204

Videotapes, *see also* Videotaping
  advantages/disadvantages, 204–205
  planning-videotaping, 204
  and self-talk, 202

Videotaping
  and bibliotherapy, 203
  high-needs child, 203
  as monitoring tool, 203

peer models, child learning, 203–204
post-traumatic stress disorder, 202–203

Visual representation, *see* Graphic representation

Vocabulary, 75–76

Vygotsky, Lev, 214

W

Watson, John B., 26, 27, 128

Web(s), 259–59. *See also* Webbing
with developmental approach, 261

Webbing, 244, 257
as developmentally appropriate planning, 257–58
purpose of, 260
and "web" development, 258–59

Week by Week: Documenting the Development of Young Children, 110

Weikart, David, 218

The Wild Boy of Aveyron, 25

Working files, and office observation, 66–68

Writing
as confidential recording, 81
opportunities for observing and, 85
physical description and uses, 92–93
physical description of child, 91–93
rough notes re observations, 81
rough notes to good copy, 82–83, 84–85
self-evaluation of, 89–90
sharing, 89–90
tape recorder alternative to, 201
unique style for ECE, 80–81
and wellness reports, 93

Wylie, S., 245, 248

Z

Zimmerman, 264